ROUTLEDGE LIBRARY EDI
WOMEN'S HISTORY

WOMEN AS MOTHERS IN
PRE-INDUSTRIAL ENGLAND

WOMEN AS MOTHERS IN PRE-INDUSTRIAL ENGLAND

Essays in memory of Dorothy McLaren

Edited by
VALERIE FILDES

Volume 17

LONDON AND NEW YORK

First published in 1990

This edition first published in 2013
by Routledge
2 Park Square, Milton Park, Abingdon, Oxfordshire OX14 4RN

Simultaneously published in the USA and Canada
by Routledge
711 Third Avenue, New York, NY 10017

First issued in paperback 2014

Routledge is an imprint of the Taylor and Francis Group, an informa company

British Library Cataloguing in Publication Data
A catalogue record for this book is available from the British Library

ISBN: 978-0-415-63337-6 (Volume 17)
ISBN: 978-0-415-75252-7 (pbk)

Publisher's Note
The publisher has gone to great lengths to ensure the quality of this reprint but
points out that some imperfections in the original copies may be apparent.

Disclaimer
The publisher has made every effort to trace copyright holders and would
welcome correspondence from those they have been unable to trace.

WOMEN AS MOTHERS IN PRE-INDUSTRIAL ENGLAND

ESSAYS IN MEMORY OF DOROTHY McLAREN

Edited by Valerie Fildes

ROUTLEDGE
London and New York

First published in 1990
by Routledge
11 New Fetter Lane, London EC4P 4EE
Simultaneously published in the USA and Canada
by Routledge
a division of Routledge, Chapman and Hall, Inc.
29 West 35th Street, New York, NY 10001

Typeset by LaserScript Limited, Mitcham, Surrey
Printed and bound in Great Britain by Mackays of Chatham PLC, Kent

British Library Cataloguing in Publication Data

Women as mothers in pre-industrial England:
essays in memory of Dorothy McLaren.
1. England. Motherhood, Social aspects, history
I. Fildes, Valerie A. II. Series
306.8'743'0942

Library of Congress Cataloging in Publication Data

Women as mothers in pre-industrial England: essays in memory of
Dorothy McLaren/edited by Valerie Fildes
p.   cm. — (The Wellcome Institute series in
the history of medicine)
Bibliography: p.
Includes index.
1. Women—England—History.
2. Motherhood—England—History.
3. McLaren, Dorothy. I. McLaren, Dorothy.
II. Fildes, Valerie A. III. Series.
HQ1599.E5W63   1989
306.874'3'0942—dc20
89-10474
CIP

ISBN 0-415-02488-9

Contents

Contents

Tables

Figures

Contributors

Patricia Crawford is Associate Professor of History at the University of Western Australia, where she teaches women's history. Her publications include several pioneering studies of women in seventeenth-century England and she is the author of *Denzil Holles 1598–1680* (Whitfield Prize, 1980) and editor of *Exploring Women's Past* (Sydney, 1984). She is currently writing a book on women in seventeenth-century England.

Valerie Fildes trained and worked as a nurse before obtaining a first degree and Ph.D. in Human Biology at the University of Surrey. She has carried out research on infant care and paediatrics prior to 1800 at the Wellcome Institute for the History of Medicine and is the author of *Breasts, Bottles and Babies: A History of Infant Feeding* (Edinburgh, 1986) and *Wet Nursing. A History from Antiquity to the Present* (Oxford, 1988). She is currently researching infant feeding practices in the nineteenth and early-twentieth centuries at the ESRC Cambridge Group for the History of Population and Social Structure.

Fiona Newall studied Geography at Clare College, Cambridge, and carried out the research for her Ph.D. at the ESRC Cambridge Group for the History of Population and Social Structure. She is currently a research fellow at the Social Policy Research Unit, University of York.

Linda Pollock has been a Wellcome fellow, and research fellow and college lecturer in history at Churchill College, Cambridge. She is the author of *Forgotten Children. Parent–child Relations*

1500–1900 (Cambridge, 1983), *A Lasting Relationship. Parents and Children Over Three Centuries*, (London, 1987), and the forthcoming *The Meditations and Medical Practices of Lady Grace Mildmay* (1989). She has completed the research for a two-volume work on family relationships among the propertied ranks of sixteenth- and seventeenth-century society, and is currently teaching history at Tulane University, New Orleans.

Mary Prior was born in China, educated in New Zealand, and came to England in 1959. After the death of her husband she became a mature student and was awarded a D.Phil. from the University of Oxford. She has worked part-time for the Open University and the Oxford University Department of External Studies. She is the author of *Fisher Row: Oxford Fishermen, Bargemen and Canal Boatmen 1500–1900* (Oxford, 1982) and editor of *Women in English Society 1500–1800* (London, 1985).

Robert Schnucker obtained degrees from Northeast Missouri State University, Dubuque Theological Seminary, and the University of Iowa. He teaches at Northeast Missouri State University and is currently director of the Thomas Jefferson University Press and edits several scholarly journals. He is the author of numerous articles and works on social history and history of education.

Adrian Wilson studied preclinical medicine at the University of Adelaide, where he was awarded a research degree in medical science, and researched the history of childbirth for a history D.Phil. at the University of Sussex. His forthcoming book *A Safe Deliverance* embodies this research and also some years of post-doctoral study and teaching in the Wellcome Unit for the History of Medicine, Cambridge. He has worked on the history of gender, medicine, and science in early-modern England and, with T. G. Ashplant, on historical epistemology. He is currently a research fellow in the Department of Social History, University of Leicester.

Abbreviations

Add.	Additional
Am. Hist. Rev.	*American Historical Review*
Am. J. Dis. Child.	*American Journal for the Diseases of Children*
Ann. Démog. Hist.	*Annales de Démographie Historique*
Annales ESC	*Annales d'Economies, Sociétés et Civilisations*
Archaeol. Cant.	*Archaeologia Cantiana*
Bapt. Quart.	*Baptist Quarterly*
Berks Old & New	*Berkshire Old and New*
BI	Borthwick Institute
BL	British Library
BodL	Bodleian Library
Bull. Hist. Med.	*Bulletin of the History of Medicine*
Bull. Soc. Soc. Hist. Med.	*Bulletin of the Society for the Social History of Medicine*
CCCC	Corpus Christi College, Cambridge
CCRO	Chester City Record Office
Child & Fam.	*Child and Family*
Compar. Civil. Rev.	*Comparative Civilisations Review*
Compar. Stud. Soc. Hist.	*Comparative Studies in Society and History*
Cont. & Change	*Continuity and Change*
Crim. Just. Hist.	*Criminal Justice History*
CUL	Cambridge University Library
DNB	*Dictionary of National Biography*
DRO	Devon Record Office
Dugdale Soc. Occ. Pap.	*Dugdale Society Occasional Papers*

DWL	Dr Williams Library
Econ. Hist. Rev.	*Economic History Review*
Eighteenth Cent. Stud.	*Eighteenth Century Studies*
ERO	Essex Record Office
Fem. Stud.	*Feminist Studies*
GL	Guildhall Library
Glasg. Med. J.	*Glasgow Medical Journal*
GLRO	Greater London Record Office
Herts Count.	*Hertfordshire Countryside*
Hist. & Theory	*History and Theory*
Hist. Childh. Quart.	*History of Childhood Quarterly*
Hist. Educ.	*History of Education*
Hist. J.	*Historical Journal*
Hist. Meth.	*Historical Methods*
Hist. Nurs. Grp Roy. Coll. Nurs. Bull.	*History of Nursing Group, Royal College of Nursing Bulletin*
Hist. Today	*History Today*
Hist. Workshop J.	*History Workshop Journal*
HL	Huntington Library
HRO	Hertfordshire Record Office
Hum. Biol.	*Human Biology*
Int. J. Wom. Stud.	*International Journal of Women's Studies*
J. Biosoc. Sci.	*Journal of Biosocial Science*
J. Fam. Hist.	*Journal of Family History*
J. Hist. Ideas	*Journal of the History of Ideas*
J. Hist. Med	*Journal of the History of Medicine and Allied Sciences*
J. Interdisc. Hist.	*Journal of Interdisciplinary History*
J. Med. Ren. Stud.	*Journal of Medieval and Renaissance Studies*
J. Psychohist.	*Journal of Psychohistory*
J. Relig. Hist.	*Journal of Religious History*
JRL	John Rylands Library
J. Roy. Soc. Med.	*Journal of the Royal Society of Medicine*
J. Sex Res.	*Journal of Sex Research*
J. Soc. Arch.	*Journal of the Society of Archivists*
J. Soc. Hist.	*Journal of Social History*
KAO	Kent Archive Office
Kroeber Anthrop.Soc.Pap.	*Kroeber Anthropological Society Papers*

LAO	Lincolnshire Archive Office
Law Hist. Rev.	*Law and History Review*
LJRO	Lichfield Joint Record Office
Loc. Popul. Stud.	*Local Population Studies*
Lond. Rev. Books	*London Review of Books*
LPL	Lambeth Palace Library
LSG	Library of the Society of Genealogists
Mat. Child. Hlth	*Maternal and Child Health*
Med. Hist.	*Medical History*
Mid. Chron.	*Midwives' Chronicle*
Mid. Hist.	*Midland History*
Mid. Hlth Vis. Comm. Nurs.	*Midwife, Health Visitor and Community Nurse*
MUL	Manchester University Library
NLS	National Library of Scotland
North. Hist.	*Northern History*
Nott. Med. Stud	*Nottingham Medieval Studies*
NRO	Northampton Record Office
NUL	Nottingham University Library
Nurs. Times	*Nursing Times*
OED	*Oxford English Dictionary*
ORO	Oxford Record Office
P & P	*Past and Present*
Path. Ann.	*Pathology Annual*
Phil. Pub. Aff.	*Philosophy and Public Affairs*
Popul. Dev. Rev.	*Population and Development Review*
Popul. Stud.	*Population Studies*
PRO	Public Record Office
Scient. Am.	*Scientific American*
SCL	Sheffield Central Library
Scot. Hist. Soc. Miscel.	*Scottish History Society Miscellany*
ScotRO	Scottish Record Office
Sixteenth Cent. J.	*Sixteenth Century Journal*
Soc. Hist.	*Social History*
Soc. Rev.	*Sociological Review*
SomRO	Somerset Record Office
StaRO	Stafford Record Office
Stud. Church Hist.	*Studies in Church History*
Stud. Eighteenth-Cent. Cult.	*Studies in Eighteenth-Century Culture*
Trans Camb. Bibliog. Soc.	*Transactions of the Cambridge Bibliographical Society*

Abbreviations

Trans Hist. Soc. Lancs Chesh.	*Transactions of the Historic Society of Lancashire and Cheshire*
Trans Roy. Hist. Soc.	*Transactions of the Royal Historical Society*
Univ. Pittsburgh Law Rev.	*University of Pittsburgh Law Review*
WCA	Westminster City Archives
WIL	Wellcome Institute Library
Wilts Rec. Soc.	Wiltshire Record Society
WRO	Warwick Record Office

Dorothy McLaren

Dorothy McLaren left school at the age of 15 and it was not until her children were grown up that she entered academic life. After gaining a degree in history from the University of Reading she embarked on a study of 'Stuart Caversham: a Thames-side community in Oxfordshire during the seventeenth century', for which she was awarded a Ph.D. in 1975. It was during her research for this thesis that she first noted the differences in childbearing and lactation habits between wealthy and poor women in the community. Her interest in the reasons for these differences was to lead to her spending the last 10 years of her life in detailed research into the lives of women in seventeenth-century England, at first in Oxfordshire and Buckinghamshire and later in Somerset. By reconstituting small communities and using both historical and modern physiological evidence to explain her findings, she identified and explained the connection between breastfeeding, marital fertility, and child spacing in pre-industrial England.

That lactating women are less likely to conceive had been known for centuries. Both physicians and ordinary men and women were well aware of the connection between breast-feeding and fertility. During the twentieth century, however, this concept had received the attention of doctors and physiologists who demanded concrete proof. Thus, scientific opinion on the existence of this link fluctuated according to the current state of research. It is only in the last few years that the contraceptive effect of breastfeeding has been fully accepted. Just 6 years ago it was possible for an eminent medical scientist, when asked his opinion of the latest published evidence on lactation and fertility, to state that he did not believe it because he had worked on it 20 years before and had found no evidence that breastfeeding suppressed fertility at that time. Not surprisingly, historians and historical demographers followed the views of the scientific community when trying to explain historical changes in fertility. Thus, when Dorothy first produced her interpretation of the effect of maternal breastfeeding and wet nursing on fertility and birth intervals, reactions from historians tended to be hostile, ranging from polite interest, through disbelief, to, in at least one instance, open attack after presenting a paper on the subject. However, time was to vindicate her theory. Growing scientific and demographic evidence resulted in the acceptance of the concept that natural, frequent breastfeeding does have a contraceptive effect, particularly in the first few months after birth. Dorothy's last published work, 'Marital fertility and lactation 1570–1720', not only provided impressive historical evidence of the important role of lactation in the lives of women in pre-industrial England, but also listed the developing beliefs of both scientists and historical demographers about the significance of lactation amenorrhoea. Today her pioneering work on the subject is fully accepted.

Shortly before her death in a car accident in 1985, Dorothy pinpointed another gap in the historiography of women in seventeenth-century England: their central and important role as mothers. She did not live to write the book she planned on English women as mothers in this period. It seemed fitting, therefore, that a volume in her memory should concentrate upon the subject area she had identified, and largely utilize the type of evidence she sought and employed to such good effect: the detailed personal and local records of English women and their families.

This book is dedicated with affection and respect to Dorothy McLaren, 1922–85.

Publications of Dorothy McLaren

'The marriage act of 1653: its influence on the parish registers', *Popul. Stud.* 28 (1974), 319–27.

'Fertility, infant mortality and breast-feeding in the seventeenth century, *Bull. Soc. Soc. Hist. Med.*, 20 (1977), 12–15.

Dorothy McLaren

'Fertility, infant mortality and breastfeeding in the seventeenth century', *Med. Hist.*, 22 (1978) 378–96.

'Nature's contraceptive. Wet nursing and prolonged lactation: the case of Chesham, Buckinghamshire 1578–1601', *Med. Hist.*, 23 (1979), 426–41.

'The individualism of good mothering', *Bull. Soc. Soc. Hist. Med.*, 24 (1979) 36–8.

'Emmenologia: a curse or a blessing?', *Bull. Soc. Soc. Hist. Med.*, 25 (1979), 65–7.

'Disease and dirty water in West Somerset in the late nineteenth century', *Bull. Soc. Soc. Hist. Med.*, 35 (1984), 35–6.

'Marital fertility and lactation 1570–1720', in M. Prior (ed.), *Women in English Society 1500–1800* (London, 1985), 22–53.

Introduction

Although an increasing amount of work is being published on the lives of English women in the pre-industrial period, research on their role as mothers remains at an early stage. Yet, as the essays in this volume will show, the preparation for, and the experience and the results of, motherhood were central to the existence of women in all classes of society.

Patricia Crawford's chapter introduces the concept of maternity in the seventeenth century and outlines the expectations and experience of being a mother. Despite the patriarchal influences which shaped society's ideas about maternity, the role presented both problems and delights and, for many women, was the most fundamental and rewarding experience of their lives. She sets the scene for the chapters of Linda Pollock and Adrian Wilson, which detail the experience of pregnancy and the ritual of childbirth respectively. Pregnancy could be a time of happy expectation, but also of dread of the forthcoming confinement. It could progress uneventfully but potential hazards, such as miscarriage, had to be watched and prepared for. To varying extents, women had to adapt their way of life to the biological demands of impending motherhood. Childbirth itself was central to women's lives. Truly a rite of passage, it was a time for women alone. Although apparently shaped by patriarchal ideology, childbirth was an occasion for women to come together to form a support system, both for the labouring woman and for the continuity of female culture and social existence.

Once a woman became a mother her role had only just begun. For many, child rearing occupied most, or all, of the remaining years of their lives. How to discipline children was a recurring problem, especially in Puritan families, and Robert Schnucker's chapter shows that attitudes towards childhood discipline were relatively constant over time, and that discipline was primarily regarded as the prerogative of the father.

In a period when it was relatively common for children to lose one or both parents before reaching maturity, mothering by surrogates, such as wet nurses, parish nurses, and other caretakers, was an important feature of English society. Fiona Newall reconstructs some of the families in a rural parish to examine the socio-economic status of families who cared for other people's children, or whose own children were cared for by others. She demonstrates that women who mothered parish children were of lower status than women whom parents employed to care for their offspring; but she also shows that the view, based largely on French evidence, that foster mothering resulted in a high mortality of infants does not appear to be true for England. Valerie Fildes's chapter carries forward this theme by examining the children who were abandoned in London and Westminster and were cared for by foster mothers employed by parishes and institutions. Although frequently maligned, the evidence that a large proportion of nurses murdered or mistreated their infant charges is tenuous. Looking at abandonment from the woman's point of view, this chapter shows that mothers who were forced to resort to this act were not necessarily 'unnatural' or devoid of maternal feelings or love for their children.

Mary Prior's chapter uses the previously unexplored source of poems of conjugal love to show changes in women's view of marriage and family. She echoes a recurring theme in this volume, that patriarchal values shaped attitudes to marriage and motherhood. Yet women did not submit passively to male ideas of maternity. Being a mother was, and is, a continual process; ever changing and constantly developing; subject to influences from both family members and society. Each pregnancy, each birth, and each child was different, and needed to be handled as such within the accepted norms of society, regardless of the status of the women.

It is hoped that these essays will serve only as an introduction to how women faced and experienced their unique and central role as mothers in pre-industrial England. Much more remains to be discovered.

Valerie Fildes

1

The construction and experience of maternity in seventeenth-century England

Patricia Crawford

I

The continuance of human society has always depended upon woman's ability to give birth: an obvious point, but one frequently overlooked. Without woman's reproductive labour, society would cease to exist. Since reproduction is essential, all societies have an interest in controlling it. In no society known to us are women allowed to give birth however and whenever they choose. Because of women's potential maternal function, society has an interest in attempting to regulate female lives: that is, a woman's social existence is influenced by her maternal potential, irrespective of whether or not she actually gives birth. Motherhood is more than a social construct, however: it is part of woman's unique biological functioning.[1]

Despite the importance of motherhood for women and for human society, it attracted comparatively little interest from historians until recently. There could be many reasons for this, not least of which may be a separation between the 'private' world of women and children and the 'public' world of men. Historians saw the lives of women and children as of little historical importance or interest, and assumed that they changed relatively little over time. Of course there was always some interest in domestic life of the past, but more from amateur historians and the reading public. However, the development of social history in the twentieth century has brought the mass of the population more into view. Social historians writing of the family and childhood have focused attention upon women's roles as wives and mothers in the past. This scrutiny was not initially particularly favourable to mothers.

Ariès developed a thesis about the discovery of childhood in the early-modern period which has exercised a powerful influence on much subsequent writing. Childhood, he argued, was recognized as a separate life stage only in the early-modern period.[2] Lawrence Stone has condemned mothers along with fathers as unloving parents. 'Children were brutally treated, even killed', he wrote, and documented a horrendous picture of parental neglect in the early-modern period.[3] Only in the eighteenth century, argues Randolph Trumbach, were aristocratic women more interested in being mothers than wives.[4] The most recent studies of the early-modern family are more positive. Ralph Houlbrooke and Keith Wrightson present a happier picture of families in early-modern times, but they do not distinguish between mothers and fathers as parents.[5] Another issue recently debated is the maternal instinct: was it inherent in all women or the product of a particular historical period? 'Good mothering', according to Edward Shorter, 'is an invention of modernization.' He argued that in traditional societies mothers viewed the development and happiness of infants younger than 2 with indifference.[6] Elizabeth Badinter also concluded that the 'maternal instinct' was not a natural one, but rather a later development.[7] However, other scholars, such as Betty Travitsky and Brigitte Niestroj, date the focus on good mothering earlier, to the Renaissance period.[8]

Of more consequence than the development of social history for the history of motherhood has been the international women's movement of the 1960s and 1970s, which has raised questions about women's roles in society, the boundaries between the private and the public sphere, and about the low valuation placed on many aspects of women's lives. Feminists have drawn attention to the central importance of motherhood in their own societies, and have subjected it to various kinds of sociological and personal analysis.[9] The ideology of motherhood has been discussed in terms of capitalist oppression, which makes women seem the natural rearers as well as bearers of children.

The women's movement has affected the writing of history. Writers of women's history initially concentrated on recovering information about the lives of women in the past and making them visible. This celebratory phase of women's history was widely criticized. Lawrence Stone, in a 1985 review, pronounced Ten Commandments for women's history, the first of which was

'Thou shalt not write about women except in relation to men and children.'[10] This, he implied, was more honoured in the breach than in the observance. In his terms, writing about motherhood instead of parenthood appears to be the narrowest kind of women's history which leaves women in a vacuum. Furthermore, tracing the history of maternity could seem to be like maternity itself, something which only women do. Of fascinating interest to women, it would be of only limited interest to men. However, Stone's position caricatures the objectives and practices of women's history, and denies the essential claim of feminist history that women have had a separate historical experience. Just as men have a history as fathers, distinct from the history of parents, so maternity has a history separate from the history of the family.[11]

Over the last 20 years, women's history has developed, both in method and in scope. To focus upon women is a political redirection: woman ceases to be the object of male study, and becomes a subject.[12] This questions the primacy of men's experiences. The history of maternity, which comprises both childbirth and female-specific child rearing, rightly focuses primarily on women, and secondarily on men's observations and directives.[13] Whether a woman mothers within or outside a family, her experiences are affected by her society. A history of maternity directs attention to the significant aspects of society which influence the circumstances in which women conceive, give birth, and rear their children. Such an analysis raises questions about the relationship between gender and power: to what extent was an ideology of motherhood part of the means by which men attempted to keep women subordinate? 'Women's history', the process of making women the subjects of their own story, thus challenges existing accounts of motherhood written from the perspective of men. It invites us to re-examine the past and the histories which are made of it, as part of the longer-term goal of rewriting our histories and putting the 'private' experience of motherhood into the 'public' arena. However, the history of motherhood is not just about men's attempts to control women, for motherhood is also a unique female experience. It is the purpose of this chapter to show, first, how maternity was socially constructed in seventeenth-century English society and, second, how women themselves experienced maternity.

II

The biological experiences of maternity – parturition and lactation – were socially constructed in early-modern England, and child rearing was defined as likewise natural to women. The ways in which men developed an ideology of the good woman in seventeenth-century England are reasonably familiar, but some brief discussion is necessary here. Men had a great deal to say about motherhood, and their medical treatises, sermons, domestic advice books, and handbooks for justices are the major sources to be used for an account of the ideology of maternity.[14] While the focus of their attention was on motherhood, the underlying issue was female sexuality. Divines and medical practitioners all shared the same assumptions: women were the disorderly sex, and their sexuality was to be controlled so that they bore children only within marriage, and then only to their lawful husbands.[15]

Medical theories were increasingly published in English during the sixteenth and seventeenth centuries, so that people could understand the biological processes related to reproduction, or 'generation', as it was termed.[16] Treatises originally published in Latin thus became more generally accessible. Popular medical texts were reprinted, even into the twentieth century in the case of one work, *Aristotles Masterpiece.*[17] Most people derived their understanding of reproduction from a mixture of medical theories, and, during the seventeenth century, the gap between the theories of the educated élite and those of the general populace widened. An outline of the main theories shows how medical 'knowledge' gave a social meaning to the biological process, and distinguishes social implications of certain of these theories.

The onset of menstruation showed a women to be fertile and was thought to be necessary for conception. After the menarche, she developed seed in her blood and longed for sex because she wanted to be a mother. Frustrated of her desire, she might sicken and turn green. Men were convinced that women were biologically driven to sexual intercourse: women 'snatch the seed from them', said Lemnius in the sixteenth century, 'as hungry dogs do at a bone'.[18] They wanted to be mothers: 'Sterility or Barrenness hath in all Ages and Countries been esteemed a Reproach'.[19]

There were several theories about the process of conception. Earlier in the century one popular theory posited that a child was conceived from a mixture of both male and female seed emitted during intercourse. Accordingly, since female sexual pleasure was generally accounted necessary for conception, in the first half of the seventeenth century it followed that a husband wanting children would consider his wife's sexual pleasure. On the other hand the woman who pleaded rape would not succeed in her plea if she conceived, because she was deemed to have consented.[20] Lemnius's sixteenth-century treatise, translated into English in 1658, referred to another theory about conception which, he argued, had adverse consequences for maternal affection. 'Some Bawds', he said, try to persuade women that

> Mothers afford very little to the generation of the child, but onely are at the trouble to carry it, . . . as if the womb were hired by men, as Merchants Ships are to be straited by them; and to discharge their burden, . . . women grow luke-warm, and lose all humane affections towards their children.[21]

Some thought that the male seed organized matter in the female's womb, shaping a child. Later in the seventeenth century there was a major controversy over theories of pre-formation: either the child was already in the male sperm – and illustrations of what was seen under the microscope revealed tiny homunculi – or the foetus was contained within the female ovum which was like a box within a box from the time of Eve. The woman nourished the child in her womb with her blood, and gave to it her character. Her imagination was believed to shape the child's features, although deformities could be a punishment for parental sin. Printed bills advertising the exhibition of monstrous children frequently blamed the mother: for example, a child was born with 'ruffs' because its mother had followed the fashions in dress:

> And ye O England whose womankinde
> in ruffes do walke so oft
> Parsuade them stil to bere in minde,
> This childe with ruffes so soft.[22]

A mother had not finished her work when she delivered, but was urged to continue to transmit her qualities of character by suckling her baby herself.

Preachers taught their congregations that the ideal good woman was the good mother. The Bible was the basic authority in this, as in other areas of life. Concepts of motherhood were deeply embedded in the metaphorical discussion of Church and State. Thus, for example, the true Church was a mother, the false a whore.[23] More directly, Scripture said that the woman was saved by childbearing (1 Timothy, ch.2, v.5). A curse upon a woman made her barren. To prevent conception or procure an abortion was murder.[24] The pain of childbirth was both a consequence and a punishment for Eve's transgression.[25] Scripture said that the godly desired sons rather than daughters.[26] Divines advanced arguments from the Bible to prove that a mother ought to nurse her own child, and reinforced their case with practical observations. 'Commonly such children as are nursed by their mothers prosper best', observed Gouge. 'Mothers are most tender ouer them, and cannot indure to let them lie cry out, without taking them up and stilling them'.[27]

Protestantism has been said to enhance the status of women as wives and mothers. This was certainly an argument advanced by the reformers in an attempt to win and to hold converts. They recognized that for women there were losses in the new faith. Whereas the Catholic Church had allowed certain kinds of supernatural aid to women in childbirth, such as the loan of the girdle of a saint, the Protestant Church offered only prayer.[28] Protestants went further than some Catholic critics of the cult of the Virgin Mary: Peter Heylin, an Anglican divine, objected to the way in which Catholics pictured Mary in their churches: 'If they must needs have her in the estate of glory . . . or of honour . . . let them disburden her of her Child.'[29] Protestant theologians taught that a woman was created for maternity, and that in caring for her children she was serving the Lord.[30] Nevertheless, Protestant ministers continued to affirm, as had Catholic priests earlier, that in motherhood, as in all else, women should be subject to male authority. Indeed, as Lyndal Roper has shown in her analysis of Luther's teachings, the authority of a husband in the household was strengthened after the Reformation. Any woman whose sexual desires were not directed towards marriage and motherhood was labelled unnatural, and there was no longer a role for the confessor to define what was acceptable behaviour in the household.[31] In a case-study of one Protestant family, the Henrys in later seventeenth-century England, I have argued that maternity was valued less highly than certain religious activities, such as preaching and teaching the messages of salvation. A wife's care for her children, family, and worldly matters might even impede her own salvation.[32] Protestantism changed certain emphases in the Christian faith, but did not challenge the basic premiss that women were inferior, and therefore should be subject to men. In the long run male authority in the household was enhanced.

Although society was strongly pro-natalist, motherhood was approved only within marriage. Powerful disincentives discouraged maternity outside wedlock. The law defined such children as bastards and as incapable of inheritance. Justices of the Peace were directed to punish the parents with a whipping and confinement to the house of correction for a year.[33] Families also played a large part in the control of female sexuality, and those with most wealth controlled their daughters more strictly than those of lower social status. Daughters of the peers and gentry were more likely to be virgins at marriage. Those of wealthy yeomen, who could provide dowries, had good chances of marriage. As for the daughters of small husbandmen and labourers, historians have pointed out that a dowryless state and greater sexual licence were connected.[34] A girl who was pregnant was unlikely to be able to force her child's father to marry her without the backing of family and friends. Not all pregnant women who failed in their quest for marriage were treated alike. The level of prosecution of pre-nuptial pregnancy varied according to economic circumstances. Martin Ingram, in his study of Wiltshire in the years 1600–40, has shown that in the populous partly industrialized area the rate of presentment was 60–75 per cent. However, in the more sparsely populated uplands country, only about 7 per cent of the cases were presented, and this was more likely if the offenders were poor. Margaret Spufford has argued that this selective prosecution was not a new pattern, for from the thirteenth century, humble people were more likely to be fined for adultery and fornication.[35] The justices of the secular courts who administered the laws relating to bastardy were more concerned about the cost of maintenance of the illegitimate child than the sinfulness of the sexual activity, for if the child died, or the parents were able to maintain it, then the punishment was abated. A couple who married before a bastardy order was made or who produced a child within $7^{1}/_{2}$ months of marriage were to be punished for no more than incontinency.[36]

It was not sufficient for a woman to restrict her sexual activity to her years of matrimony: her only sexual partner was to be her husband. The law deemed all children born in wedlock to be legitimate, unless a husband could prove otherwise.[37] If a wife was sexually unfaithful, a husband had grounds for a separation, or even, so one divine early in the seventeenth century asserted, a divorce.[38] Scripture justified a harsh attitude to adultery, so in 1650 the Parliament attempted to bring the law of the land into harmony with the law of God by introducing the death penalty for adultery. By definition, adultery was a crime committed only by married women. (A married man who engaged in sexual activity with a woman other than his wife was guilty of fornication, which carried a lesser penalty.)[39] Although the death penalty was apparently rarely inflicted, wives who transgressed were strongly criticized. Class differences affected the double standard. Property and inheritance coloured men's attitudes, as an example from a parliamentary debate in 1656 illustrates. Members had no trouble in empathizing with Edward Scot, who petitioned for a divorce on the grounds of his wife's adultery. Even though they thought that Scot was mentally unstable, 'his wife ought not to abuse him'. 'It is fit the gentleman should be relieved, that bastards may not inherit his estate', said Sir Thomas Wroth. 'It is a sad case to have such a wife', continued Mr Robinson, 'and to have a posterity put upon him that is none of his own.'[40]

Keith Thomas has explored the reasons for the double standard of sexual morality in England.[41] Although he concluded that it was not entirely due to men's preoccupation with legitimate children, this was undoubtedly a factor. Furthermore, the double standard was part of the means by which men controlled women's sexuality. For a man of higher social status, extra-marital sex was condoned. There was rarely proof of his guilt. While the ratio of sexual activity to pregnancy was probably low, it was harder for the woman to evade the consequences of her sexual intercourse.[42] Puritan divines attempted to argue that men were as guilty as the women, but with little success. A man who got a maid with child remained a nine-day wonder, as an anonymous pamphleteer bitterly remarked, while the woman was harshly censured.[43]

The Anglican Church inherited rituals associated with childbirth from the Catholic Church. Protestants continued the Catholic ritual of the churching of women, but stressed that it was a thanksgiving service rather than a purification rite.[44] Baptism was far more significant. If the baby seemed likely to die at birth, the Catholic Church had allowed the midwife, who was licensed by the clergy, to administer baptism.[45] However, Protestant theologians were not agreed that baptism was absolutely necessary for the infant. Calvin argued that God had extended his promise to the seed of the faithful, so the unbaptized children would not be damned. Since 'Christ did not command women, or men of every sort, to baptise', baptism by women disrupted proper order in the Church, which was more critical than any fears about the fate of the newly born child.[46] However, the Anglican bishops were prepared to tolerate private baptism by women in cases of emergency, and the influential Bishop Richard Hooker wrote against the Anabaptist view that baptism by women was no more 'then any other ordinarie washinge or bathinge'. Although the matter remained controversial, midwives in England continued to baptize infants in emergencies.[47] The clergy also administered another rite, that of burial, which gave them the opportunity to enunciate society's ideals about good women. Many of their printed funeral sermons paid public tribute to ideals of motherhood: 'As A Mother! Care, Tenderness, and Providence'. High praise was given to the woman who was 'a tender hearted Mother to her children'.[48] Published lives of godly women usually attested to their careful education of their older children.[49]

The biological bond between a mother and her child was understood to be a natural bond. A mother should breastfeed her child herself because 'this is so naturall a thing that euen the beasts will not omit it', observed John Dod and Robert Cleaver in 1606.[50] Contemporaries also assumed that child rearing, a social process, was likewise biologically determined and natural to women: 'The Care and Education of Children, both with respect to their Bodies and Minds, is by Nature given all along to the Mother, in a much greater Proportion than to the Father.'[51] Men recounted anecdotes to reassure themselves about the infallible nature of the maternal instinct. Sir Hugh

Cholmley, for example, told how babies who were not their own were offered both to his mother and later to his wife: each time biology triumphed, and 'it was pretty and admirable to see how, by the instinct of nature, she had found out her own child'.[52] A mother who claimed that she could not love her children was diagnosed as insane.[53]

Contemporaries usually judged that a mother was responsible for the care of children under the age of 7. Even bastards were usually kept with their mothers until that age. The justices preferred not to send children to the house of correction with their mothers unless they were sucking, but in practice there was usually no choice.[54] However, the law authorized anyone to take vagrant children of about 4 or 5 years of age from their mothers, 'whether they be willing or not'. Once the child had been bound before the justices or certain witnesses, neither mother, father, nor nurse was allowed to steal the child back.[55] Sometimes a parish paid a mother to be a nurse to her own child rather than take the child into care.[56] Poorer children were to be kept with their parents until they were 7, but after that age they were to be put to learn some kind of service in a household.[57] If mothers had feelings about this, they were not recorded.

In the upper levels of society, maternal education for boys was confined to their earlier years. After about the age of 7, boys from the gentry were usually entrusted to the care of a schoolmaster or tutor. 'Leave the boys to the father's more peculiar care', the Marquis of Halifax advised his daughter, 'that you may with the greater justice pretend to a more immediate jurisdiction over those of your own sex.'[58] Although mothers were responsible for the education of daughters, they were subject to paternal authority. Even a radical social reformer during the Civil Wars, Gerrard Winstanley, accepted the need for patriarchal authority: if 'the father of a family be weak...wanting the power of wisdom and government', then children were not to be left to the authority of a mother but rather were to be put into others families to be instructed under fatherly authority.[59] In practice, a widow was usually appointed guardian to her children, or obtained their wardship, although certain kinds of behaviour could deprive her of control of her children. When the widow of his friend, the Duke of Buckingham, reverted to Roman Catholicism, Charles I took the children from her.[60]

12

While most images of motherhood in early-modern England were positive, others were ambiguous or negative. Some popular wisdom was contemptuous: 'None but fools were fit to beare children.'[61] Satirists mocked what they considered were exaggerated claims to respect for maternity:

And as for her Pain and Peril of Child-bearing, I do no more wonder at it, than at the laying of a great Eg, by a Hen, or a Goose, the ordinary effect of Nature, no more, notwithstanding all their Tittle-Tatle.[62]

Such satire reveals, indirectly, that the community did respect childbearing women.

A newer source of hostile comment on mothers came increasingly from medical practitioners. In their attempts to distance themselves from the unqualified, and to establish medicine as a profession, they tried to discredit women's traditional knowledge as midwives as foolish. The debate between the confident professional doctors and the midwives contributed to a devaluing of women's traditional skills.[63] Doctors also sought to replace women's authority in matters maternal with their own methods grounded in 'scientific' knowledge.

Hostility was also projected on to surrogate mothers, especially stepmothers. Maternal mortality rates were high, and many men, especially wealthier ones, married more than once.[64] The stepmother was much feared in early-modern society as it was believed that she would alienate a father's affections and prefer her own children. Fairy stories, such as Cinderella, depicted her in a threatening guise as a danger to the child's life and happiness. Other fairy tales conjured with maternal figures: some revealed fear of their power.[65]

To sum up, a powerful ideology of the good mother as caring for children under patriarchal direction existed in early-modern England. The gender division of labour was rigid on the issue of the rearing of children under 7: it was women's work, and it was their natural function. Men in turn were expected to exercise authority over their families, to support them financially, and to play a role in the education of older children.

III

Ideology shaped the context within which women became mothers in early-modern England, but women responded creatively to being mothers. This section focuses on some of the evidence about women's experiences of maternity, concentrating on the time from sexual intercourse to the earliest months of the child's life. Sources for a study from the female perspective are more than usually difficult, but although they are less numerous than those for male ideas about maternity, female records do survive. There are printed writings by women, and unpublished diaries and autobiographies.[66] Among the papers of wealthier families, there are women's letters and also some commonplace books. Only recently have social historians begun to explore these family archives for the rich material they contain about many aspects of personal life. Although the evidence about motherhood is biased towards the wealthy and the literate, information about women of lower social status is contained in the records of the secular and ecclesiastical courts.

Women's maternal experiences were varied. Wanted, unwanted, biological and social, their motherhood was mediated by their social level and influenced by their family situation, economic circumstances, and religious beliefs. We have no way of separating their attitudes to the biological from the social experience. Yet as the contemporary midwife Jane Sharp observed, women's desire for children was recognized as nearly universal: 'To conceive with child is the earnest desire if not of all yet of most women.'[67]

Although most married women would spend their time childbearing and rearing, the number of children they bore was affected by their social status and also by their attitude to wet nursing. At the upper levels of society, girls married at around 20 in the late sixteenth century, about 2 years later at the end of the seventeenth century. These women were less likely to be engaged in economic production, and consequently more emphasis was placed on their reproductive labour. Those who could afford to hire wet nurses bore more children than the rest of the population, although fewer infants may have survived. A woman in the middling or lower ranks of society, on the other hand, was more likely to marry in her mid-twenties. The mean age at marriage rose from 26 to 26.5 years later in the seventeenth century.[68] Vivien Brodsky Elliot found that in London, the daughters of wealthy tradesmen married at a mean age of 20 while migrant women married at around age 24.[69] Once married, a women would on average bear a child every couple of years, or, if she sent her child out to nurse, perhaps once a year. Ceasing to give birth around her early forties, she would remain responsible for children until she was in her later fifties. Should she live to be a grandmother, she would probably help her own daughters with their maternal responsibilities. From all this experience, many women gained knowledge about child rearing, but how this experience was evaluated by themselves and their society remains to be assessed.

About one-third of the population was poor. Contemporaries recognized that to be 'overcharged with many young children' was a cause of poverty, and that 'the poore do most of all multiply'.[70] A poor woman who married in her mid to late twenties may have enjoyed a relatively satisfactory time after the birth of her first child, but the arrival of a second and subsequent children could drag the whole family below the poverty line. In some cases, a wife's wage-earning capacity would be decreased by her pregnancies and child-care responsibilities, so that the family would depend increasingly on the wages of the husband; and if he disappeared or died, the mother and children would find themselves in a desperate situation.[71] Some women were able to turn their maternity to financial advantage, as they used their skills in nursing and child rearing to earn a wage.[72] Families in poverty were eligible for relief, but this varied from parish to parish, and as the numbers of those in poverty multiplied during the seventeenth century, the Poor Law was increasingly inadequate. Contemporary publications described the destitution of widows, and illustrated the temptations to which their poverty exposed them. Such was the unhappy story of Mary Goodenough, sentenced to death in 1692 for infanticide. She allowed a neighbour sexual favours in return for 'necessary maintenance' for herself and her two children. When her illegitimate baby was born, she did not struggle to preserve its life, and was found guilty of murder. 'It was for want of Bread she said', recorded a contemporary author, who castigated her neighbours for their lack of charity. 'If her Modesty made her asham'd to beg, did not her meagre Look, her starved Children, her meanly furnish'd House and Table beg from you?'[73] Compassion for maternity in this instance had failed to materialize. Increasing poverty at the end of the century was causing growing concern.

Women's experiences of motherhood take us into a female world. From the diaries and letters of literate women – most of whom had a servant to assist them – we can see how much time and energy women at the upper social levels devoted to their mothering. Autobiographies frequently reveal that their authors' adult lives were structured around the rhythms of their pregnancies, childbearing and child rearing.[74] While it is difficult to separate the tasks involved in child rearing from those of housekeeping, it is clear that women's days and nights were filled with attending to their children and their households. The letters and diaries of literate women reveal networks of support and advice. Surviving commonplace books contain, in addition to recipes for cookery and aids for beauty, remedies for specifically female conditions such as complications in pregnancy and lactation. Several women published advice on maternal matters for the benefit of their own sex. The Countess of Lincoln wrote a whole pamphlet urging women to breastfeed their own babies in 1622.[75] The first female almanack writer, Sarah Jinner, published advice on reproduction in 1659. She recommended two other works to her readers as 'modestly treating of generation', so that 'our Sex may be furnished with knowledge'.[76] Other female almanack writers followed her lead. The first midwife to publish advice for her own sex was Jane Sharp in 1671,[77] and in the following year another female author, Mary Trye, also promised help for female-specific disorders.[78] A number of printed bills survive in which female medical practitioners in London advertised their services, chiefly for the treatment of female disorders and childhood complaints.[79] These sources reveal women's desire to understand and consequently to control their reproductive experiences. Their attitudes were always affected by the social context, their own previous reproductive history, and their desire or fear of pregnancy. It was very difficult for women to break the nexus between sexuality and reproduction.[80] Sarah Jinner put it bluntly in her almanack for 1659: more women would embark on sexual activity at the time of a predicted eclipse 'were it not for fear of the rising of the Apron'.[81] 'Beware of the sollicitations of the flesh, for they will undo you', Hannah Wolley warned under cook-maids.[82]

Pregnancy in early-modern times was notoriously difficult to detect. Surviving evidence in medical casebooks and treatises indicates that women viewed the cessation of menstruation as the most usual sign. (A girl or woman who never menstruated would be deemed incapable of childbearing.) Frances Howard, for example, who consulted Simon Forman in 1597, 'supposes herself with child . . . she hath not had her course'.[83] 'My wife after the absence of her terms for seven weeks', wrote Samuel Pepys, 'gave me hopes of her being with child'.[84] Anne Steele, an unmarried woman, based her knowledge of her pregnancy on the evidence of other women. She told the justices in 1690 that 'she knowes her self to be now with child, & so she is told by divers women who have examined her condition'.[85]

Not all women welcomed the signs of pregnancy. Although Alan Macfarlane claims that 'Children born in wedlock were welcome', married women who had too many children already, or who feared for their lives in childbirth, may have viewed their pregnancies with a range of negative emotions.[86] Spinsters had special cause to fear pregnancy. They faced the risk of dismissal from employment, social disgrace, and even physical punishment. Many consequently sought a solution to their situation in marriage. From the number of pregnant brides – about one-third – historians have argued either that women needed to prove their fertility before men would marry them, or that their pregnancy precipitated an intended marriage.[87] Some examples of the latter survive in the quarter-sessions records: in 1651 Anne Barker was questioned by the justices in Exeter for her pre-marital pregnancy. She was a servant to John Reeve, who put her trundle bed at his bed's foot, where he used her 'constantly and familiarily every week'. When she, 'weepinge & cryinge', told him that she was quick with child by him, he 'puffinge & stamping, bid her be quiett, & content, & say nothinge, nor cry'. When her state could be concealed no longer, he agreed to marry her 'if her mother and brother would do something for her', but he concluded, 'it would bee the undoinge of him, but a makinge of her'.[88] Women with family and kin to support them had a better chance of forcing men to marry them. Similarly, in the religious sects, where, despite contemporary tales of sexual licence to the contrary, a strict personal morality was upheld, there are examples of the congregation exerting considerable persuasive force upon unwilling putative fathers, as the following account of a Baptist congregation at Bristol in 1679 illustrates. The congregation sent two women members of the church to a servant girl, Mary Smith, who was reported to be with child by her master, one Ship, a widower. Subsequently, when two brethren confronted the man, he did not deny his paternity but refused to marry her. Mary answered the summons to attend 'with great shame and weeping, and covering her face', and was excommunicated. After disciplining her, the congregation returned their attention to Ship. One of the elders went again with a pastor, confronted him while he was at his plough, accompanied him into his house, and argued with him over Scriptural texts. He was finally brought to consent to marriage.[89]

There are contemporary records of women who failed in their quest for legal matrimony.[90] 'Oh Susan, what shall I doe?' was the response of a blacksmith to his lover's declaration of her pregnancy. 'Tradinge is soe bad I cannot live heere.' Susan Draper came before the justices in Exeter as a bastard bearer in 1652.[91] From similar records it is clear that single women and widows sometimes considered abortion, and presumably some successfully avoided maternity by this means.[92] If a woman did give birth to an illegitimate or unwanted child, she might abandon it as a foundling. By the seventeenth century, this carried less danger of detection in towns than in the country. Infanticide was the unhappy solution adopted by some women, for which the penalty, if they were convicted, was death. Malcolmson's fascinating study of eighteenth-century infanticide shows how women concealed their pregnancies, gave birth secretly and silently, and finally disposed of their babies.[93] Sexual misconduct could weaken a woman's chances of legitimate marriage. In the 1650s, one man's defence against a charge of paternity was to attack the woman's sexual morality: she was a women of ill fame with three bastards living.[94] Yet a few unmarried mothers were so undeterred by all the negative social pressure against illegitimacy that they continued to bear children without matrimony, as we can see from one woman's account to the justices in 1599. Joan Grobbyn said that she was lately delivered of her third bastard child,

> begotten upon her as she affirms and confesses by one Thomas Wyatt, late servant to John Vaucher of Salisbury. She says that one Battyn, a joiner, deceased, is the father

of the first child, a son yet living, and that she does not remember the father of the first child, a daughter, because he was a stranger to her.[95]

When a couple was childless, this was usually considered to be the wife's 'fault'. A childless woman was labelled a barren woman, and many echoed the cry of Rachel in the Old Testament: give me children, or else I die (Genesis 30.1). Barren wives lacked social status and respect, and the higher their social position, the unhappier was their lot. Catherine of Braganza, the wife of Charles II, failed to bear an heir: a contemporary observed that 'as the whole happiness of her life was centred on this single blessing, ... she had recourse to all the fashionable specifics against barrenness'.[96] Katherine Villiers, who was already a mother, wrote to her husband in the 1620s of her disappointment at failing to become pregnant: 'I woold I had bine so hapy.'[97] Elizabeth Walker recounted that her parents were in despair when they had no child after 5 years of marriage.[98] The diary of one young woman, Sarah Savage, is a poignant record of her prayers to the Lord about 'a Particular matter'. Married in 1687 to a widower with a child, for 2 years she recorded in her diary her longing to be 'a fruitfull vine' if the Lord saw good. She experienced an upsurge of hopes every 4 or 5 weeks, followed by a bitter struggle to reconcile herself to disappointment.[99]

There was a female lore on matters related to pregnancy and birth, starting with advice about conception. Commonplace books contain suggested cures for childlessness. In Johanne St John's book of 1680 one remedy for barrenness came with a strong recommendation: 'Mrs Patrick conceived twice with it & she advised it to one that had been 9 years marryd on whom it had the same effect.'[100] Pepys talked with a group of women after a dinner in July 1664 about 'my not getting of children' and they merrily gave him ten points of advice, some of which they stressed seriously, especially the instruction that the couple should lie in bed with the head lower than the feet.[101]

Gentlewomen knew that they were expected to bear sons to inherit name, title, and estates. A daughter, however, was at least a sign that the couple was fertile: 'this child, though a daughter, was very welcome both to her and her husband, because it gave them hope of further issue'.[102] 'Although it be a girle that God hath sent', wrote Thomas Chichely to his daughter on the birth of her child in 1671, 'yet it is a very great blessing. I remember a saying of yor Grandfather Russell who said in time it would [turn?] to a boy.'[103] Wives were expected to continue childbearing until they produced sons. Mary Henry would have been glad to bear a son, after three daughters, her husband told his father.[104] Nor, in the families of the gentry, was one son enough. The Earl of Rutland congratulated Bulstrode Whitelocke on the birth of his first son and jocularly suggested that his wife should not be afraid to have more.[105] A few women's letters of apology and excuse announcing the birth of daughters survive. Lady Hatton, mother to a daughter in 1678, told her husband that she would gladly have laid down her life to procure him a son.[106] Among themselves, women discussed the means of determining the sex of their children. Sarah Jinner's almanack recommended Lemnius's work, *The Secret Miracles of Nature*, to her readers as 'modestly treating of generation . . . and by Art, to get a Boy or Girl, which they desire most'.[107]

To bear no child at all was unfortunate, but to bear too many children could also be so, and some women wanted to limit their family size. In 1672, after 12 years of pregnancies, miscarriages, and childbirth, Elizabeth Turner recorded in her diary her fear that she was 'breeding' again, 'which was matter of great trouble & disquiet to me'.[108] Methods of family limitation were restricted, and little contraception was under exclusive female control. Abstinence from sexual activity was condemned by the clergy, who taught that couples owed each other 'due benevolence', and by medical advisers, who argued that it was bad for health.[109] Women exchanged suggestions about reducing male sexual drive. Mary Holden prescribed a diet in her almanack book that will 'make a man no better than an eunuch'.[110] They attempted to control their own fertility by the use of pessaries and to procure abortions by various means, such as decoctions of herbs. Abortion and infanticide, despite all their attendant risks to reputation, health, and life, were at least methods under women's control.[111] Further, it has been argued by McLaren and Fildes that women were aware of the contraceptive effect of prolonged lactation, and certainly there is evidence to support this hypothesis towards the end of the seventeenth century.[112] Earlier in the century, since advice books urged men to refrain from intercourse with their breastfeeding wives, it may not have been so obvious that lactation rather than abstinence limited conceptions.[113] Under male control was the technique of withdrawal, a sin in Onan, and, so the clergy taught, a sin in all other men.[114] Gossiping together at a poor woman's lying-in, two ladies were not sure whether the husband who gave his wife too many children or none at all was the better, but did not consider the company convenient for sharing their joking.[115]

There was a female lore about ante-natal care. Women discussed the effects of their own longings and imagination upon their unborn babies. Alice Thornton attributed her son's birthmark to a fright which she had had during pregnancy.[116] The role of Providence as a direct agent in human affairs caused profound anxiety to some women. When Elizabeth Turner miscarried in October 1662, she wrote 'I know not what ocationed But am jealous least it may be a punishment of some particular sin.'[117]

Childbirth was the female rite of passage *par excellence*. The midwife played an important role. On her knowledge and skill other women depended.[118] The midwife's loyalty was divided, however, for she was sworn to threaten the refusal of her services if the name of the father of an illegitimate child was not divulged. Midwives could also be witnesses against a mother if they were called on to testify in cases of infanticide as to whether a child was born alive or dead.[119] There are many examples of a woman choosing her midwife and of anxiety when she gave birth without her. Sometimes a woman let her midwife go to attend another woman in labour. Elizabeth Cholmley was so charitable that she allowed the midwife who had been with her for 10 years to go to another woman with whom she should have been, despite the opposition of her husband.[120] Women appreciated a midwife's services: in 1584 Jane Magham of Hull, a widow, bequeathed four sheep to her midwife in her will.[121] In addition, female relatives helped each other. Diaries show that many mothers, such as Elizabeth Joceline and Sarah Savage, travelled to be with their daughters at their lyings-in,[122] and sometimes women of higher social status than the woman giving birth would also attend.[123] Up to the mid-seventeenth century, the presence of any man at a childbirth was unusual. Women's modesty required all female attendants. More than one midwife would be summoned if the case were difficult.[124] Male physicians would attend only in the last resort, which, as Adrian Wilson argues, militated against their giving effective help.

Caesarian sections were usually fatal to the mother. After the Chamberlens discovered the use of the obstetric forceps, although this was kept as a family secret, women found that babies could be delivered in difficult cases and that their own lives could be saved. Consequently, they were more willing to summon medical aid. Wilson argues that this advance led women to change their attitudes to male participation in the management of childbirth during the seventeenth century.[125] However, it is important to remember that there was a strong body of female opinion in favour of female attendants. Notions of modesty were inculcated from an early age, so that dislike of 'groaping doctors' remained.[126] Besides, physicians were either too expensive or too far away for the majority of women.

Many women approached childbirth with fear. The words of the preachers, that women should expect and prepare for death, were not encouraging. A few women were not optimistic. Katherine Stubbes told her husband, neighbours, and friends that her forthcoming child 'woulde bee her death', and another gentlewoman, Elizabeth Joceline, secretly bought a new winding sheet.[127] Although Schofield has argued that, in fact, maternal mortality rates were not very high, a 6 to 7 per cent risk of dying in childbed, no pregnant woman could be sure that she would be among the fortunate survivors. Besides, attendance at the childbeds of other women where horror stories were exchanged was, as Sara Mendelson has shown, a means of equitably distributing one woman's terror to her female acquaintance.[128] The sources of help were charms, talismens, prayer, and the aid of medical practitioners. Anne, Viscountess Conway reckoned that she conceived on 12 May 1658. She secured the services of a midwife and a nurse, and borrowed an eagle stone, 'esteemed of great virtue in hard labour' which she wore on her arm for a while. Labours lasted for varying lengths of time and outcomes. Women secured the services of trusted midwives and prayed for a safe delivery, but it could all be to no avail. Anne Hulton, pregnant herself, saw her friend die in childbirth: 'it did much affect me with cares and thoughts about another world, which had been too little minded by me'.[129] Elizabeth Walker's eighth child was a stillborn son, after which she suffered depression for 3 months.[130] Nor were women's worries for themselves alone. Elizabeth Turner was relieved when her child was born 'not onely free from deformity but a goodly lovely Babe'.[131] She, like some other gentlewomen, noted all her children's births in her diary.[132]

After the pains of childbirth, mothers suffered grief if their babes died. The infant mortality rate was high in the first year of life, and the first 36 hours were the most dangerous.[133] Although historians have repeatedly quoted Montaigne to demonstrate that parents were indifferent to the loss of their children in infancy, there is much evidence to contradict this impression of parental callousness.[134] In particular, there are many examples of women suffering deep grief at the death of their babies. Anne Hulton gave birth to her first child on 29 July 1695, 'A day never to be forgotten; wherein I felt the bitter fruits of the sin of my grandmother Eve'. Near to death herself, she survived but her child did not. 'O Adam, Adam! what hast thou done! My comforts are taken away before I had well received them: was it all lost labour?' She consoled herself with the hope 'that Heaven is something fuller for my babe.'[135] The widespread recognition of a mother's grief for the death of her child was poignantly attested to by Mary Cary's description of her view of an ideal society in 1651, the first item in which was that 'No infant of days shall die while they are young . . . . They shall not be afflicted for the loss of their children.[136] As Mendelson has pointed out in her study of Mary Rich, contemporaries had no trouble in believing that parents suffered such deep grief at the deaths of their children that they could die themselves.[137]

A mother knew that her baby's survival depended upon success in feeding. Infant feeding has recently received detailed historical attention in the work of Dorothy McLaren and Valerie Fildes, but here some brief comments on women's experiences are needed.[138] We know that many mothers were anxious about their ability to nurse their own infants. A gentlewoman, Elizabeth Turner, who had 'apprehended much difficulty by reason of the weakness of my head & little milke', thanked God that her child was content.[139] Wealthier women's correspondence contains details about the feeding of their children. In 1678 Alice Hatton wrote to her brother 3 days after her sister-in-law had given birth to a daughter:

> her breasts very well a gret deall of Milke & like to be a very good Nurs . . . she is mightely pleased att being a nurse but ye Child dos not like sucking so well as feeding wth a

spoone . . . my poore sister is conserned ye child will not
suck she has sent for a pupy dog to draw her breast.[140]

The crucial point was that the child was healthy, as Abigail
Harley told her husband in 1669: the nurse was not well but 'my
bedfellow thrives amaine as he may well do, for he grows a
terrible sucker by night'. In some wealthier families, a wet nurse
was employed, as also for those who were unable to feed their
own babies. 'I understand thy breasts still payne thee', wrote Sir
Thomas Baskerville to his wife in the 1590s. 'I pray therefor lett
som french nurse feed thy son.'[141] Fildes argues that the practice
of wet nursing was increasing during the later seventeenth and
early eighteenth centuries. The wet nurses were from the lower
levels of society, but not the very poorest.[142] Unlike the
elaborate instructions which medical writers offered about the
selection of wet nurses, women gave each other practical advice
about the choice of a nurse, and valued women who were kind
to their charges.[143] A wet nurse reassured Sir Symonds D'Ewes
and his wife that 'I thank God, haue my helth and am wel and
haue good store of milke'.[144] Some wealthier women also had
compassion for the wet nurse and her child. The Countess of
Lincoln urged mothers to breastfeed: 'bee not accessary to that
disorder of causing a *poorer woman to banish her owne infant,* for
the entertaining of *a richer womans child*'.[145] However, in practice
wet nurses probably did not banish their own babies, for some
became wet nurses after their own infants were weaned. In one
case, correspondence revealed that the wet nurse had her child
at home with her until it broke out in a rash. The nurse sent it
to quarantine with her own mother, so it would not infect her
nursling.[146]

Practical advice about weaning was exchanged among
women. Mothers were counselled to take account of factors
such as the health and age of the child, the weather, and the
cycle of the moon. Such advice could be conveyed with
scepticism: 'when you wean him let it bee in ye old of ye Moon',
wrote Sarah Savage to her daughter Hannah in the early
eighteenth century, 'when ye memory is more weak – which old
Mrs Starky adviz'd – & I thot there was someth[ing] in it – tho'
others are otherwise minded'.[147]

Although religion was important in providing a framework of
meaning for many women's sorrows in maternity, there were
mixed reactions to the involvement of the Anglican clergy in the

rituals associated with childbirth. Katherine Chidley claimed that even if a baby was born dead, priests wanted money for reading a dirge over it. She also objected to the practice of churching 'before the mother dare goe abroade . . . that the Sun shall not smite her by day, nor the Moone by night'. Church court records indicate that she was not alone in her dislike of the ceremony: in Essex in 1598 one woman said that churching was 'like unto of a sow with pigs following her or like to a bitch that went to salt'.[148] Probably the majority of women submitted without protest.[149] Women also had views about baptism, and some participated in the controversies on the subject. The Baptists maintained that only believers, which meant those of years and understanding, could be baptized. However, in a few sectarian congregations, a child consecration ceremony was developed in response, it seems, to maternal demand. A hostile pamphleteer described how, in a congregation of Independents and Baptists in the 1650s, a woman was troubled that her unbaptized children were no better than heathen. Consequently, around 1651, Thomas Ewins, the teacher of the congregation, devised a special service for the mother who 'desired that her Children might also be presented to the Lord by Prayer'. Ewins thought that 'any godly Woman, a Member of a Congregation' should attend church both to give thanks on her own behalf and to present her child to the Lord. The name could be entered into the congregation's book of names.[150] In more secular contexts, the naming of the child might be a family matter, in which mothers would be involved to various degrees.

Surrogate motherhood of various kinds was common in early-modern England. Those who found themselves stepmothers did not have an easy time. Since they had no biological link with their stepchildren, it was assumed that they would have no love for them. Families gloomily predicted that if children were motherless, they would have a stepmother 'who in all probability wil less befriend them'.[151] In practice, despite the general belief that stepmothers were ill-disposed to their stepchildren, women's experiences varied. A few women have left records of their conscientious attempts to mother their stepchildren, but not all were happy. Elizabeth Turner's relationship with her stepdaughter Betty deteriorated over the years. The girl, who was in 1668 'a goad in my side and pricks in mine eyes', became increasingly spiteful and envious in her stepmother's view. In 1674 the Turners became step-parents to two orphaned nieces and a nephew, which 'great charge' she said was a burden in their declining years. Two years later Betty married, and Elizabeth recorded her prayers for the girl's happiness 'notwithstanding her continued hatred & mallignant endeavour towards mee & mine'.[152] Other stepmothers were happier: Lady Gorges's stepchildren 'pay'd her the same duty as iff she had been there own mother', said Lady Elizabeth Delaval.[153] In 1659 Mary Rich, Countess of Warwick, promised to care for her husband's three nieces 'as if thy had been my own', and she urged her husband, 'even during the life of her son', to make noble provision for the girls.[154] A poem by Bathsua Makin of 1664 mourned the death of Lady Elizabeth Langham and praised her surrogate motherhood:

A mother; though not hers, nor partial
She loved, as if they had been natural.[155]

Wet nurses were also surrogate mothers with varying relationships with their charges. Although there were economic rewards – the pay was better than for some other female occupations, and it was work which was possible for mothers who were not especially poor – there were also pleasures in caring for the children. Some nurses were deeply attached to the babies and retained a life-long interest in their welfare.[156] The role of mother-in-law (confusingly, often referred to as a 'step-parent') was not one in which women seemed as comfortable as that of mother. There were conflicts of theory: a child's marriage partner was to be loved as one's own, yet women had been taught that only for those children they had borne would they experience natural love.[157] Grandmother was a happier role, and one for which some women longed. The daughter of Margaret, Countess Dowager of Cumberland, was for some time without a child after marriage, but finally Lady Margaret 'had the happiness which she had so often and generally prayed for, which was to see herself first of all a grandmother'.[158] Lady Anne Clifford, in her turn, rejoiced in her numerous grandchildren.[159] Women enjoyed sharing in the care of their grandchildren, and wrote with pleasure of their grandchildren's activities.[160] Indeed, it was in old age, especially as grandmothers, that wealthier women enjoyed most social respect. Thus, for example, correspondence around 1630 addressed to Lady Joan Barrington, widow of the godly and widely respected Member of Parliament, Sir Thomas Barrington, attests to her powerful position in her family and wider society.[161]

The sorrows, problems, and joys of maternity were all subjects about which women wrote, as can be seen from the correspondence in one godly Nonconformist household. The 'tediousness of nursing we owe to sin', reflected one. Maternity was a selfless occupation: it offered more to others than to the woman herself, but religion provided comfort: we are raising children for God. They listed among the mercies that their families had received, the preservation of their children 'from the perils of infancie'.[162] And as their children grew older, mothers were concerned with the education of their children as well as their physical survival. Successful child rearing here depended upon adaptation to the child's temperament as well as to its age and sex. Although this theme is beyond the scope of this chapter, the relationships of mothers with their eldest sons were often different from those with other sons, and their bonds with their daughters differed again.

IV

The daily tasks of maternity were recognized as women's business: among themselves, they exchanged information and advice. None of their experience was particularly relevant to men's daily activities. Not surprisingly, men knew little about maternal knowledge, and they were inclined to dismiss women's talk as 'gossip'. Nor did children necessarily esteem their mothers. Paternal authority overshadowed them. The general tenor of public comment was that because mothers were gentle and loving, so fathers were the more respected as the children grew up. Of the two parents, Gouge observed, 'the mother is lesse regarded'. His explanation was in terms of greater maternal tenderness for her children: 'familiarity breedeth contempt'.[163] Doubtless, children were sensitive to their fathers' greater authority in both the family and the outside world.

Yet if patriarchal authority was the more highly esteemed, this does not mean that contemporaries devalued motherhood in daily life. Men recognized that there was a female culture about pregnancy, birth, and the successful rearing of infants. It was not a culture from which men were excluded: husbands and fathers often shared the news of women's maternal experiences, and supported women in their parenting. Furthermore, as we have seen, men acknowledged maternal influence and appealed to it in matters of favour and patronage: 'Pray dear Niece use all yr power & interest as a Mother to perswade him to grant my request', wrote one seeker of her son's parliamentary interest.[164] As for mothers themselves, they placed a high valuation on their role. For them, the family was the world, they measured their life stages in terms of its rhythms, and it was a space that they made their own. Their letters reveal that their children gave them great joy and pleasure as well as grief. They wrote of the amusing sayings of their offspring: 'the little ones say their father is gone to buy some babies for them'.[165]

Women's publications and private writings show that they valued their maternal experiences highly. In 1610, the gentlewoman Elizabeth Grymeston prefaced her publication of her prayers and meditations for her son with a powerful statement:

> My dearest sonne, there is nothing so strong as the force of loue; there is no loue so forcible as the loue of an affectionate mother to her naturall childe: there is no mother can eyther more affectionely shew her nature, or more naturally manifest her affection, than in aduising her children out of her own experience.[166]

Despite the social code of silence and self-effacement, the strength of her maternal feeling allowed Elizabeth Grymeston to retain the status of a good woman while acting in a radical way by publishing her work. As another author of maternal advice, Dorothy Leigh, declared, 'motherly affection' overrode all fears of censure. A mother's love was beyond the bounds of reason. To save her children's souls, 'will not a Mother venture to offend the world'.[167] Women wrote autobiographies, diaries, and family histories for the sake of their children, or so they claimed. Rachel, Countess of Westmorland, bequeathed her instructions for a good life to her children in a manuscript book: 'tho I know myself so unfitt to apeare among so maney wise & Larned parsons yett I am unwilling my Children should think I negleckted eather prayers or advise to make them both happey here or here after'.[168] Although this evidence comes from literate women from the upper social levels, other women, less socially exalted, later in the century showed that they too valued their maternity. Women thanked God for their children, said one of the middling sort, Hannah Wolley.[169] Elizabeth Walker, a minister's wife, 'considered children as the nursery of Families, the Church and Nation'.[170]

Maternity was a unique experience from which women claimed authority. As the Quaker Rebecca Travers testified, 'none but a tender Mother can tell what it is to have Hopeful Children so soon taken from them'.[171] Perhaps she was right, for subsequently historians have found it hard to recognize women's grief at the deaths of their children. Because they were charged with the daily care of their children, and the running of the household, women developed practical knowledge of children's behaviour. Personal experience was the basis for female authority on the matters maternal. 'If it were mine', was the refrain in one woman's letters to her sister-in-law, she would not wean the child, but she would change the nurse, having found a brown ruddy complexioned nurse the best.[172] Maternity gave women knowledge. As Quaker women declaimed, 'we which have been Mothers of Children and Antient Women in Our Families, do know in the Wisdom of God, what will do in Families'.[173] Maternal authority could be used beyond the household to justify intervention in the wider world.

Thus, although patriarchal ideology shaped the changing social context in which women gave birth and cared for their children, biological and social motherhood offered women an important personal and social role. Creating life, women valued themselves and many found in their maternity their most rewarding human experiences.

Acknowledgements

I wish to thank my friends for references and comments, especially Sara Mendelson, Mary Prior, Lyndal Roper, and the editor, Valerie Fildes.

Notes

1. A. Rich, *Of Woman Born. Motherhood as Experience and Institution* (London, 1977); P. L. Berger and T. Luckmann, *The Social Construction of Reality. A Treatise in the Sociology of Knowledge* (London, 1967).

2. P. Ariès, *Centuries of Childhood* (Harmondsworth, 1962).

3. L. Stone, *The Family, Sex and Marriage in England, 1500–1800* (London, 1977).

4. R. Trumbach, *The Rise of the Egalitarian Family: Aristocratic Kinship and Domestic Relations in Eighteenth-century England* (New York, 1978), 3–4.

5. R. A. Houlbrooke, *The English Family 1450–1700* (London, 1984); Keith Wrightson, *English Society, 1580–1680* (London, 1982), 89–118; A. Macfarlane, *Marriage and Love in England. Modes of Reproduction 1300–1840* (Oxford, 1986), does not usually distinguish between mothers and fathers as parents either.

6. E. Shorter, *The Making of the Modern Family* (London, 1976), 168.

7. E. Badinter, *The Myth of Motherhood: An Historical View of the Maternal Instinct* (London, 1981).

8. B. S. Travitsky, 'The new mother of the English Renaissance: her writings on motherhood', in C. N. Davidson and E. M. Broner (eds), *The Lost Tradition. Mothers and Daughters in Literature* (New York, 1980), 33–43; B. H. E. Niestroj, 'Modern individuality and the social isolation of mother and child', *Compar. Civil. Rev.*, 15 (1987), 21–40.

9. For example, B. Friedan, *The Feminine Mystique* (New York, 1963); N. Friday, *My Mother/My Self. The Daughter's Search for Identity* (New York, 1977).

10. L. Stone, 'Only Women', *New York Rev. Books*, 11 April 1985, 21.

11. G. Lerner, 'Review essay: Motherhood in historical perspective', *J. Fam. Hist.*, 3 (1978), 297–301.

12. See, for example, J. W. Scott, 'Gender: a useful category of historical analysis', *Am. Hist. Rev.*, 91 (1986), 1053–75.

13. Rich, *Of Woman Born*.

14. See also M. Laget, 'Childbirth in seventeenth- and eighteenth-century France: obstetrical practices and collective attitudes', in R. Forster and O. Ranum (eds) *Medicine and Society in France. Selections from the Annales, Economies, Sociétiés, Civilisations* (Baltimore, 1980), 137–9.

15. N. Z. Davis, 'Women on top', in her *Society and Culture in Early Modern France* (Stanford, 1975).

16. This paragraph is based upon I. Maclean, *The Renaissance Notion of Woman* (Cambridge, 1980); A. McLaren, *Reproductive Rituals. The Perception of Fertility in England from the Sixteenth Century to the Nineteenth Century* (London, 1984); A. Eccles, *Obstetrics and Gynaecology in Tudor and Stuart England* (London, 1982); P. Crawford, 'Attitudes to menstruation in seventeenth-century England', *P & P*, 91 (1981), 47–73.

17. J. Blackman, 'Popular theories of generation: the evolution of *Aristotle's Works*. The Study of an Anachronism', in J. Woodward and D. Richards (eds) *Health Care and Popular Medicine in Nineteenth Century England: Essays in the Social History of Medicine* (London, 1977), 56–88.

18. L. Lemnius, *The Secret Miracles of Nature* (London, 1658), 23. See also N. Fontanus, *The Womans Doctour* (London, 1652), 134, 193, for women's desire for men's seed.

19. J. P., *The Fruitful Wonder: or, a Strange Relation from Kingston upon Thames* (1674), 1.

20. M. Dalton, *The Country Justice* (London, 1655), 351. In the next century, R. Burn, *The Justice of the Peace and the Parish Officer* (2 vols, London 1755), 315–16, questioned Dalton's argument about conception.

21. Lemnius, *Secret Miracles of Nature*, 9–10.

22. BL, Huth Collection 50, esp. 34, *The True Description of a Childe with Ruffes*, 1566.

23. For example, S. Marshall, *The Strong Helper...A Sermon Before the Honorable House of Commons* (London, 1645), 30: 'it is their Mother, in whose womb they have laine, whose breasts they have sucked'. W. Charke, *An Answer to...a Iesuite* (London, 1579), sig. B8.

24. W. Whately, *Prototypes, or, the Primarie Precedent Presidents out of Genesis* (London, 1640), 2; W. Whately, *A Care-cloth: or a Treatise of the Numbers and Troubles of Marriage* (London, 1624). 52; G. Mackenzie, *The Laws and Customs of Scotland* (Edinburgh, 1678), 156.

25. T. Bentley, *The Monument of Matrones* (London, 1582), vol. 3, 95.

26. C. Hooke, *The Child-birth or Womans Lecture* (London, 1590), n.p.

27. W. Gouge, *Of Domesticall Duties* (London, 1622), 512–13. See also P. Crawford, '"The sucking child": adult attitudes to child care in the first year of life in seventeenth-century England', *Cont. & Change*, 1 (1986), 23–51.

28. *Letters and Papers, Foreign and Domestic, of the Reign of Henry VIII*, vol. 10, Visitation of monasteries. Among the items lent to pregnant women were listed the girdles of St Bernard, of St Mary and St Alred (p. 139), a finger of St Stephen (p. 140) and a ring of St Ethelred (p. 143).

29. Erasmus criticized the excessive respect paid to the Virgin; P. N. Brooks, 'A lily ungilded? Martin Luther, the Virgin Mary and the Saints', *J. Relig. Hist.*, 13 (1986), 137; [P. Heylin], *A Voyage of France* (London, 1673), 29.

30. See esp., Gouge, *Domesticall Duties*, 282–94. Other examples include W. Perkins, *Christian Oeconomie* (London, 1609), 134–5; H. Newcome, *The Compleat Mother* (London, 1695).

31. L. Roper, 'Luther: sex, marriage and motherhood', *Hist. Today*, 33 (1983), 33–8. For a fascinating discussion of the impact of the Reformation on Catholic theology of motherhood, see C. W. Atkinson, '"Your Servant, My Mother": the figure of Saint Monica in the ideology of Christian motherhood', in C. W. Atkinson, C. M.

Buchanan, and M. R. Miles (eds), *Immaculate and Powerful. The Female in Sacred Image and Social Reality* (Boston, Mass., 1985), 152–8.

32. P. Crawford, 'Katharine and Philip Henry and their children: a case study in family ideology', *Trans. Hist. Soc. Lancs Chesh.*, 134 (1984), 39–73.

33. Dalton, *The Country Justice*, 40–2; R. Kilburne, *Choice Presidents...Relating to the Office and Duty of a Justice of the Peace* (London, 1685), 45–6.

34. M. Spufford, 'Puritanism and social control?', in A. F. and J. Stevenson (eds), *Order and Disorder in Early Modern England* (Cambridge, 1985), 48.

35. M. J. Ingram, 'Ecclesiastical justice in Wiltshire, 1600–1640, with special reference to cases concerning sex and marriage' unpublished D. Phil. thesis, University of Oxford, 196, ch. 6; Spufford 'Puritanism and social control?', 42.

36. W. Shepherd, *The Whole Office of the Country Justice of Peace* (London, 1650), 65; Bod., MS Eng Misc e 479, Manuscript notes in H. Townshend, *The Compleat Justice* (London, 1661), 48, indicate that a bastard child of parents able to keep it and not be a charge to the parish was outside the statute 18 Eliz. 2.

37. W. Shepherd, *An Epitome of all the Common and Statute Laws of this Nation Now in Force* (London, 1656), 180.

38. W. Whately, *A Bride-bush* (London, 1619). He recanted his views publicly in 1624.

39. K. Thomas, 'The Puritans and adultery: the Act of 1650 reconsidered', in D. Pennington and K. Thomas (eds), *Puritans and Revolutionaries. Essays in Seventeenth-century History Presented to Christopher Hill* (Oxford, 1978), 257–82, esp. 261.

40. J. T. Rutt (ed.), *Diary of Thomas Burton, Member in the Parliaments of Oliver and Richard Cromwell* (4 vols, London, 1828), vol. 1, pp. 204–6.

41. K. Thomas, 'The double standard', *J. Hist. Ideas*, 20 (1961), 195–216.

42. Ingram, 'Ecclesiastical justice in Wiltshire', 229–38.

43. M. Tattlewell and J. Hit-him-Home, *The Womens Sharpe Revenge* (London, 1640), 88, 120, 133–4.

44. K. Thomas, *Religion and the Decline of Magic. Studies in Popular Beliefs in Sixteenth and Seventeenth Century England* (London, 1971), 38–9, 59–61.

45. J. Donnison, *Midwives and Medical Men. A History of Inter-professional Rivalries and Women's Rights* (New York, 1977), 5–8.

46. J. Calvin, *Institutes of Christian Religion*, Book 4, ch. 15, sections 20–22, (Philadelphia, 1980), vol. 21, ed. J. T. McNeill, 1320–3.

47. W. S. Hill (ed.) *The Folger Library Edition of The Works of Richard Hooker*, vol. 2, *Of the Laws of Ecclesiastical Polity* (Cambridge, Mass., 1977), Book 5, ch. 62.1 (vol. 2, 268–89); Thomas, *Religion and the Decline of Magic*, 55–6.

48. O. Stockton, *Consolation in Life and Death...A Funeral Sermon...of Mrs Ellen Asty* (London, 1681), 3; E. Barker, *A Sermon*

Preached at the Funeral of . . . Lady Elizabeth Capel (London, 1661), 32; also *Two Sermons Preached at the Funerals of Mrs Elizabeth Montfort and of Dr Thomas Montfort Respectively* (London?, 1632).

49. S. Clark, *The Lives of Sundry Eminent Persons* (London, 1683); see Katherine Clark, Elizabeth Wilkinson.

50. J. Dod and R. Cleaver, *A Plaine and Familiar Exposition of the Ten Commandments* (London, 1606), 196.

51. *Considerations upon the Institution of Marriage* (London, 1739), 6.

52. *The Memoirs of Sir Hugh Cholmley* (London, 1787), iii. 53.

53. M. MacDonald, *Mystical Bedlam. Madness, Anxiety and Healing in Seventeenth-century England* (Cambridge, 1981), 83–4.

54. Shepherd, *Whole Office*, 96; W. Shepherd, *A Sure Guide for His Majesties Justices of the Peace* (London, 1663), 253; J. Keble, *An Assistance to Justices of the Peace*, (London, 1683).

55. Keble, *Assistance to Justices*, 480–1.

56. Edwin Freshfield (ed.), *The Account Book of the Parish of St Christopher le Stocks in the City of London 1662–1685* (London, 1895), 12, 27, 31; Christ's Hospital admitted children from the parish and sometimes sent them back to mothers to nurse; *Admissions Register of Christ's Hospital 1552–1599* (London, 1937), 175, 145, 171, 154, 190, 131, original MS in Guildhall Library MS 12/818/1–3.

57. Shepherd, *Sure Guide*, 253.

58. G. Savile, Marquis of Halifax, 'Advice to a daughter', J. P. Kenyon (ed.), *Complete Works* (Harmondsworth, 1969), 291.

59. G. Winstanley, *The Law of Freedom and Other Writings*, ed. C. Hill (Cambridge, 1982), 329.

60. *Calendar of State Papers Venetian*, vol. 23, 377; vol. 24, 150.

61. HRO, Panshanger MS, Commonplace book of Sara Cowper, D/EP F37, 'Woman', no.17. I owe this reference to the kindness of Dr Sara Mendelson.

62. *The XV Comforts of Rash and Inconsiderate Marriage ... Done Out of French* (London, 1682), 54.

63. P. Chamberlen, *A Voice in Rhama* (London, 1647), sig. A2; Donnison, *Midwives and Medical Men*, chs 1 and 2.

64. About one quarter of all seventeenth-century marriages were remarriages for the bride or groom; Stone, *Family, Sex and Marriage*, 56.

65. B. Bettleheim, *The Uses of Enchantment. The Meaning and Importance of Fairy Tales* (New York, 1977), 66–73 and *passim*.

66. P. Crawford, 'Checklist. Women's published writings, 1600–1700', and S. H. Mendelson, 'Stuart women's diaries and occasional memoirs', in M. Prior (ed.) *Women in English Society, 1500–1800* (London, 1985).

67. J. Sharp, *The Midwives Book* (London, 1671), 93.

68. E. A. Wrigley and R. Schofield, *The Population History of England* (Cambridge, Mass., 1981), 255; Peter Laslett, *The World We Have Lost* (2nd edn, London, 1971), 85–6; Stone, *Family, Sex and Marriage*, 46–54.

69. V. B. Elliott, 'Single women in the London marriage market: age, status and mobility, 1598–1619', in R. B. Outhwaite (ed.), *Marriage and Society. Studies in the Social History of Marriage* (London, 1981), 80–100.

70. *An Ease for Overseers of the Poore* (Cambridge, 1601), 25–6.

71. A. Clark, *Working Life of Women in the Seventeenth Century*, (London, 1919), 64–92; M. F. Roberts, 'Wages and wage-earners in England: the evidence of the wage assessments, 1563–1725', unpublished D. Phil. thesis, University of Oxford, 1981, ch. 7, The sexual division of wage labour.

72. V. Fildes, *Breasts, Bottles and Babies: A History of Infant Feeding* (Edinburgh, 1986), 159–62.

73. *Fair Warning to the Murderers of Infants Being an Account of the Trial ... of Mary Goodenough* (London, 1692), 4.

74. Mendelson, 'Stuart women's diaries', 195.

75. E. Clinton, Countess of Lincoln, *The Countesse of Lincolnes nurserie* (Oxford, 1622).

76. S. Jinner, *An Almanack and Prognostication for the Year of Our Lord, 1659* (London, 1659), preface to the reader.

77. Sharp, *The Midwives Book.*

78. M. Trye, *Medicatrix, or the Woman-physician* (London, 1675).

79. P. Crawford, 'Printed advertisements for women medical practitioners in London, 1670–1710', *Bull. Soc. Soc. Hist. Med.*, 35 (1984), 66–70.

80. Cp. Stone, *Family, Sex and Marriage*, 483, who claims that 'human sex takes place mostly in the head'.

81. Jinner, *Almanack, 1659*, preface to reader.

82. H. Wolley, *The Gentlewomans Companion* (London, 3rd edn, 1682), 301.

83. A. L. Rowse, *Simon Forman: Sex and Society in Shakespeare's Age* (London, 1974), 226–7.

84. R. Latham and W. Matthews (eds), *The Diary of Samuel Pepys* (11 vols, London, 1970–1983), vol. 1, 1. See also Crawford, 'Attitudes to menstruation', 69–70.

85. ORO, QS 1690, Ea/16; see also McLaren, *Reproductive Rituals*, 46.

86. Macfarlane, *Marriage and Love*, 51.

87. P.E.H. Hair, 'Bridal pregnancy in rural England in earlier centuries', *Popul. Stud.*, 20 (1966), 233–43; P.E.H. Hair, 'Bridal pregnancy in earlier rural England further examined', *Popul. Stud.*, 24 (1970), 59–70.

88. DRO, Q/SB Box 58, 22.

89. R. Hayden (ed.), *The Record of a Church of Christ in Bristol, 1640–1687* (Bristol, 1974), 213–16.

90. Quarter Sessions records in particular contain information about illegitimate maternity.

91. DRO, Q/SB Box 59, 33.

92. See also ibid., Box 58, 21, Deborah Brackley, 1651; McLaren, *Reproductive Rituals*, 89–112.

93. R.W. Malcolmson, 'Infanticide in the eighteenth century', in

J. S. Cockburn (ed.), *Crime in England 1550–1800* (London, 1977), 187–209.

94. P. Slack (ed.), *Poverty in Early-Stuart Salisbury* (Devizes, 1975), 23.

95. DRO, Q/SB, Box 59, 1653.17.

96. A. Hamilton, *Memoirs of the Comte de Gramont*, trans. P. Quennell, (London, 1932), 302–3. In the previous century, Mary Tudor's need for an heir was said to be 'the foundation of everything'; H.F.M. Prescott, *Mary Tudor* (London, 1953), 307.

97. BL, Harleian MS 6987, f. 120v.

98. A. Walker, *The Holy Life of Mrs Elizabeth Walker* (London, 1690), 12.

99. CCRO, Diary of Sarah Savage, 22 May 1687 and *passim*; P. Crawford, 'Attitudes to pregnancy, from a woman's spiritual diary, 1687–8', *Loc. Popul. Stud.*, 21 (1978), 43–5.

100. WIL, MS 4338, W. IIa; see also MS 501, p.553, to help conception, and BL, Sloane MS 3859, 'barrenness'.

101. Latham and Matthews (eds), *The Diary of Samuel Pepys*, vol. 1, p. 222 (26 July 1664).

102. J. O. Halliwell (ed.), *The Autobiography and Correspondence of Sir Simonds D'Ewes* (2 vols, London, 1845), vol. 1, p. 416.

103. JRL, MUL, Legh of Lyme correspondence, Thomas Chicheley to Elizabeth Legh, 28 Oct. 1671.

104. DWL, Henry MS 90.7.18, Matthew Henry to Philip Henry, 4 April 1693.

105. BL, Add. MS 37343, f. 32.

106. NRO, Finch Hatton MS 1468. See also M. Slater, *Family Life in the Seventeenth Century: The Verneys of Claydon House* (London, 1984), 82–3. Algernon, Earl of Northumberland, wrote to the Countess of Leicester in 1636, 'The haueing of an other Girle, I thought so little considerable, that I made no Haste in acquainting you with it;' Arthur Collins, *Letters and Memorials of State* (London, 1746), 450. I owe this reference to the kindness of Judith Richards.

107. Jinner, *Almanack, 1659*, preface to reader.

108. KAO, F 27, Journal of Elizabeth Turner, 5 May 1672.

109. Gouge, *Domesticall Duties*, 130.

110. M. Holden, *The Womans Almanack for the Year...1688* (London, 1688), 9.

111. McLaren, *Reproductive Rituals*, ch. 4.

112. D. McLaren, 'Nature's contraceptive. Wet nursing and prolonged lactation: the case of Chesham, Buckinghamshire 1578–1601', *Med. Hist.*, 23 (1979), 426–41; Fildes, *Breasts, Bottles and Babies*, 107–8.

113. Crawford, 'Sucking child', 30.

114. Gouge, *Domesticall Duties*, 130; Thomas Hilder, *Conjugall Counsell* (London, 1653), 17–18.

115. JRL, MUL, Legh family of Lyme, Sara Fountaine to Richard Legh, 20 March [1681?].

116. C. Jackson (ed.), *The Autobiography of Mrs Alice Thornton* (Durham,1875), 140.

117. KAO, Journal of Elizabeth Turner, October 1662.

118. M. E. Wiesner, 'Early modern midwifery: a case study', in B. A. Hanawalt (ed.), *Women and Work in Preindustrial Europe* (Bloomington, Indiana, 1986), 110.

119. J. M. Beattie, *Crime and the Courts in England, 1660–1800* (Oxford, 1986), 120–1.

120. *Memoirs of Sir Hugh Cholmley*, 41. Lady Anne Waller was very distressed at the death of her midwife, 'one that had bin long carefull and very loving to me', two days before her baby was due; *Harcourt Papers*, vol. 1. p. 177.

121. BI, Borthwick Prob. Reg. 22 pt 11, f. 538v., Will of Jane Magham, prob. date 22 May 1584. I owe this reference to the kindness of Claire Cross.

122. Bod., Diary of Sarah Savage, 96–7, 11 April 1716. DWL, Henry MS 4.29, 1707; A. Macfarlane (ed.) *The Diary of Ralph Josselin, 1616–1683* (London, 1976), 615. A. Macfarlane, *The Family Life of Ralph Josselin, a Seventeenth-century Clergyman. An Essay in Historical Anthropology* (Cambridge, 1970), 85, 115, 116, 117, 155. See also Mendelson, 'Stuart women's diaries', 196–7.

123. Walker, *Holy Life of Mrs Elizabeth Walker*, 179–82; C. Severn (ed.), *Diary of the Rev. John Ward* (London, 1839), 102.

124. See, for example, account for moneys disbursed for Elizabeth Smith at the time of her delivery, for two midwives as well as a doctor and nurse; ORO, QS 1687, Ea/21.

125. A. Wilson, 'Participant or patient? Seventeenth century childbirth from the mother's point of view', in R. Porter (ed.), *Patients and Practitioners. Lay Perceptions of Medicine in Pre-industrial Society* (Cambridge, 1985), 137; see also his 'Childbirth in seventeenth- and eighteenth-century England', unpublished D. Phil. thesis, University of Sussex, 1982.

126. *The accomplisht physician, the honest apothecary, and the skilful chyrurgeon* (London, 1670), 37.

127. P. Stubbes, *A Christal Glasse for Christian Women* (London, 1591), 4–5; E. Joceline, *The Mothers Legacie to her Unborne Child* (London, 1624), sig. a5.

128. R. Schofield, 'Did the mothers really die? Three centuries of maternal mortality in "the world we have lost"' in L. Bonfield, R. M. Smith, and K. Wrightson (eds), *The World We Have Gained. Histories of Population and Social Structure* (Oxford 1986), 259; Mendelson, 'Stuart women's diaries', 196–7.

129. M. H. Nicholson (ed.) *Conway Letters. The Correspondence of Anne, Viscountess Conway, Henry More, and Their Friends, 1642–1682* (London, 1930), 152–3, 154. J. B. Williams, *Memoirs of the Life and Character of Mrs Savage* (London, 1821), 286.

130. Walker, *Holy Life of Mrs Elizabeth Walker*, 63, 93. See also MacDonald, *Mystical Bedlam*, 77–8, 81–5, 159–60.

131. KAO, Journal of Elizabeth Turner, September 1676; NRO, MS West Misc. 35, 'Book of advice to the children...written by several Lady Westmorlands and their ancestors in the early 17th century'; Anne, wife of Sir William Waller, thanked God for her child 'which

was born with all itts parts and limbs'; E. W. Harcourt (ed.), *The Harcourt Papers* (7 vols, Oxford, 1880–1905), vol. 1, 173.

132. For example, F.W. Bennitt (ed.), 'The diary of Isabella, wife of Sir Roger Twysden, Baronet, of Royden Hall, East Peckham, 1645–1651', *Archael. Cant.*, 51 (1939), 117; NRO, MS West. Misc 35, Book of Lady Westmorelands.

133. R. Schofield and E. A. Wrigley, 'Infant and child mortality in the late Tudor and early Stuart period', in C. Webster (ed.), *Health, Medicine and Mortality in the Sixteenth Century* (Cambridge, 1979), 61–96; R. Schofield, 'Comment on infant mortality', *Loc. Popul. Stud.*, 9 (1972), 49.

134. Stone, *Family, Sex and Marriage*, 105.

135. Williams, *Memoirs of the Life and Character of Mrs Savage*, 287.

136. M. Cary, *The Little Horns Doom* (London, 1651), 289–90.

137. S. H. Mendelson, *The Mental World of Stuart Women: Three Studies* (Brighton, 1987), 88.

138. Dorothy McLaren's doctorate was awarded in 1975 and subsequently she published 'Fertility, infant mortality and breastfeeding in the seventeenth century', *Med. Hist.*, 22 (1978), 378–96; 'Marital fertility and lactation 1570–1720', in M. Prior (ed.) *Women in English Society, 1500–1800* (London, 1985), 22–53; Fildes, *Breasts, Bottles and Babies*, esp. part II. On feeding, see also Crawford, 'Sucking child', 29–37.

139. KAO, Journal of Elizabeth Turner. For further examples of mothers' comments on their breastfeeding, see Crawford, 'Sucking child', 32–3.

140. NRO, Finch Hatton MS 1480, Alice Hatton to brother, 15 May [1678].

141. BL, Portland loan 29/76, Abigail Harley to her husband Sir Edward, 30 November 1669; BL, Harelian MS 4762, f. 16.

142. Fildes, *Breasts, Bottles and Babies*, 153–5, and chs 5–7, *passim.*

143. Crawford, 'Sucking child', 34–5.

144. BL, Harleian MS 382, f. 182, 10 May 1639.

145. Clinton, *The Countesse of Lincolnes Nurserie*, 19 (original emphasis).

146. BL, Harley papers, Portland loan 29/76, 3, Abigail Harley to her husband Sir Edward Harley, 8 November [16]80; for further evidence about nurses' attitudes, see Crawford, 'Sucking child', 34.

147. DWL, MS Henry 4.25, Sarah Savage to Hannah Whitton, 2 April 1734.

148. K. Chidley, *The Justification of the Independent Churches of Christ* (London, 1641), 57; F. G. Emmison, *Elizabethan Life: Morals and the Church Courts Mainly from Essex Archdiaconal Records* (Chelmsford, 1973), 160.

149. J. Boulton, *Neighbourhood and Society. A London Suburb in the Seventeenth Century* (Cambridge, 1987), 197.

150. T. L. Underwood, 'Child dedication services among British Baptists in the seventeenth century', *Bapt. Quart.*, 23 (1969), 166–9.

151. NUL, letter book of the Earl of Clare, Ne C 15 404, p. 272 (21 November 1631).

152. KAO, Journal of Elizabeth Turner, 14 July 1672.

153. D. G. Greene (ed.), *The Meditations of Lady Elizabeth Delaval Written Between 1662 and 1671* (Durham, 1978), 74–5.

154. T. Croker (ed.), *Autobiography of Mary, Countess of Warwick*, (Percy Society, 1848), 28–31. One of the attractions of a suitor to Anne Rich was 'the nearness of the neighbourhood' in which she would live. A. Walker, *The Virtuous Woman Found* (London, 1678), 93.

155. B. Makin, in M. R. Mahl and H. Koon (eds), *The Female Spectator: English Women Writers Before 1800* (Bloomington, Ind., 1977), 125.

156. For examples, see Crawford, 'Sucking child', 36.

157. William Gouge, for example, had strictures upon those parents who visited a daughter when their son-in-law was out: Gouge, *Domesticall Duties*, 326.

158. J. P. Gilson (ed.), *Lives of Lady Anne Clifford Countess of Dorset, Pembroke and Montgomery (1590–1676) and of Her Parents Summarized by Her Self* (London, 1916), 28–9.

159. Ibid., 61. Margaret rejoiced when a grandson was born to bear her 'noble father's name', and when a granddaughter was named after her: ibid., 57.

160. BL, Add. MS 42,849, f. 50.

161. A. Searle (ed.) *Barrington Family Letters, 1628–1632* (London, 1983).

162. Williams, *Memoirs of the Life and Character of Mrs Savage*, 310, 285, 314, 329; see also Crawford, 'Katharine and Philip Henry', 49–57.

163. Gouge, *Domesticall Duties*, 275.

164. JRL, MUL, Legh of Lyme correspondence, W. Russell to E. Legh, 8 October 1695.

165. BL, Portland loan 28/83,3, Brilliana Stanley to her brother, Edward Harley, 10 January [1660].

166. E. Grymeston, *Miscelanea. Medidations. Memoratives* (London, 1610), sig. A3; Crawford, 'Women's printed writings', 221–2, 268–9.

167. D. Leigh, *The Mothers Blessing* (London, 1616), 10.

168. NRO, West. Misc. MS 35, f. 45v.

169. H. Wolley, *A Supplement to the Queen-like Closet* (London, 1674), 140.

170. Walker, *Holy Life of Mrs Elizabeth Walker*, 66.

171. Rebecca Travers, in Joan Whitrowe, *The Work of God in a Dying Maid* (London, 1677), 5.

172. BL, Harleian MS 383, ff. 39,45, 55.

173. *A Living Testimony from the Power and Spirit of Our Lord Jesus Christ in Our Faithful Womens Meeting* (London, 1686), 3.

2

Embarking on a rough passage: the experience of pregnancy in early-modern society

Linda A. Pollock

Going with child is as it were a rough sea, on which a big-belly'd woman and her infant floats the space of nine months: and labour, which is the only port, is so full of dangerous rocks, that very often both the one and the other, after they are arriv'd and disembark'd, have yet need of much help to defend them against divers inconveniences which usually follow the pains and travail they have undergone in it.[1]

I

Among the propertied élite of early-modern England, children were a desired but, for many, a difficult-to-procure commodity. In addition to a mean level of childlessness of almost 19 per cent, the family size of the landed ranks declined between 1590 and 1740. The cohort born in the late seventeenth century failed to reproduce itself and during the early Hanoverian period, the nobility tended towards extinction.[2] Thus, much anxiety surrounded any new match: would it found a new generation? Lady Savile's comment 'I would fain hear you were bringing your husband the most acceptable present' to her stepdaughter who was still not pregnant almost a year after her marriage, embodied the fears of the élite.[3] Conception eluded many young couples, as Simonds D'Ewes discovered. He mourned in 1629:

our hopes, not only in our own fears, but in opinion also, were almost turned into despair; for we had now been

partakers of the nuptial rites about two years, and yet had
as little expectation of issue as in the first eight months of
our continence next after marriage.[4]

A baby of either sex would be welcome as testimony to the
procreative potential of the union; a son, given the difficulty the
aristocracy encountered in producing male heirs, would be
even better.[5]

Pregnancy, however, was more than a matter of mere
reproduction; it was also a public symbol of sexual intimacy in a
marriage and affirmation of the contentment of the two parties
involved.[6] Bridget Croft's anxiety over the marital disharmony
of Theophilus, Earl of Huntingdon, was somewhat assuaged on
being informed of the birth of his son:

> if I had bin to chews his name it should have bin yt wch has
> signified a peacemaker, but whatsoever his name is, as his
> first begining in ye womb did begin in a better agreement,
> so I hope he will in ys his birth and continuance with you,
> so unight your hartes in affection as nothinge shall ever
> seperate ym.[7]

Pregnancy was the more eagerly looked for by interested parties
when a couple had considered a permanent estrangement. The
Marquis of Hamilton and his wife decided to try again with their
marriage after a period apart. Three months after their reunion
Mary's sister, Katherine Manners, Countess of Denbigh, joyfully
confided the success of the reconciliation to her brother: 'the
good nuse you will now here of your sister's great belay will
amase you as it has done all use here but now all oure feres is at
an end'.[8] Children cemented a match, bonding the couple
more firmly and making separation and the disruption of family
alliances more unlikely.

In addition, a fruitful marriage was not only testimony to the
couple's physical uniting; it was also proof of an impregnation,
that is of the sexual act successfully performed. It was a vindicat-
ion in particular of the husband's expertise.[9] Because of the pre-
vailing belief that a woman's pleasure during intercourse was
essential to conception, advice literature cautioned men on the
importance of foreplay and caresses in arousing their wives.[10]
Childless marriages could cast a slur on the husband's sexual
prowess. Lord Paget teased Mary Jones, the wife of his steward:

I am sorry to heare no newes of your being with childe; I am afraide Roger Jones is worthy the blame, for I thinke you very fruitful were you well handled. I intend to bee att my house by Michaelmas where if I finde you still barren, I will take some paines with you myselfe.[11]

Thus, when a wife did conceive it was a matter for self-congratulation on the part of her spouse. After the birth of his son Sir Edward Nicolls boasted to his friends 'yt he had but 2 bouts with his wife for it and it came according to ye last bout'.[12] Ultimately, however, barrenness was believed to be the fault of the woman. If a male was capable of erection he was presumed potent; if he achieved penetration and ejaculation and yet conception did not occur, then it was assumed that the woman was infertile.[13]

Pregnancy when it did ensue was a matter for rejoicing – as much as a visible demonstration of the man's virility, the woman's fertility, and the happiness of the marriage, as for the wanted progeny. Yet the pleasure induced by the prospect of a child, especially from the woman's perspective, was not unalloyed: conceiving, carrying the child to term, and successfully giving birth to a healthy infant without impairing the well-being of the mother were viewed as stages on a hazardous journey, fraught with obstacles and dangers from beginning to end.

II

Consummation itself was not always straightforward. It could be delayed, as in the case of Lewis Boyle, Viscount Kinalmeaky, because the husband was afflicted with venereal disease. He bewailed his plight to his brother-in-law 'I am not in ye way of all flesh, would I have never been in any, yr most sweet sister had not been now a maid.'[14] Other couples met with unforeseen impediments. Theophilus, Earl of Huntingdon, had been unable to penetrate his bride of two months and consulted his uncle Arthur Stanhope for advice. The letter in reply is a unique document which, because of the light it sheds on sexual relations in early-modern society – for example, the ignoring of the taboo on sex during menstruation as well as the emphasis on patience – is worth quoting in full.

I feare you will find it difficult and troublesome anuffe to make and enter the breach in my ladyes c: but I am the most concerned for my poore lady when she comes to push a pike with you. God Almighty if it be his ages [aegis?], will facillitate and hasten the compleatinge of that soe good and necesary a worke and to that end I beseeche you punctually to observe the honest drs directions, which I hope my lady will both be patient and agent in likewise and give mee leave to give you this farther directions of my owne wch I hope may be usefull to you in this buisnes. And that is in the first place that you finger my lady espetially att this time now she has her flowers for I assure you those parts are most apt to delate and widen when she is in thatt condition, and the most probable time to gett yr p: in to her. Next I advice you, that you have always ready by the bedside in a glas bottle some oyle of lillies or oyle of swete almonds or plane sallet oyle for salinge, and twine them gently up and downe the part espetially where you find it stratest; and when you thinke you have made roome anuffe that the head of yr pintle may enter, just when you are ready to spend and not before, that yr seede begins to come, then thrust quicke and hard. And [I] would alsoe advice you to let my lady take sometimes once or twise in a week in the evening a glister made of nothinge but a pint of new milke the yoke of two eggs and two large spoonefulls of glister sugar, and soe let it be adminstred lukewarm and let her take this espetially at night or in the mornings before you have some hopes and intend to enter her. Beleive me my lord there is not any thing that be properer for my lady, by reson of her constant costiveness; which makes her excriments presse soe hard upon that partt, that it will very much hinder your interance and soe you may remember ye dr told you. Soe much for the fucking partt; hoping yt now you haveing used two fingers ere longe you will not onley make way for three but for yr p:; alsoe when you have one past the strates I doubt not but you will come where you will find otian anuffe, too deepe for your rudder to feale the bottom were it as long againe as it is.[15]

Presumably the instructions were acted upon since 2 years and 3 months later, Elizabeth gave birth to a son.

Once consummation had been accomplished, the next hurdle confronting the couple was that of ascertaining if conception had occurred. The medical treatises of the period dwell at length on the problem of determining whether or not a woman was pregnant. A variety of tests and symptoms were suggested ranging from bodily signs such as full breasts, a closed cervix and swollen veins in the neck, through mental manifestations such as strange longings and food cravings, to empirical diagnosis by urine tests.[16] The cessation of menstruation was cited as a sign but was not seen as the most important factor. Indeed, Francis Mauriceau, one of the most influential man midwives of his time, considered that 'many women are themselves deceived, concluding themselves with child, from the staying of their courses'.[17] Notwithstanding the amount of attention accorded to the topic of deciding when a woman was carrying a child, the professionals undoubtedly had difficulty in diagnosing pregnancy, as the letter from Edward Conway to his brother-in-law in 1658 reveals:

> We have thoughts oftentimes in my wife's sickness, perhaps she may be breeding; but the excessive increase of her distemper, with many other reasons, so interrupted it, that they served only to torment. At last seeking but sincerely her satisfaction, we had recourse to the best doctors and midwives to be resolved, but they have plunged us into the greatest uncertainty; for they assured us with much confidence that, according to their art, she is not so.

Edward and Anne thought she must be pregnant – 'it appears evident to sense' – but because of the professional diagnosis, remained uncertain until the birth of Heneage 5 months later.[18]

Since their letters and diaries frequently refer to the time they thought they would be brought to bed, most women had some means of deciding when they had conceived.[19] Certainly, they were not always sure of the time of the birth. Sabine Johnson did not know when her labour would commence: 'to appoint the time, it lies not in me, and whether it shall be before Whitsuntide or after, Our Lord knoweth, for I stand in doubt'.[20] At other times they may have miscalculated. Elizabeth Isham gave birth earlier than she had anticipated, admitting she 'was deceived in her reckoning'.[21] Generally, though, women were reasonably accurate in their predictions. It appears they relied on four factors for determining conception and the stage of gestation: amenorrhea, quickening, the size of the abdomen, and increasing pains as the woman neared confinement. These factors were not always accorded the same weighting by the medical writers of the period.

Despite the lack of emphasis placed on the ceasing of menstruation by medical writers and midwifery tracts, women did perceive this as heralding a pregnancy. Jane Hook informed her Aunt: 'I think Madam that I am with child, because I have not had them but once which was a mounth after I had been here.'[22] Likewise, the onset of menstruation was evidence that they had not conceived. Sir Archibald Johnston noted in his diary: 'This night my wyfe told me somthing of hir auen flouers coming on hir now at the turne of the moneth, which shew that shoe was not with chyld.'[23] Amenorrhoea indicated a possible conception; women's suspicions of their condition received further corroboration once the child was felt to move, at about the fourth month. Anne Clifford informed her husband and her sisters she was pregnant when she 'was quick with child'.[24]

Once the fact of conception had been determined, the time of the birth was estimated. Unlike the popular medical literature which stated that a child could either be born at 7 months or at 9,[25] 40 weeks was regarded by women as the normal gestation period. As Hugh Cholmley commented in 1624, 'My wife would not be persuaded but she went full forty weeks.'[26] When the foetus quickened, women were more confident in foretelling the date of parturition. Anne Meautys, at the end of July 1630, wrote 'I am now with child; my time if God permit me life, will bee about Crismas, yt I shall lie ine'.[27] Married couples gauged the proximity to delivery by the size of the woman's abdomen. Unton Dering grew 'so bigge', her husband decided she must be brought to bed within 6 weeks.[28] The onset of pains was considered to be the final indicator of the nearness of the confinement. As Anne Meautys wrote to her mother-in-law, 'I groe very bige and full of paines expecting continually ye houre when it shall please God to send mee a safe delivery and to meake mee a glead mother.'[29]

The ability to diagnose the onset of pregnancy is an integral part of adequate antenatal care, since otherwise it could be no more than a 'last minute preparation for labour'.[30] The evidence discussed above reveals that women in early-modern society – often at variance with the opinions expressed in the referential literature – could judge the time of conception, the stage of gestation, and the imminence of the birth. This being the case, how was pregnancy experienced and managed in this period?

III

With regard to health in general, being a woman in early-modern society was not an enviable position. As Michael MacDonald has stated, 'Women sought medical treatment more often than men because they were more often ill.'[31] Medical practitioners considered women to be particularly prone to disease, 'subject to fevers and ill vapors arising from a malfunctioning menstrual cycle, to hysteria resulting from a diseased womb, and to general bad health'.[32] Married women could add to the ailments endured by all their sex, those induced by reproduction and child care. The nonconformist preacher Richard Baxter has provided us with a doleful synopsis of the life lying in wait for fertile wives:

> Women especially must expect so much suffering in a married life, . . . Their sickness in breeding, their pain in bringing forth, with the danger of their lives, the tedious trouble day and night which they have with their children in their nursing and their childhood.[33]

Baxter's gloomy prophecy seems to have been fulfilled. Richard Napier, for example, treated 1,286 women for mental illness and 748 men. Over a fifth of Napier's female patients also complained of a gynaecological or obstetrical illness, and the fear, stress, and illness caused by difficult births contributed to the mental disorders of eighty of them.[34] In spite of the strictures of writers like Mauriceau that pregnancy should be viewed as a 'neuter estate', that is as a condition precariously balanced between sickness and health, and not as an illness;[35] in the opinion of women who experienced pregnancy it was indisputably 'un mal de neuf mois'.[36] Rather than associating childbearing with a sense of well-being and joy, pregnancy in the sixteenth and seventeenth centuries was correlated with physical discomfort and mental unease.

The letters and diaries of the period contain much information on the indispositions suffered by women with child.
Alethea Talbot, for instance, always found it a trying time, her
mother observing on one occasion 'I besech our Lord send hir
much comfort of hir children for she breeds them very
painfully'.[37] References to a comfortable pregnancy are few and
it is clear that for many women, sickness and pain were the
customary accompaniments of the reproductive process.[38]
Charles Lyttelton's wife was subject to frequent bouts of nausea,
as he grumbled she was 'soe continually sick with (I think)
breeding, that she can do nothing but puke'.[39] Ralph Montagu
noted of his spouse, believing she may have conceived, 'my wife
has bin indisposed and sick these two moneths just as she used
to be when breeding'.[40] A respite may have been gained after
the third or fourth month. Cicelea Hatton was at that stage in
'better health' and Alice Thornton recalled that when she was
expecting her first child 'I was exceeding sickly in breeding, till
I was with quicke childe; after which I was very strong and
healthy.'[41] However, the reprieve for many was of short
duration, and as the time of the birth drew near, the woman's
torments intensified. Sir Gilbert Gerard was relieved that his
heavily pregnant wife was 'as well as a woeman in her case may
bee growing unwieldy and full of paines'.[42] Moreover, women in
the third trimester of gestation were apparently more
susceptible to infection.[43] Jane Boys, for example, was 'very ill of
ye yellow janders' for the last 2 months of her pregnancy.[44]
Because of this discomfort the onset of labour, although feared,
was welcomed as marking the return to health. So reasoned
Frances, Lady Hatton remarking hopefully, 'I have not stired
out of my chamber this 3 weeks for I have never been well and
am troubled in a most violent manner with a great cough but I
trust in God when I am once brought abed I shall be cured of
all my illnes.'[45]

Indeed, a healthy mother, rather than being a cause of
satisfaction, could be a disquieting indication that the foetus
was not thriving. Frances Hatton at an early stage in her
pregnancy was perturbed about her good health: 'I am very well
and never was as fat in my life, makes me fear yt my child does
not thrive I doe so much'.[46] That pregnancy was routinely
associated with illness can be seen from the extracts in
Archibald Johnston's diary concerning his wife in 1654. She had
been ailing for several weeks but Johnston was not unduly

worried since they both believed her to be with child. However, once it was clear that this was not the case, Johnston's alarm about her condition increased 'this morning finding my wyfe's auen to be on hir and that therby it apeared shoe was not with chyld, I begoud to aprehend mor seriously the daungerousnesse of hir condition'.[47]

Pregnancy was a source not only of bodily distress but also of mental foreboding. Women in that condition were susceptible to bouts of melancholy. Mary Verney, 4 months pregnant, confessed: 'I am soe extreamly opressed with mellencollick that I am almost ready to burst.'[48] Sarah Fountaine, pregnant with her third child, lamented that 'the condition I am now in occasions many a dolefull thought'.[49] Above all, the impending birth loomed large in their fears. Jane Hook, supposing that she may have conceived, entreated her Aunt 'to be earnest in your prayeres to God for me that he would prepare me and help mee to undergoe whatsoever he shall be plesed to exercise me withal that I may indur his hand pasiently and meekly'.[50] The thought of her approaching labour continued to haunt her, and she begged her Aunt once more: 'I beseech you for Christ sake remember me by nam in your ernest prayeres, that God would be please[d] to fit me for the day of tryall and that I may not faint in the day of my affliccion.'[51]

Historians have long made do with citing the action of Elizabeth Josceline as well as the attitude of Jane Josselin to depict the dread with which women regarded confinements.[52] In contradiction, new demographic research suggests that these women may not have been typical. Utilizing parish family reconstitutions, Roger Schofield calculates that the maternal mortality rate in the past was about 1 per cent. Since this risk was present at every delivery, women would run a cumulative risk of dying in childbed of 6 to 7 per cent during their procreative careers. As Schofield points out, this was no greater than the chance a woman had of dying every year from infectious disease and other causes. He therefore concludes that 'in the distant past women will have known of others who died giving birth to a child; but they may also have considered it such a rare event that there was little risk that the tragedy would befall them'.[53] Notwithstanding the relatively low maternal mortality rate, it is still possible that childbirth was imbued with dread. Childbirth was a very conspicuous *single* cause of mortality and a fate which a prospective mother had several long months to contemplate.

Moreover, women could fear not merely that the birth would prove fatal but also 'the painfulnesse of that kinde of death'.[54] Their attitude towards death in childbed was less likely to be shaped by the statistical risk of encountering problems and more by the knowledge that once a problem arose, death was almost certain.

Having witnessed or at least been informed of the death of others from childbirth, women were aware that their survival could not be guaranteed. Many anticipated and sought to prepare themselves for death. Lady Massingberd counselled her daughter:

> Child, You now draw nere yr time for childbead . . . I hope you will doe very well yett none can foerse [foresee] how it may plese ye Lord to deall with you. Ye safe dylevery in childbearth is God's one work. Pray spare as much time as you can for meddetation and prayer to acquaint yrself with God.[55]

An approaching confinement aroused apprehension in all family members. Dorothy Norcliffe fretted about her daughter, 'I begin to have many fears about my pore Nina, yt is but a few days to hir time.'[56] James Lawes-Wittewronge was similarly perturbed for his sister:

> I daly pray for my sister's safe delivery being much concern'd for her, and am the more trobled till I hear of her wellfare because I have some lice against my shirt which use to boad me noe good, I know 'tis a foolish thing to be superstitious, but [I] can't help it.[57]

Expectant mothers themselves were obviously afraid. Richard Chaworth was disturbed to receive a letter from his niece – 'ready to lye downe' – which she regarded as her 'last will...with many such mortifyed passages which troubled me not a little'.[58] The fact that they had successfully given birth previously did not appear to allay their misgivings. Lucy, Countess of Bedford tried to reassure her friend Jane, Lady Cornwallis, 5-months pregnant with her fourth child,

> itt trobels me more to hear how aprehensive you are of a danger it hath pleased God to carry you so often safely

48

through, and so I doubt not will againe, though you may do yourselfe and yours much harme, by those doubtings and ill companions for all persons, and wors for us splentick creatures. Therfore, dear Cornwallis, lett not this melancholy prevale with you to the begetting or nourishing of those mistrusts [wch] will turne more to your hurt than that you feare, which I hope will passe with safety and end to your comfort.[59]

What is of note here is that Lady Cornwallis was reproved not for fearing she may die in childbirth but for fearing this when she had given birth successfully several times before.

In conclusion, expecting a child in early-modern society was an uncomfortable condition, bringing pain and anxiety to the prospective mother. The maternal mortality rate was certainly lower than we may have thought but to women, their relatives and spouses, the prospect of not surviving a birth was very real. What were the instructions imparted and followed to alleviate discomfort and ensure as far as possible that the pregnancy terminated in the safe delivery of a living child?

IV

Prescriptive writers placed the main responsibility for pre-natal care on the mother. William Gouge advised that as soon as a woman realized she was pregnant, she should take extra care of herself so that the child would be carried to term and be safely delivered. Since the child was carried within her body, the mother, by attending to her own well-being, would also be looking after the child's.[60] Childbearing women were entreated to be more than usually solicitous of their welfare. Ralph Montagu wished his wife 'to be as careful as may be of herself in case she should be breeding'. In practice, this vigilance took the form of restricting the activities of teeming women as well as specifically catering for their condition. Ante-natal care undoubtedly existed in early-modern society,[62] but it was governed by different assumptions from those underpinning modern-day care. There was no concept of an abnormal pregnancy differing from a normal one and no routine ante-natal care designed to distinguish between these:[63] instead, the management of women with child was intended to prevent spontaneous

abortions. Accordingly, the advice given in the printed works –
operating from the premiss that all pregnancies were potential
miscarriages[64] – stressed moderation in all things.

The dietary regime to be adhered to during pregnancy was in
keeping with this aim. The mother was to ensure that she took
in enough nutrients to sustain the foetus, otherwise it would
leave the womb in search of nourishment, but not too much
food which may suffocate the baby. A temperate diet was best,
one which provided adequate nourishment for the mother and
foetus while minimizing digestive difficulties and avoiding foods
that might bring on dangerous situations such as constipation,
vomiting, terms, and fluxes.[65] Pregnant women were to avoid
salty and spicy foods, pulses, and strong alcohol. Alcohol was
undoubtedly recommended, especially wine 'well temper'd
with water',[66] but strong drink was considered inappropriate for
a prospective mother. In a letter to Henry Fletcher, John Locke
advised that 'as to drink, ye smallest is always ye best'; 'strong
liquors' were 'gently to be quitted' if they were the woman's
accustomed beverage.[67]

It is difficult to ascertain whether this advice was followed
since information on nutrition during pregnancy is both scarce
and miscellaneous. Anne D'Ewes 'took some small sustenance'
on a fast day in 1634 when she was pregnant.[68] Lady Barbara
Compton asked Walter Bagot for venison for her daughter for
'many times, great-bellied women think of such novelties'.[69]
Some pregnant women were unable to digest their food. Anne,
Countess of Leven at mid-term received the following letter
from her mother:

> I am very sory you are still so much troubled wt the collick.
> I fear you eat too much fruit or heavy meats both wch are
> very ill for you. I never found aniething to me so much
> good as a gentle glister wch they never stand to give after
> one is wth quick chylde. You never told me if you use to
> vomet yr meat. I intret you strive against it for it [will]
> destroy yr stomach and give you perpetuell paines.[70]

Indeed, women were grateful if eating did not lead to bouts of
nausea. Elizabeth Mordaunt gave thanks to God 'that I have bin
abel to ete mete without being very ill after it'.[71] About all that
can be deduced from these snippets is that allowance, in the
sense of non-fasting as well as the satisfying of food cravings, was

made for the condition of pregnancy and that it was believed that certain foods could make a woman ill.

In other areas, however, evidence can be found to support the view that steps were taken to reduce the risk of miscarriage. Pregnancy frequently led to a curtailment of the woman's normal activities. Elizabeth Hatton was concerned that her daughter-in- law Cicelea, 5 months pregnant, was not resting as much as she should: 'I would by noe means have her work [sew] now because it is not good for her.'[72] Travelling was particularly frowned upon because riding on horseback or in a jolting coach threatened to dislodge the foetus. Elizabeth Isham could not visit her father because of 'my present condition, my burthen, disabling mee for travell'.[73] Women, anyway, found travelling uncomfortable as they increased in girth. Ann Dering completed her journey successfully but commented: 'I doe finde myselfe to grow apace and I think if I had not come downe when I did I should hardly have endured ye jorny.'[74] These precautionary measures could be carried to extremes in those cases in which a woman felt she was in particular danger of miscarrying. In this situation, women confined themselves to their rooms. Lady Anne Clifford was ill at 4 months during her second pregnancy and from then on stayed in her chamber, resolutely refusing even to cross the threshold until her child was born.[75] Lady Frances Hatton was 'content to be a prisoner to hir condition; and is perswaded to begin hir lying in three quarters of a year before hand, which caution will I hope be so successfull, as abundantly to answer all the trouble of it'.[76] In pursuing this course of action, women were rejecting professional wisdom. John Locke, for example, counselled Henry Fletcher about his wife Margaret:

> If she be with child let her not do as is usually wth women of [her] condition, mew herself up in her chamber for fear of miscarrying, much lesse confine herself to her bed. This makes ye body and spirite weak which is one great cause of miscarriage.

Locke recommended bleeding about the fourth month of gestation as a more effective precaution against spontaneous abortion.[77]

Midwives and doctors could be consulted if any problems arose, either in deciding whether a woman was or was not pregnant or if a miscarriage had occurred. Lady Brilliana Harley miscarried in 1639 and a doctor was sent for 'who gave me some directions'.[78] For normal preventive care, however, home remedies and charms were relied upon. Aelites, or eagle's stone – a pebble with a small pebble rattling within it – was reputed to ward off miscarriage. Anne Conway was lent a large one and 'in pain wore it upon her arm a good while'.[79] Home medicine could even be preferred to that obtained from professional practitioners. When Ann Windsor heard that her sister-in-law was in danger of miscarrying, she urged her brother to ensure that his wife took 'good strengthening things. Kitchin phisick I beleive is more proper for her than the Dr's filthy phisick which will poison her body, if she take too much off it.'[80] That professional practitioners were not involved in regular ante-natal care can be deduced from the fact that they were sought generally as the birth approached and would have been with the mother for, at the most, the last 2 weeks of pregnancy. Joan Thynne, anticipating her confinement to be about Easter, commenced searching for a midwife to be with her then on the third of March 1596.[81] Sir Hugh Cholmley's wife in 1625 had a midwife with her for 10 days before the birth of her child.[82] The proper management of pregnancy was primarily the responsibility of the woman and her husband. Midwives were sent for as 'the tyme drawes nye at hand', their function being to supervise the birth rather than the pregnancy.[83]

Childbirth is commonly viewed as a female affair and undoubtedly women consulted their mothers, sisters, and close female friends for advice during the pregnancy, and wished for their presence at the birth.[84] Even so, husbands were not superfluous to the reproductive process once it was underway but had their own part to play. According to the moralists, husbands were to be particularly sympathetic to and tender of their wives when they were carrying a child. As William Gouge put it, 'Husbands also in this case must be very tender over their wives, and helpfull to them in all things needfull.'[85] A few, at least, took such instructions to heart. Edward Dering wrote to his wife Unton in 1630: 'God in heaven blesse thee, and oure hopefull burthen, for I cary in my heart ye paynes thou sufferest for me.'[86] The husband's role extended beyond that of offering love and support, to ensuring that adequate provisions were made for the birth.

Careful preparations for the woman's lying-in seems to have been the norm and those cases in which the husband was negligent in this duty aroused concern and criticism.[87] In 1590, Elizabeth Molys was anxious about the condition of her daughter whose 'intollerabley badd husband' refused to make suitable provision for her delivery. Elizabeth requested her daughter's mother-in-law to pressurize her son

> to allowe and provyde for her that ys mete for a woman in her case, and that she maye be accompaned wth suche honest matrons as maye be for her saffetie for yt ys evident that he hathe no car for the preservacon of her lyffe.[88]

Thomas Peyton warned Henry Oxinden that his daughter Margaret Hobart, aged 18 and pregnant with her first child, was not being looked after properly: 'there is a daughter of yours I heare towards lying in and her husband minds it as much as my cowes calving . . . shee is as unprovided [for] as one that walkes the highwaies'.[89] Married women, as decent honest matrons, were entitled to appropriate arrangements being made for their confinement.

Although men may have been excluded from the delivery room, women wanted their husbands to be at home when they were brought to bed. Sabine Johnson in 1546 requested her husband to return in time for her labour, adding: 'What a great comfort it shall be to me to have you here at that time.'[90] Husbands themselves could be eager to be with their wives. Lady Godolphin thought her son cancelled an intended visit to her because of 'his hastie zeale to his great belly which he is come timely enough to see layed downe'.[91] The evidence available to us strongly suggests that husbands were expected to be, and frequently were, near at hand at the birth of their children.[92]

V

References to pregnancy in this period are few and far between except for the subject of miscarriage. Is this because the risk of spontaneous abortion was higher in the past?[93] Robert Fogel suggests that it was. He argues that the traditional diet of the upper ranks, rich in alcohol and salt, not only contributed to the high mortality of peers after the age of 40 but also adversely affected the development of children in the womb. He claims that the high consumption of alcohol – estimated at between 3 and 9 ounces of absolute alcohol daily – resulted in an increased incidence of late foetal deaths.[94] There is some support for Fogel's thesis: contemporaries condemned the consumption of strong drink by pregnant women, believing, for example, that the drinking of too much alcohol while pregnant or breastfeeding was one of the main causes of childhood rickets.[95] The moralists and medical writers were preoccupied with the problem of miscarriage, and personal papers provide many instances of miscarrying women. The question that should be asked, though, is whether these abortions were spontaneous or induced.

We know that women did not reproduce at their biological maximum. In the seventeenth century the marital fertility of the upper ranks was about the same as or even slightly higher than that of the population at large, as one would expect from their reliance on wet nurses.[96] However, between 1550 and 1724 the number of children born per married couple decreased from nearly five children to three or four. Total fertility, that is the number of children ever born, is influenced by patterns of nuptiality and mortality. Hollingsworth's calculations reveal that women who married under the age of 25 would produce about six children in the seventeenth century, whereas women who married between 25 and 34 would give birth to between three and four. The percentage of women who married over 25 did increase from 15.2 per cent for the cohorts born between 1600 and 1624 to 22.3 per cent for those born between 1675 and 1699. The mean age at first marriage for women also rose slightly during this period from 23 in the sixteenth century to 24 in the seventeenth. The high mortality levels of the peerage mitigated against large families, but as these levels changed little between 1600 and 1750, mortality cannot explain the decline in family size.[97] Despite the alterations in nuptiality which would affect total fertility, both Stone and Hollingsworth suspect that some method of family limitation was employed by the peerage by the mid-seventeenth century and that this too contributed to the decline in family size.[98]

Recent research has demonstrated that the concept of controlling family size did exist in early-modern society: conception could be prevented through the mechanisms of maternal breastfeeding and restricting coitus as well as by the use of herbal contraceptives and the technique of coitus interruptus.[99] In practice, none of these methods was entirely reliable and a woman could conceive even though the prospect of another pregnancy was unwelcome. Alice Thornton, convalescing after a severe illness, was dismayed when she discovered she was carrying her ninth child: 'if it had been good in the eyes of my God I should much rather (because of that [her illness]) not to have been in this condition'.[100] Women in her situation had two options: they could either resign themselves to their fate or they could try to terminate the pregnancy.[101]

Abortion was within the bounds of possibility, but it was condemned by moralists and medical practitioners.[102] More significantly, private medical books often contain recipes for abortion. At times a recipe can be explicitly described as an abortifacient as in the case of the Jerningham family medicinal receipt book which contains instructions for a concoction 'to cause miscarriage'. This was composed of sowbread and fabers syrup of birthwort roots and the resultant liquid was 'a great secret' which 'forces away the birth dead or alive as allso the afterbirth'.[103] At other times the information was disguised as either a remedy to 'bring on the terms' or as one intended to remove a 'false conception'.[104] Elizabeth Freke, in her medicinal recipe book, described a drink 'to prevent miscarrying in a breeding woman'. It consisted of a mixture of nutmegs, cinnamon, cloves, mace, ginger, aniseed, and licorice in water, sweetened with sugar, and was to be drunk as often as possible: 'This hypocrass soe taken will strengthen the body and preserve conception iff itt be true; iff nott itt will bring itt away with ease and saffty and has done many women good to my knowledge and is a very good medycyne.'[105]

Information on procuring an abortion was therefore available to those seeking to terminate a pregnancy, but before we conclude that unwanted pregnancies could be dealt with in this period, we must ascertain how effective these remedies were likely to be. Women of the past, because of nutritional deficiencies, or pelvic deformities resulting from rickets in childhood, or uterine muscles weakened by long labours, may have been more 'abortion-prone' than healthy women today. Consequently, abortifacients of limited efficiency could have wrought the desired result.[106] Elizabeth Frekes's spicy potion described above seems a dubious provoker of miscarriages, although as pregnant women were regularly warned not to eat spicy food for this very reason, it is probable that this was the intention of the recipe. It is likely that the mixture was nauseating: women were to drink as much as 'your stomack will beare', and so could procure an abortion through severe vomiting.[107] Other abortifacients were more efficacious. Mixtures containing rue or savin – herbs familiar to early modern society – were likely to procure an abortion at a late stage of gestation since they promote uterine contractions, causing the foetus to be expelled.[108] Recipes which suggested rubbing ointments on to the abdomen could cause the foetus to be aborted as a result of the physical massage.[109] What is significant is that these remedies were not hidden in 'obscure medical treatises'[110] but were kept by women in their private medical books, presumably because they thought they might require recourse to such knowledge.

It seems reasonable to deduce that abortion was possible, but did it occur? For those couples involved in illicit affairs, Quaife concludes 'attempted abortions were widespread and often successful'.[111] It is more difficult to determine whether or not married couples made use of abortifacients. The most explicit reference to abortion I have come across for the early-modern period is in a letter from Margaret, Countess of Wemyss to her daughter Anna, Countess of Leven in c.1698, in which she wrote: 'I hear you have been taking a little physick, I hope it will do you good. I should have been sory if you had so soon fallen with child before you recover some more strength.'[112] Such admissions are all too rare. However, an examination of the cited miscarriages of married women may shed some light on whether these abortions were spontaneous or induced.

Some miscarriages, as in the case of Sarah Henry, were a source of dismay or, as in the case of the wife of Robert Sibbald who in 1677 lost the baby she was carrying after falling down the stairs, genuine accidents;[113] others, we have reason to be more sceptical about. Catherine Finch, Countess of Winchelsea, was unhappy to discover she was with child again in 1676. She was in Venice and her husband intended to travel to London to try and sort out some of their financial difficulties. She grumbled to her sister

I shuld have bene very glad to had gone along with him into England, considering the condition I feare I am in. I did but just begine to suspect it at his goeing away, but now am more cartaine of my being with child, 'tis a sad trouble to mee to bee soe at this distance from you all.

Catherine miscarried a month later and was able to join her husband.[114] In another instance, Lady Cavendish lost her baby when she ignored the warnings against violent exercise during pregnancy.[115]

Miscarriages which jeopardized the life of the mother may further strain our credulity. Up until the third month of gestation there is no medical reason why spontaneous abortion should be so painful and hazardous.[116] A woman who experienced a perilous early miscarriage may have employed an abortifacient. Anne Meautys reported to her mother-in-law in 1641:

I have bine very dangerously ill; I was gone with child three mounths; att ye end of which time I did miscarrie, and was in yt extremetie, yt those yt were about mee, did not thinke I should have escaped.[117]

After the third month, abortions (spontaneous and induced) are risky, but because 80 per cent of spontaneous abortions occur by this stage, we should expect fewer instances.[118] Moreover, some of the herbal abortifacients which terminated a pregnancy at a late stage of gestation, about the fifth month, did have unpleasant or even fatal side-effects.[119] Although we cannot be sure, it is possible that Bridget Osborne, who 'had the misfortune to miscarry of a very fine boy with great hazard of her owne life', had brought about the miscarriage herself.[120]

There are also several examples of women miscarrying if they had recently given birth to a child (see Table 2.1). Although women who conceive again very soon after childbirth or an aborted pregnancy have a slightly greater chance of early miscarriage, and multiple pregnancies are more prone to miscarry than single, these cases also suggest that abortion was resorted to if the birth intervals were too short.[121]

Finally, we may also be suspicious of a series of miscarriages towards the end of a woman's procreative career. A woman who has borne many children, especially if she has endured lengthy labours, is more susceptible to miscarry.[123] Nevertheless, when, as in the case of Jane Josselin, the miscarriages took place as soon as she realized she was pregnant – at one stage on three consecutive occasions – we should at least entertain the hypothesis that abortifacients were being used.[124]

Table 2.1 Examples of suspect miscarriage

Name	Date	Description of miscarriage
Sarah Godfrey	1613	Miscarried of twins in second pregnancy having given birth 5 months earlier to twins
Sarah Godfrey	1614	Miscarried in third pregnancy 10 months after previous miscarriage
Elizabeth Cholmley	1636	Miscarried at 10 weeks, in sixth pregnancy c.6 months after giving birth to a child
Barbara Drummond	1659	Miscarried at c.22 weeks in her second pregnancy having conceived within 3 months of previous birth
Katherine Patrick	1681	Miscarried in third pregnancy, 8 months after previous birth

Sources: See note 122.

At the moment it must be conceded that the above analysis amounts to little more than conjecture and speculation. A systematic examination of the timing and incidence of miscarriage among the upper ranks – an investigation which is beyond the scope of this chapter – may allow us to discover if abortion was a preferred mode of family limitation, at least by women.[125] The implication of this chapter that it was so is in contradiction to recent demographic research in the area. Chris Wilson has argued that contraception and abortion did not play a large part in controlling family size in early-modern England. The lower English fertility level, he suggests, was a result of the long birth intervals caused by maternal breastfeeding.[126] The two points of view can be reconciled if abortion is not seen primarily as a mechanism for hindering the birth of another child but as a measure taken to preserve the long-term health of the mother. Certainly, women preferred to be well and with full strength before embarking on the trials and tribulations of childbearing. The Countess of Manchester, to give one example, hoped her niece would 'gaine a perfitt health before she proove with child'.[127] As McLaren points out, inducing abortion was a frightening prospect, but then, as the extracts in this chapter vividly illustrate, so was pregnancy. If abortion was mainly employed when a woman had conceived again too soon, the effect of this would be compatible with the demographic record delineated by Wilson.

VI

This chapter has examined the procuring, experience, and management of pregnancy for the élite of early-modern society. Women rarely enjoyed the period of gestation, beset as they were with sickness, pain, and fear. Pregnancy was viewed through the prism of miscarriage: as a difficult, uncomfortable, and potentially dangerous condition which, unless tended with care, was destined to end prematurely. Thus, ante-natal care in the sixteenth and seventeenth centuries had different goals, in keeping with the opinions of the medical world and perceived perils of pregnancy, from that of today. For the most part, ante-natal care was the responsibility of the expectant parents rather than professional practitioners. The chapter has also speculated on the incidence of miscarriage, suggesting that many were induced abortions. Children were undoubtedly sought but too many too soon endangered the health of the mother.

In pursing this topic, light has been shed on facets of the relationship between referential literature and actual behaviour. Women and their husbands often rejected the advice of the printed works. Nevertheless, the rejection of professional wisdom was selective and not total. If women were procuring abortions, then it suited them to accept the view that it was important for a woman's health to restart periods if they had stopped. The cessation of menstruation was regarded as dangerous by the medical writers because a woman's body would not be able to rid itself of its noxious humours.[129] From this standpoint it was not only justifiable but desirable that remedies 'to bring on the terms' abounded. However, since women did regard amenorrhoea as a sign of conception they were aware that by exciting 'the terms', they were in reality procuring an abortion. It is inconceivable that they failed to comprehend that medicine intended to provoke menstruation was in actuality expelling a foetus. By resorting to such measures, women increased the miscarriage rate. In so doing, they fed the preoccupations of the referential literature and confirmed the prevalent attitude that any pregnancy could all too easily terminate in spontaneous abortion: that is, women not only manipulated the current ideology to their own advantage, but in turn their actions reinforced certain aspects of it. Their behaviour was underpinned by different assumptions and yet it supplied the empirical basis for the erroneous perceptions of the medical writers. Thus, if ideas have a history, then it cannot be one divorced from the experience which legitimated some ideas at the expense of others.

Acknowledgements

The research for this chapter was financed by research awards from the Economic and Social Research Council (award number GOO232047), the British Academy, and the Henry E. Huntington Library. I would like to thank Gillian Craig, Valerie Fildes, and Roger Schofield for their helpful advice and pinpointing of errors on earlier drafts of the chapter. I am also grateful for the constructive criticism of Barbara Donagan, Ian Gentles, and Barbara Harris.

Notes

1. F. Mauriceau, *The Diseases of Women with Child, and in Childbed,* first pub. 1668, Facsimile (New York, 1985), 244.

2. T. H. Hollingsworth, 'The demography of the British peerage', *Popul. Stud. Suppl.,* 18 (1965), 45–7, 71. L. Stone and J. F. Stone, *An open élite? England 1540–1880* (Oxford, 1984), 96–7. It should be noted that both these studies deal with the peerage only; as yet we have no demographic study of the gentry. For the purposes of this chapter, it has been assumed that the population history of the gentry will be similar to that of the aristocracy. This chapter is concerned only with the propertied élite of early-modern society.

3. E. Newton, *Lyme Letters 1660–1760* (London, 1925), 19 (1663). See also Charles Montagu to his brother Edward in 1613 'Wee had rather here of my sister's thickning'; NRO, Montagu of Boughton MS, vol. 3, fo. 92.

4. J. O. Halliwell (ed.), *The Autobiography and Correspondence of Sir Simonds D'Ewes, Bart* (London, 1845), 417.

5. Between the cohort of owners born in the last half of the sixteenth century and those born in the first half of the eighteenth, the proportion leaving no male heir rose from 26 per cent to 52 per cent. Stone, *An Open Élite?*, 101.

6. Arthur Stanhope to the Earl of Huntingdon after his marriage, 1672: 'I doubt not to see you the fondest and lovingeste couple in the world when my deare p: has beene up to the hilts in her c:. HL, Hastings MS HA 12503.

7. HL, Hastings MS HA 1779 (1674).

8. WRO, Fielding MS CR 2017, vol. C1, fo. 36 (1630–1).

9. For an analysis of the stress placed on virility as an important facet of masculinity in the nineteenth century, see J. Weeks, *Sex, Politics and Society. The Regulation of Sexuality Since 1800* (London, 1981).

10. A. Eccles, *Obstetrics and Gynaecology in Tudor and Stuart England* (London, 1982), ch. 5; A. McLaren, *Reproductive Rituals: the Perception of Fertility in England from the Sixteenth Century to the Nineteenth Century* (London, 1984), 19–21.

11. StaRO, Paget MS D603/K/2/1 (c.1636).

12. NRO, Isham MS IC 749 (1672).

13. McLaren, *Reproductive Rituals*, 38.

14. WRO, Fielding MS CR 2017, vol. C2, fo. 117 (c.1640).

15. HL, Hastings MS HA 12503 (1672).

16. Eccles, *Obstetrics and Gynaecology*, 58–61; J. Sharpe, *The Midwive's Book*, first pub. 1671, Facsmile (New York, 1985), 102–4. The urine tests involved inspecting a woman's urine for worms after 3 days – if they were present she was pregnant; or immersing a needle in the urine and if red spots appeared on the needle after 24 hours, the woman had conceived.

17. Mauriceau, *Diseases of Women with Child*, 31; Sharpe, *Midwive's Book*, 102.

18. M. H. Nicolson, *Conway Letters. The Correspondence of Anne, Viscountess Conway, Henry More and Their Friends, 1642–84* (London, 1930), 92.

19. Women knew the date of conception with surprising accuracy. Lady Clifford described her sister as travelling into town '13 weeks gone with child'; V. Sackville-West (ed.), *The Diary of the Lady Anne Clifford* (London, 1923), 60 (1617).

20. B. Winchester, *Tudor Family Portrait* (London, 1955), 101 (1546).

21. NRO, Isham MS IC 583 (1666). Women could also be completely deceived about their pregnancies. For examples of false pregnancy, see the letters of James Lawes-Wittewronge about his sister, HRO, Lawes-Wittewronge MS D F28 (6/4/1689 to 8/6/1689); and the false pregnancy of Honor Lisle, M. St Clare Byrne (ed.), *The Lisle Letters* (6 vols, Chicago, 1981), vol. 4, 68, 134, 148–9, 150.

22. A. Searle (ed.), *Barrington Family Letters 1628–1632* (London, 1983), 172 (1630). Jane Josselin diagnosed her pregnancies from at least the second month: A. Macfarlane, *The Family Life of Ralph Josselin, a Seventeenth-century Clergyman. An Essay in Historical Anthropology* (Cambridge, 1970), 83.

23. D. Fleming (ed.), *Diary of Archibald Johnston of Wariston 1650–54* (Scottish History Society, 1919), 238 (1654). Similarly, Sarah Henry realized she had not conceived when she menstruated; P. Crawford, 'Attitudes to pregnancy from a woman's spiritual diary', *Loc. Popul. Stud.*, 21 (1978), 43–5.

24. Sackville-West (ed.), *Diary of Lady Anne Clifford*, 107 (1619). See too Halliwell (ed.), *Autobiography of Simonds D'Ewes*, 420 (1629).

25. Eccles, *Obstetrics and Gynaecology*, 33; Sharpe, *Midwive's Book*, 146. Mauriceau, *Diseases of Women with Child*, 33, was one of the few authors to disagree with this line of reasoning.

26. H. Cholmley, *The Memoirs of Sir Hugh Cholmley* (no pub. given, copy in CUL, pressmark S450.b.78.2), 40.

27. ERO, Neville MS D/DBy C23/2 fo. 33 (1630).

28. KAO, Dering MS U3350 C2, fo. 24 (1630); see also fo. 43 (1634).

29. ERO, Neville MS D/DBy C23/2 fo. 57 (1637); also fo. 50 (1627).

30. A. Oakley, *The Captured Womb. A History of the Medical Care of Pregnant Women* (Oxford, 1984), 17.

31. M. MacDonald, *Mystical Bedlam. Madness, Anxiety and Healing in Seventeenth Century England* (Cambridge, 1981), 38. For a lurid account of all the ills to which female flesh was heir, see E. Shorter, *A History of Women's Bodies* (London, 1983).

32. H. Smith, 'Gynecology and ideology in seventeenth-century England', in B. Carroll (ed.), *Liberating Women's History* (Urbana, 1976), 99.

33. R. Baxter, *A Christian Directory*, 2nd edn (1678), cited in H. Smith, *Reason's Disciples. Seventeenth-century English Feminists* (Urbana, 1982), xiv.

34. MacDonald, *Mystical Bedlam*, 36, 108.

35. Mauriceau, *Diseases of Women with Child*, 48.

36. The phrase was used to describe Lady Frances Hatton when she was pregnant in c.1678. NRO, Finch Hatton MS FH 4338.

37. LPL, Talbot MS 3205, fo. 141.

38. Cicelea Hatton did inform her husband, 'I am very well and my child for I feel it very strong within me.' More commonly, however, women suffered many ailments when pregnant. For a description of the trials endured by Jane Josselin, see L. M. Beier, 'In sickness and in health: a seventeenth-century family's experience', in R. Porter (ed.), *Patients and Practitioners. Lay Perceptions of Medicine in Pre-industrial Society* (Cambridge, 1985), 104–7 and Macfarlane, *Family Life of Ralph Josselin*, 84. For other examples of the discomfort caused by pregnancy, see L. Pollock, *A Lasting Relationship: Parents and Children over Three Centuries* (London, 1987), 22–6.

39. *Correspondence of the Family of Hatton* (2 vols. London, 1878), vol. 1, 54 (1667).

40. NRO, Montagu of Boughton MS vol. 4, fo. 255 (c.1674).

41. BL, Add. MSS 29571, fo. 107 (c.1667); *The Autobiography of Mrs Alice Thornton of East Newton, County York* (Durham, 1875), 84 (1652).

42. Searle (ed.), *Barrington Family Letters*, 191 (1631).

43. R. Schofield, 'Did the mothers really die? Three centuries of maternal mortality in "the world we have lost"', in L. Bonfield, R. M. Smith, and K. Wrightson (eds), *The World We Have Gained. Histories of Population and Social Structure* (Oxford, 1986), 254. See also J. Loftis (ed.), *The Memoirs of Anne, Lady Halkett and Ann, Lady Fanshawe* (Oxford, 1979), 137 (1658).

44. WRO, Newdegate MS CR 136 B48 (early-seventeenth century).

45. NRO, Finch Hatton MS FH 4394 (c.1678).

46. NRO, Finch Hatton MS FH 1465 (1678).

47. Fleming (ed.), *Diary of Archibald Johnston*, 238 (1654).

48. F. P. Verney, *Memoirs of the Verney Family* (2 vols, London, 1892), vol. 1, 349 (1647).

49. Newton, *Lyme Letters*, 100–1 (1681).

50. Searle (ed.), *Barrington Family Letters*, 172 (1630).

51. Ibid., 173 (1630).

52. Elizabeth Josceline bought a winding sheet for her burial once she felt the foetus move within her, anticipating that she would not survive the birth: E. Josceline, *The Mother's Legacie to Her Unborne Childe*, ed. J. Haviland, repr. 3rd edn of 1625 (Edinburgh and London, 1852), preface. Jane Josselin was 'oppressed with fears' about her confinements: Beier, 'In sickness and in health', 104–5; Macfarlane, *Family Life of Ralph Josselin*, 84.

53. Schofield, 'Did the mothers really die?', 259–60. Since upper-rank women on average had one or two fewer children than women lower down the social scale, their risk of death in childbirth would be proportionately smaller.

54. Josceline, *Mother's Legacie*, preface. For the public drama surrounding childbirth, see A. Wilson, 'Participant or patient? Seventeenth-century childbirth from the mother's point of view', in R. Porter (ed.), *Patients and Practitioners*, 129–44. For further information on the fear which childbirth produced in women, see S. Mendelson, 'Stuart women's diaries and occasional memoirs', in M. Prior (ed.), *Women in English Society 1500–1800* (London and New York, 1985), 196–7.

55. LAO, Burrell Massingberd MS B/1 (1700).

56. SCL, Bright MS BR 79 (1681).

57. HRO, Lawes-Wittewronge MS D F29 (1689).

58. NRO, Isham MS IC 328 (1653).

59. *The Private Correspondence of Jane, Lady Cornwallis* (London, 1842), 85 (1623).

60. W. Gouge, *Of Domesticall Duties* (London, 1622), 505; R. V. Schnucker, 'The English Puritans and pregnancy, delivery and breast feeding', *Hist. Childh. Quart.*, 1 (1974), 638–9.

61. NRO, Montagu of Boughton MS vol. 4, fo. 246 (1673).

62. For reviews of ante-natal care in the early-modern period, see Eccles, *Obstetrics and Gynaecology*, ch. 7; McLaren, *Reproductive Rituals*, ch. 2; Schnucker, 'The English Puritans', 637–58; R. V. Schnucker, 'Elizabethan birth control and Puritan attitudes', *J. Interdisc. Hist.*, 5 (1975), 655–67.

63. This is a point made by Oakley, *The Captured Womb*, 11–12. She argues further (p. 16) that there was no concept of ante-natal care until the twentieth century. Such a stance can be supported only if one insists that the care must be provided by professionals, an anachronistic viewpoint. Oakley also claims that pregnancy has been redefined by obstetricians in this century in order to abolish any

idea of its normality; today all pregnancies are potentially pathological. This in fact is not a redefinition since the medical writers of the early-modern period also viewed all pregnancies as potentially pathological, requiring, if not professional routine care, at least the careful following of a specified regime.

64. M. K. Eshleman, 'Diet during pregnancy in the sixteenth and seventeenth centuries', *J. Hist. Med.*, 30 (1975), 23–40.

65. Ibid., 29–30.

66. Mauriceau, *Diseases of Women with Child*, 51.

67. NLS, Fletcher MS 17851/132 (late-seventeenth century).

68. Halliwell (ed.), *Autobiography of Simonds D'Ewes*, 102 (1634).

69. StaRO, Bagot MS MF 9 1.a.145 (1666). Jane Josselin while pregnant also experienced food cravings, in her case for fresh cherries: Macfarlane, *Family Life of Ralph Josselin*, 84.

70. ScotRO, Melville MS GD26/13/401/22 (1695).

71. *The Private Diary of Elizabeth, Viscountess Mordaunt* (Duncairn, 1856), 230 (c.1660).

72. BL, Add. MSS 29571, fo. 76 (c.1667).

73. NRO, Isham MS IC 580 (1668); see also Newton, *Lyme Letters*, 113 (1684).

74. KAO, Dering MS U3350 C2 fo. 9 (c.1626); see also A. Wall (ed.), *Two Elizabethan Women: Correspondence of Joan and Maria Thynne, 1575–1611* (Wilts Rec. Soc., 1983), 14 (1596).

75. Sackville-West (ed.), *Diary of Lady Anne Clifford*, 112 (1619).

76. NRO, Finch Hatton MS FH 4331 (c.1678).

77. NLS, Fletcher MS 17851/132 (late seventeenth century). Professional advisers were not in agreement on this point: for example, Mauriceau, *Diseases of Women with Child*, 115, instructed abortion-prone women to stay in bed.

78. T. T. Lewis (ed.), *Letters of the Lady Brilliana Harley* (London, 1854), 78 (1639). Eccles, *Obstetrics and Gynaecology*, 61, also notes that professional help was virtually limited to the correction of disorders if they arose.

79. Nicolson, *Conway Letters*, 154 (1658).

80. NotRO, Saville MS 221/97/7, fo. (1659). For examples of home treatments for pregnancy see those contained in the medicinal receipt book of Elizabeth Freke, BL, Add. MSS 45718, ff. 228, 235, 238.

81. Wall (ed.), *Two Elizabethan Women*, 14 (1596).

82. Cholmley, *Memoirs*, 41 (1625).

83. D. Gardiner (ed.), *The Oxinden Letters 1607–1642. Being the Correspondence of Henry Oxinden of Barham and His Circle* (London, 1933), 24 (1625); see also SomRO, Phelips MS DD/PH 224/33 (1641).

84. Wilson, 'Participant or patient?', 133–4. For examples of women inviting their sisters and mothers to attend the birth, see Winchester, *Tudor Family Portrait*, 103 (1550); Searle (ed.), *Barrington Family Letters*, 188–9 (1631).

85. Gouge, *Domesticall Duties*, 506; Schnucker, 'The English Puritans', 639.

86. KAO, Dering MS U3350 C2 fo. 27 (1630).

87. For a detailed description of the preparations involved in an aristocratic birth, see the letters concerning Honor Lisle's pregnancy in St Clare Byrne (ed.), *Lisle Letters*, vol. 4 (1537).

88. BodL, Herrick MS C474, vol. 1, fo. 132 (1590).

89. D. Gardiner (ed.), *The Oxinden and Peyton Letters 1642–1670* (London, 1937), 186 (1653).

90. Winchester, *Tudor Family Portrait*, 101. Olivia Porter requested Endymion to be home in time for the birth of their third child and he himself apologized for being unable to leave his court duties in order to be near at the birth of their first child: D. Townshend (ed.), *The Life and Letters of Mr Endymion Porter: Sometime Gentleman of the Bedchamber to King Charles the First* (London, 1897), 22, 77 (1622 & 1624).

91. BL, Add. MSS 28052, fo. 12 (c.1666).

92. John Winthrop was in the next room when his son was born, R. C. Winthrop, *Life and Letters of John Winthrop* (Boston, 1869, 2nd edn), vol. 1, 148 (1620). See also R. A. Houlbrooke, *The English Family* (London and New York, 1984), 129.

93. In the 1970s, 15 per cent of all recognized pregnancies terminated early by spontaneous abortion: R. W. Huff and C. J. Paverstein (eds), *Human Reproduction, Physiology and Pathophysiology* (New York and Chichester, 1979), 122.

94. R. W. Fogel, 'Nutrition and the decline in mortality since 1700: some additional preliminary findings', Working paper 1802 (National Bureau of Economic Research, 1986), 68–9.

95. Cited in G. F. Still, *The History of Paediatrics*, (London, 1931), 212–13.

96. The higher fertility levels of women as a result of employing wet nurses has been stressed by D. McLaren, 'Nature's contraceptive. Wet-nursing and prolonged lactation: the case of Chesham, Buckinghamshire, 1578–1601', *Med. Hist.*, 23 (1979), 426–41 and 'Marital fertility and lactation 1570–1720', in M. Prior (ed.), *Women in English Society*, 22–53; R. A. P. Finlay, *Population and Metropolis: The Demography of London 1580–1650* (Cambridge, 1981), 133–46. Elite women who married under the age of 25 would have 6–7 children, ordinary women 5–6: Hollingsworth, 'Demography of the British Peerage', 44; E. A. Wrigley and R. S. Schofield, *The Population History of England 1541–1871. A Reconstruction* (London 1981), 254.

97. Hollingsworth, 'Demography of the British Peerage', 11–12, 29, 40, 63.

98. Ibid., 51; L. Stone, *The Family, Sex and Marriage in England 1500–1800* (London, 1977), 66.

99. McLaren, *Reproductive Rituals*, ch. 3; J. Noonan, *Contraception. A History of its Treatment by the Catholic Theologians and Canonists* (Cambridge, Mass., 1966); Schnucker 'Elizabethan birth control', 655–67.

100. *Autobiography of Mrs Alice Thornton*, 164–5 (1667). See also the example of Mary Rich: T. C. Croker (ed.), *The Autobiography of Mary Countess of Warwick* (Percy Society, 1848), 32–3 (c.1632).

101. Infanticide, a possible third choice, was not a viable option for married women. As far as we can tell, infanticide was mainly confined to illegitimate children. K. Wrightson, 'Infanticide in European history', *Crim. Just. Hist.*, 3 (1982), 1–20.

102. Gouge, *Domesticall Duties*, 506. For a review of the methods and possible extent of abortion, see Eccles, *Obstetrics and Gynaecology*, ch. 8; McLaren, *Reproductive Rituals*, ch. 4; Schnucker, 'Elizabethan birth control', 655–67.

103. StaRO, Jerningham MS 3/H/3/1, fo. 65 (late-seventeenth century).

104. For example, N. Culpeper, *Complete Herbal and English Physician*, Facsimile of 1826 edn (Hong Kong, 1976), 222, gives a recipe 'to help those whose courses are stopped' which contains the abortifacient rue. See also the published seventeenth-century receipt book of Jane Mosely: J. Mosely, *Derbyshire Remedies*, (Derbyshire Museum Service, 1979), p. W.

105. BL, Add. MSS 45718, fo. 238 (mid-seventeenth century).

106. This point has been noted by G. Devereux, *A Study of Abortion in Primitive Societies* (rev. edn, New York, 1976), 27–8; G. R. Quaife, *Wanton Wenches and Wayward Wives. Peasants and Illicit Sex in Early Seventeenth-century England* (London, 1979), 118.

107. BL, Add. MSS 45718, fo. 228 (mid-seventeenth century). Devereux, *Study of Abortion in Primitive Societies*, 37, points out that some drugs procured abortion by acting as an irritant on the gastrointestinal tract.

108. Shorter, *History of Women's Bodies*, 184–7; Quaife, *Wanton Wenches and Wayward Wives*, 118.

109. Devereux, *Study of Abortion in Primitive Societies*, 36–7.

110. The quotation is taken from Stone, *Family, Sex and Marriage*, 422.

111. Quaife, *Wanton Wenches and Wayward Wives*, 120.

112. ScotRO, Melville MS GD26/13/401/40 (c.1698). See also the example of Mary Fitton who, pregnant and unmarried, was sent a suggestive note by her mother in which she was warned against the taking of harsh physic in case it resulted in abortion, Schnucker, 'Elizabethan birth control', 655.

113. Crawford, 'Attitudes to pregnancy', 43–5; F. P. Hett (ed.), *The Memoirs of Sir Robert Sibbald (1661–1722)* (London, 1932), 71–2 (1682).

114. SCL, Bright MS Br 79a (1676).

115. NUL, Cavendish MS, Portland letters PW1 78 (mid-seventeenth century).

116. N. Jeffcoate, *Principles of Gynaecology* (London and Boston, 1975, 43rd edn), 188–9.

117. ERO, Neville MS D/DBy C23, fo. 100.

118. Jeffcoate, *Principles of Gynaecology*, 188, 193.

119. Savin could prove fatal and ergot would cause severe headaches and diarrhoea: Shorter, *History of Women's Bodies*, 187.

120. BL, Osborne MS add 28 050, fo. 50 (1686).

121. Jeffcoate, *Principles of Gynaecology*, 191.

122. The entries in Table 2.1 were taken from: BL, 'Autobiography of Thomas Godfrey', Lansdowne MSS 235, fo. 3; Cholmley, *Memoirs*, 56: H. Meikle (ed.), 'The diary of Sir William Drummond of Hawthornden 1657–59', *Scot. Hist. Soc. Miscel.*, 35 (1941), 3–52, p. 33; *The Autobiography of Symon Patrick* (Oxford, 1839), 88.

123. Jeffcoate, *Principles of Gynaecology*, 191.

124. Macfarlane, *Family Life of Ralph Josselin*, 203; McLaren, *Reproductive Rituals*, 97.

125. Unlike Stone, *Open Elite?*, 97, who argues that the decision to restrict fertility lay with the husband; A. McLaren, 'Women's work and regulation of family size: the question of abortion in the nineteenth century', *Hist. Workshop*, 4 (1971), 70–81, argues that women preferred abortion since it allowed them rather than their husbands to control their fertility. A further possible avenue of exploration in the attempt to ascertain if abortion occurred on a wide scale is that of scrutinizing the evidence on mothers dying before giving birth. In the Swedish parish of Sankta Klara during the late eighteenth century, unmarried servant girls dying undelivered accounted for 60 per cent of the maternal mortality rate, indicating the possibility of lethal abortion. Schofield, 'Did the mothers really die?' 244.

126. C. Wilson, 'Natural fertility in pre-industrial England, 1600–1799', *Popul. Stud.*, 38 (1984), 225–40 and 'The proximate determinants of marital fertility in England 1600–1799', in Bonfield, Smith, and Wrightson (eds), *The World We Have Gained*, 203–30.

127. *Hatton Correspondence*, vol. 2, 5 (1681). The extracts cited from Alice Thornton and the Countess of Wemyss (notes 100 and 111) reveal a like concern with the woman's health. See also McLaren, *Reproductive Rituals*, 111.

128. McLaren, *Reproductive Rituals*, 89.

129. P. Crawford, 'Attitudes to menstruation in seventeenth-century England', *P & P*, 91 (1981), 47–73.

3

The ceremony of childbirth and its interpretation

Adrian Wilson

In this chapter I want to argue that a woman's becoming and being a mother in seventeenth-century England was suffused with political meaning; and specifically, that the ritual management of childbirth reflected the wider context of gender relations in what has been called 'the world we have lost'.[1] In order to develop this claim, which represents a shift in my own thinking about the subject of childbirth, I will describe what is known of the popular birth-ritual, and then survey some modern interpretations of that ritual. It will emerge that these interpretations exhibit a certain gender-specificity: women historians have been more willing than their male colleagues to grasp the political meaning of the 'rite of passage' surrounding childbirth. We will also see that the procedures which made up the customary ritual – procedures later condemned on medical grounds – are intelligible as rational responses to the material demands of seventeenth-century motherhood. In this respect the management of childbirth fits well with the studies on breastfeeding conducted by Dorothy McLaren, whose memory we honour in this volume.

Let us first remind ourselves of the central role which childbirth played in the lives of seventeenth-century women. In a sense a woman's whole life revolved around the act of giving birth. Not that women were continuously engaged in 'breeding': on the contrary, a typical married women could expect to give birth only four or five times after getting married in her mid- twenties.[2] Nevertheless, her life as a servant from her teenage years would have been devoted to accumulating the 'portion' she brought to marriage;[3] and marriage itself was centred upon the bearing of children. It was materially disastrous for a woman to become an unmarried mother: if her lover could not be found or 'named', she would experience not only the difficulty of supporting herself and her baby, but also a variety of pressures from the authorities of parish and manor, which might make it difficult for her own parents or relatives to assist her in her plight.[4] The loss of her 'honour' thus amounted to the loss of her means of subsistence. All the more impressive, therefore, that very few unmarried mothers seem to have resorted to infanticide to escape such difficulties.[5] Instead, such mothers either made shift as best they could to bring up their children, or 'dropped' their babies in some well-chosen place where there was a good chance that the children would be found and maintained by others: on the doorstep of a wealthy family (*Tom Jones*), on the church porch (where the parish officers would find the child), or, in London, in the vicinity of Christ's Hospital (as if to remind its seventeenth-century governors that their sixteenth-century predecessors had accepted foundling children).[6] The sometimes large numbers of foundlings, particularly in towns and especially in London, testify not to maternal 'indifference' but rather to the desperate plight of the unmarried mother.[7] Hence the willingness with which women accepted the bonds of marriage. In exchange for legal inequalities, for a vow of obedience, for conferring on the husband an absolute property in her goods, labour, and sexuality, marriage offered the mother-to-be a vital security.[8] For most women, the role of wife was the best prospect which life offered.

Thus, the key context of seventeenth-century childbirth was the material role of women within the social institution of marriage. This fundamental fact is obscured for us as historians by the particular construction of childbirth in our own society. For us, childbirth is a *medical* event, located in the medical space of the hospital, managed by medical personnel, apprehended by medical categories. Correspondingly, its history has been seen as a medical matter. What results is a double historiography: on the one hand, a dense and technical history, rich in obstetric detail and devoid of context; and on the other hand, in works of general or social history (including the history of the family), a symmetrically opposite laconic glance, dismissing childbirth in a page, a paragraph, or a mere sentence.[9] Yet different though they are, these two historiographies nevertheless share a language: the language of evaluation. We speak of childbirth as midwifery/obstetrics, and we do so in terms of welfare, efficiency, progress, improvement; in terms of cruelty, ignorance, superstition, backwardness, inadequate care. Such evaluative formulations rest upon the medical concept of childbirth and help to confirm us in our own attachment to that model.

We can begin to detach ourselves from this medical conception if we note, following Jean Donnison and Audrey Eccles, that the medicalization of childbirth was itself a historical process, a process which effectively began in the eighteenth century.[10] For seventeenth-century mothers, childbirth had many different meanings: it might become a medical event, but was not inherently so; and indeed, male medical access to childbirth was highly restricted and very much on women's terms.[11] Thus, before childbirth belonged to medicine, it belonged to women. As we shall now see, women had constructed a coherent system for the management of childbirth, a system based on their own collective culture and satisfying their own material needs.

The ceremony of childbirth

Childbirth in seventeenth-century England was a social occasion, specifically an occasion for women. In the later months of her pregnancy, the mother-to-be would issue invitations to her female friends, relatives, and neighbours. Her midwife would probably know when the birth was due; as a rule, the midwife lived in the same village as the mother, and she might well have been giving advice on the management of the pregnancy.[12] When the mother's labour pains began, there fell upon her husband (perhaps assisted by a servant or neighbour) the duty of what in East Anglia was known as 'nidgeting': that is, going about from house to house to summon the midwife and the other women to the birth.[13] Within an hour or so, the group of women would be assembled in the mother's bedroom. Meanwhile, the husband would have to make his own arrangements for passing the ensuing hours – perhaps in the parlour downstairs, talking and drinking with a group of male friends, the situation later immortalized as the setting of Sterne's *Tristram Shandy*.[14] We have no equivalent literary account of the scene upstairs, around the mother in labour, but every indication suggests that this was the precise female complement of the all-male parlour scene depicted, and richly exploited, by Sterne. With the company of women assembled, the ceremony of childbirth could begin.

What was happening in these rapid preparations was that the mother was moving into a different social space: away from the world of men (centrally, her husband) and into the world of women. It was here, within the collective culture of women, that birth belonged. If, as sometimes occurred, the labour proceeded so swiftly that the child was born before all the invited women were present, this could occasion anxiety: Ralph Josselin wrote in his diary[15] that at his wife's eighth delivery (14 January 1658), after the arrival of the midwife and nurse, 'her labour came on so strongly and speedily that . . . only 2 or 3 women more in to her, *but* god supplied all' (emphasis added). It would seem, from this and other rare fragments of evidence, that over five women were usually present. The collective character of the ritual was manifest from the onset.

The invited women often included the mother's own mother: for instance, in late October 1678 Jane Josselin rode to London to be with her daughter Mrs Elizabeth Smith at Elizabeth's first delivery.[16] As to the other women, the evidence I have so far compiled (all of it indirect) suggests that these comprised the mother's closest personal friends. Thus, some mothers apparently later felt guilty at not having invited a particular woman – which implies that the invitation was a compliment, that to omit it was a slight, and that the mother made her own choices in the matter.[17] Especially revealing is the word used to describe the invited women, its origins and its wider usage. They were known as 'gossips' and it is from this that we get our word 'gossip' – originally, a male description of what women did when they got together.[18] The word 'gossip' was a corruption of 'god-sib', or 'god-sibling' – that is, someone invited to witness the birth for the subsequent purpose of the child's baptism. It retained a usage with respect to baptism (and here could refer to men as well as to women), but by the seventeenth century had acquired a wider meaning which referred specifically to women. Thus, when Nicholas Culpeper wrote about 'the melancholy of virgins and widows', he recommended as the chief protective against this illness or ill-humour that the women should 'rejoice with her gossips' – that is, that she should take delight in the company of her female friends.[19] Such usage suggests that the collective ritual of childbirth was an integral part of a wider women's culture.

As essential as the gossips was the *midwife*, or, as she was known in some areas, the 'gracewife'.[20] Admittedly, some births did take place without the midwife. On occasion, she might not arrive in time, as when Jane Josselin gave birth in 1649 to her fifth child.[21] Again, some villages were too small to have their own midwives. The churchwardens of Dry Drayton, Cambridgeshire, replied to the visitation articles of 1662 that 'we have none . . . that practice midwifery but charitably; our neighbours as we conceive help one another'.[22] However, it is more likely that births in Dry Drayton were attended by a midwife from a neighbouring village – or perhaps that the churchwardens were simply protecting their own midwife from the considerable expense of taking out a bishop's licence in midwifery. William Harvey, arguing that midwives were too interventionist, wrote in the mid-seventeenth century that 'the business is far better managed among the poor and among those who have become pregnant in secret and are delivered in private without . . . any midwife'.[23] This seems to imply that all 'poor' women managed without midwives. Yet Harvey's friend Percival Willughby, who shared Harvey's attitude to midwives (and may in fact have been the source of this conviction on Harvey's part), had to go to some lengths to find particular stories of delivery without a midwife.[24] Indeed, other evidence shows that even unmarried mothers might well make use of a midwife: thus, in February 1668 Jane Barton, wife of Thomas, of Uttoxeter, was being 'sought for' by the consistory court apparitor, for having acted as midwife to a bastard-bearer.[25] Deliveries without a midwife, then, were rare; the presence of the midwife was the customary norm.

Etymologically, the midwife was the 'with-woman': the woman whose task it was to *be with* the mother during the delivery.[26] In practice, her tasks were more specific than this. The midwife took charge as soon as she arrived, and expected to remain in charge thereafter. It was even possible for a young and inexperienced midwife, probably of no higher than yeoman status, to defy a mother who was a lady – that is, the wife of a gentleman, a member of the ruling class.[27] *Power*, then, was a defining feature of the midwife's office. Correspondingly, the midwife was *paid* for her services, the sum depending greatly on the wealth and social standing of the mother. For the delivery of a pauper woman, the midwife might be paid 2 shillings by the parish officers; for a typical delivery in a town, perhaps 6 shillings; for delivering a gentlewoman or the wife of an aristocrat, a fee measured in guineas; for delivering the Queen, £100.[28] Daniel Fleming of Oxford always paid the midwife 10 shillings, and did so 'at my first going in to see my wife after her delivery'.[29] The midwife's remuneration did not end here, for she would later receive tips from the godparents (and possibly from others as well) at the baptism of the child. If the godfather were as wealthy as Samuel Pepys, the midwife would thereby receive another 10 shillings.[30] Beyond power and payment, the midwife probably had a further defining characteristic: it seems likely that she alone was entrusted with the *right to touch* the mother's labiae, vagina, and cervix. Certainly some midwives did handle the labiae: midwives were enjoined (by male practitioners) to investigate the state of the birth by touching the cervix; and while the gossips could and did handle the child and cut the umbilical cord, I know of no instance of a gossip's touching the mother's 'privities'.[31]

The social space of the birth, then, was a collective female space, constituted on the one hand by the presence of gossips and midwife, and on the other hand by the absence of men. It was however equally important to demarcate the *physical* space of the birth: to confer upon the room a different character, signifying its special function. This was achieved by physically and symbolically enclosing the chamber. Air was excluded by blocking up the keyholes; daylight was shut out by means of heavy curtains; the darkness within was illuminated by means of candles, which were therefore part of the standard requirements for a delivery.[32] Thus reconstituted, the room became the *lying-in chamber*, the physical counterpart of the female social space to which the mother now belonged. The flickering candlelight must have given the darkened room an atmosphere not unlike that of a rather busy and crowded little chapel. Somewhere in this room, if it had a fireplace, or perhaps elsewhere in the house, some of the gossips were preparing the mother's *caudle* – the special drink which was associated with childbirth, consisting of ale or wine, warmed with sugar and spices.[33] The mother drank the caudle to keep up her strength and spirits: no doubt the midwife instructed her on how much of it to drink and when, and the gossips kept themselves busy by maintaining the supply. (Caudle was also used as a nourishing drink for sick patients, sometimes enhanced with the yolk of an egg.[34] That it was very pleasant to taste is indicated by the manner of its use in a certain male ritual, recorded by Anthony Wood at Oxford: each freshman had to make a little speech, 'which if well done, the person that spoke it was to have a cup of caudle; if dull . . . salted drink'.[35])

As the gossips and midwife arrived, as the room and the caudle were being prepared, the birth itself was gradually advancing. However, even the entry of the child into the world was a matter of culture, not simply of Nature. The midwife had her own technique, perhaps acquired by instruction from another midwife whom she had served as a deputy, perhaps learnt by reading in a 'midwife's book': this technique she would generally have used before, and she would be convinced that it worked. Accordingly, midwives seem to have had great confidence in their own chosen methods, and those methods varied enormously.[36] There were some midwives who simply left the birth to Nature, keeping the mother warm in her bed and waiting for the delivery to proceed. Others, by contrast, stretched the labiae to dilate the passage, pulled on the child as soon as some part presented itself, and made such efforts that (in Willughby's words) 'the sweat did run down their faces, in performing of their work'.[37] The midwife might carry about with her a midwife's stool, on which the mother sat for the delivery. However, this custom, common in seventeenth-century London (and known in other localities, such as Derby), seems to have fallen out of favour with midwives by the eighteenth century.[38] There were many alternatives: the mother could lie in bed, either on her back or on her side; she could sit in another woman's lap; or she could kneel on a bolster on the floor, either with her head down (what Willughby called 'a slope, bending posture descending') or with her head supported on the lap of one of the gossips ('a slope, bending posture ascending').[39]

In a small minority of births, such differences of technique were probably consequential. The midwife had other choices to make as well: whether to extract the placenta by hand or to leave its expulsion to Nature; whether to search for a possible second child and, if a twin were found, whether to leave this or attempt to deliver it. There were also a few births (probably about one in thirty) where the delivery became obstructed or (still more rarely) where some accident such as bleeding occurred.[40] In the vast majority of deliveries, however, whatever the midwife's technique, the birth proceeded smoothly and swiftly, producing a living child in a matter of hours. If the child seemed faint or weakly, the midwife and gossips had various methods of reviving it; such expertise was apparently an important part of the midwife's work.[41] Once the child had been delivered, the 'navel-string' tied and cut (perhaps, as we have seen, by one of the gossips), and the child washed, the birth was completed by *swaddling* the child. Though the methods of swaddling (the tightness and length of the bandage, for instance) may well have varied, the fact of swaddling was one of the constant features of the management of birth. Swaddling was apparently either performed by the midwife, or at least supervised by her; once the child was swaddled, it was at last shown to the mother.[42]

With the act of swaddling, the birth was completed, but the ceremony of childbirth was only beginning: for the full childbirth ritual comprised not just the delivery itself, but the ensuing *lying-in,* a process which took some 3 weeks to a month. It was for this, as much as for the birth itself, that the room had been prepared; hence its description as the lying-in chamber. The mother had been 'brought to bed', she had completed her 'crying out'; but she was still 'in the straw', and she would remain in that state for what was called 'the month' or 'her month'.[43] In many respects the mother was now treated as if she were an invalid: above all, she was given a prolonged period of rest, in which her body could recover from the trauma of delivery. However, just as her bodily state was gradually altering, so too she shifted, in the course of 'the month', in social and physical space.

Physically, lying-in appears to have comprised three stages. At first, the mother was confined to her bed, for a period which varied from 3 days to as long as a fortnight. During this time, the room remained darkened; thus, in 1608 we find a lying-in chamber described, over 5 days after the delivery, as a 'dark lodging'.[44] Throughout this time the bed linen was kept unchanged, but the mother's 'privities' were kept clean by poultices or by bathing with herbal decoctions.[45] Then came her 'upsitting', when the bed linen was first changed; after this the mother remained in her room for a further week or 10 days, not confined to bed but still enjoying physical rest. In the third and final stage of lying-in, the mother could move freely about the house, but did not venture out of doors: this stage, too, seems to have lasted for about a week or 10 days. The *timing* of the different stages depended on the mother's perception of her physical strength. Jane Josselin was 'about the house' within 22 days of the birth of her ninth child, but after her previous delivery it had been 38 days before Ralph could record in his diary that she was 'up and down in the house, god's name be praised'.[46] Nevertheless, the *sequence* of stages seems to have been constant, so far as our fragmentary evidence suggests.

Corresponding to these shifts in physical space were a series of movements in social space. At first, only women could visit the mother, probably only in ones or twos, and perhaps only those women who had been present during the delivery itself. The 'upsitting' appears to have been an important social occasion, to judge by the examples under this word in the *Oxford English Dictionary*.[47] There is some evidence to suggest that a women's feast took place a little later, during the second stage of lying-in.[48] On the thirteenth day after one delivery, Ralph Josselin noted in his diary that his wife had been visited by some local women. Similarly, but at greater length, Samuel Sewall in New England wrote on 16 January 1702 (2 weeks after a delivery): 'My wife treats her midwife and women: had a good dinner, boiled pork, beef, fowls; very good roast beef, turkey-pie, tarts. Madam Usher carved; Mrs Hannah Greenleaf; Ellis, Cowell, Wheeler . . . ' The list of names ran on to a total of seventeen women. In addition to such group occasions, there were individual visits, during which the female guest would be invited to drink the mother's caudle. Thus, the celebratory, collective female character of the birth was continued into the process of lying-in. Correspondingly, male access to the mother was restricted: initially, only men who were the mother's own relatives could visit her, though by the final stage of lying-in this restriction was apparently relaxed.[49] It may have been easier for a man to pay a visit if he was accompanied by his wife; thus, Samuel and Elizabeth Pepys visited Betty Michell on 3 May 1667, only 10 days after her delivery.[50]

A further dimension of the lying-in transition concerned the mother's physical work. In the first stages of lying-in, it was impossible for her to perform any household tasks. Accordingly, it was standard practice for a *nurse* to be recruited.[51] A relative or friend would sometimes come to assist about the house and to look after the mother; on other occasions the nurse would be hired. Jane Josselin made use of a hired nurse after at least three of her deliveries; and on a further occasion her friend Mrs Harlakanden stayed with her, lending charitable help. As an alternative, one of the children could serve, as Penelope Mordaunt suggested her young daughter Pen could do: 'I grow very uneasy [she wrote to her husband in 1699] . . . which has made me this day send . . . for blankets and things for the child, lest I should be caught; and if I be, Pen must be nurse for I have none yet.' The hired nurse was known in the nineteenth century as the 'monthly nurse', a phrase which suggests that her services persisted for the full lying-in period. Though the term was first used from about the 1840s, the practice of employing such nurses long predated the word: the adjective 'monthly' was probably added at this time to distinguish this kind of nursing from other types, and especially hospital nursing.[52] However, the nurse might be hired for only 2 to 3 weeks; and in fact mothers were probably working at household tasks in the third stage of lying-in. This was the practical meaning of Jane Josselin's being 'about in the house' or 'up and down in the house' – as her husband Ralph made explicit on a further occasion, when he wrote (on the 29th day) 'my wife busy through mercy in the family'.[53] Yet the mother could not work out of doors; and thus, even with the help of a nurse, the husband had to carry out some of the traditional tasks of the wife. In 1570, William Kirke of Stow-cum-Quy, Cambridgeshire, admitting the charge that he had been absent from church, explained that his wife was 'lying in childbed, and also his children wanted succor, for which he was then compelled to travail in fetching meal from the mill and such other like.' This was regarded as a reasonable excuse: the case against him in the ecclesiastical court was dismissed.[54]

In addition to these progressive changes of bodily state, of physical location, of social contacts, and of involvement in household tasks, the mother's lying-in may have involved a further distinction from normal married life, a distinction in the sphere of *sexual activity*. Here our evidence is, understandably, at its most fragmentary; yet the picture which emerges is a consistent one. According to Jane Sharp's midwifery treatise, husband and wife should not have sexual intercourse until after the completion of lying-in.[55] Correspondingly, the diarist Nicholas Blundell wrote in 1704 that 'my wife's month being now out we lay together'. The only other reference to this matter which I have encountered comes from Ralph Josselin, who wrote on 8 March 1648: 'at night my wife in kindness came and lay in my bed'.

At this stage Jane Josselin was 25 days into her lying-in after the birth of her fourth child. It was another 11 days before Ralph could write in his diary: 'This day . . . my wife went to church with me; the lord be praised for this mercy in raising her up again.' Her other deliveries indicate that Jane's lying-in 'month' always lasted for over 30 days, just as it did on this occasion.[56] Here, then, it would seem that she was sleeping with her husband – whether carnally or chastely hardly matters, I suggest – earlier than the norm. The key point to observe is that Ralph Josselin recorded this as a 'kindness'. Because his wife was still lying-in, still sleeping in a separate bed, his normal conjugal rights were suspended. It is the presence of this norm, rather than the unanswerable question as to how often it was obeyed or transgressed, which is the critical point. If in this respect Josselin and Blundell were representative, then we can take the sexual prohibition outlined by Jane Sharp as genuinely reflecting popular expectations.

The end of the lying-in 'month' was marked by the ecclesiastical rite of *churching*. The churching of women had been practised in the Christian churches, both Catholic and Orthodox, for centuries. In the medieval Catholic Church, its official title was 'purification'; in 1552 the Reformed Church of England changed this to 'the thanksgiving of women after childbirth', and added 'commonly called the churching of women'. [57] In theory, the mother could not go outdoors until she was churched – which poses a curious conundrum: how did she get from her house to the church? The traditional form was that she went in the company of women – her midwife, and a number of others, presumably the same gossips who had attended the birth itself.[58] She also wore a veil: this can be interpreted as a remnant of the Catholic rubric of 'purification', and it was indeed so seen by certain Puritans; but it is also possible to regard the veil simply as a device of symbolic enclosure, suitable for the journey from house to church. Seen in this light, the journey continued the themes of the lying-in itself: physical enclosure on the one hand, and social enclosure in the company of women on the other. (Did her husband accompany her too? The evidence I have compiled on this point is conflicting; perhaps different customs obtained in different localities and at different times.[59])

Once inside the church, the woman would kneel 'in some convenient place, as hath been accustomed, or as the Ordinary shall direct'.[60] (Such was the rubric of 1662 – a flexible compromise between the pre-Reformation rule that she should kneel at the church door, and the 1552 specification that this should take place near the holy table. Some parishes had a specific 'uprising seat'/ 'child-bed pew'/ 'childwife pew'/ 'churching pew' for mothers who were about to be churched.[61]) The priest then exhorted her to 'give hearty thanks unto God' for her 'safe deliverance . . . in the great danger of childbirth', and recited to her an appropriate psalm: in the early seventeenth century, Psalm 121 (criticized by the Puritans); from 1662, either Psalm 116 or Psalm 127. There followed a *kyrie eleison*, the Lord's Prayer, three specific versicles and responses, and a concluding short prayer of thanks and supplication. Finally, the woman had to make her 'accustomed offerings' to the priest and to the parish clerk. (What was ' accustomed' varied from parish to parish; at Cheswardine, Shropshire, according to a terrier of 1722, the vicar received 4d and the clerk either 2d or two white loaves.[62]) The churching service probably took about 10 minutes. It could be held at any time, by arrangement with the incumbent, but it seems that women usually came to be churched during divine service. If this was on a Sunday, when communion was held, then as the Book of Common Prayer delicately put it, 'it is convenient that she receive the holy Communion' immediately after the completion of the churching service.

Far more is known about churching than about any other aspect of lying-in, both because the churching ritual brought the mother into contact with a male and record-keeping institution (the Church of England), and because churching was a major focus of the controversy between the ritualist established Church and its Puritan opponents. For these reasons, and because of the stigma of 'purification' which had been attached to the medieval ritual, it is easy to see churching as purely an imposition from without, as a male and clerical burden laid upon mothers. However, the significance of the churching service can only be grasped in the context of the popular ceremony of childbirth as a whole. We shall therefore return to the subject of churching a little later in this chapter, after considering the meaning of the wider ritual.

Before the mother's churching, there had occurred another ecclesiastical rite, the sacrament of *baptism*, which amounted to

the social birth of the child, its entry into the human community
– and which had traditionally taken place within a few days of
the physical birth.[63] In theory, neither the mother nor the
father had any place at baptism; instead, the three godparents
or 'sponsors' took their place. Thus, the fact that baptism was
(supposedly, at least) performed in the church, whereas the
mother was confined to the house, should not have been of any
consequence. However, mothers may have wanted to be present
at the baptism of their newborn children.[64] Some women
delayed the child's baptism until the day of their own
churching. Other families practised private baptism – baptism
at home – and made of this a cheerful family ritual, in which the
mother herself took part. In such a case, baptism was probably
delayed until at least the second stage of lying-in.[65] Pepys offers
us an example: in 1667, at the christening of Betty Michell's
child (12 days after its birth, and 2 days after Samuel and
Elizabeth had paid Betty the visit which was mentioned earlier),
they found the house 'full of his [Mr Michell's] fathers and
mothers and all the kindred, hardly any else, and mighty merry
in this innocent company; and Betty mighty pretty in bed.'
There were in fact certain links between baptism, churching,
and lying-in. Before the Reformation, the newly baptized child
was wrapped in a special 'chrisom cloth': the mother returned
this cloth to the priest as part of her offerings when she was
churched.[66] Again, as we have already seen, the midwife would
receive tips from the sponsors at the baptism – and so too would
the nurse. Indeed, W. E. Tate claimed that some baptismal fonts
had special 'midwives' seats' adjoining them.[67] Thus, the
customs surrounding baptism deserve to be considered in
relation to lying-in and churching. (This is one of many reasons
for wishing that we possessed a modern scholarly study of the
history of baptism in early-modern England.)

I have been implying that the ceremony of childbirth was
followed by women of all social classes. Yet most of the evidence
I have been citing pertains to mothers of high social status – the
wives of the aristocracy, the gentry, and what can be called the
semi-gentry.[68] Did mothers lower down the social scale behave
in the same way? Living as they did in one- or two-roomed
cottages they cannot have used a separate room; they may well
have been unable to afford the curtains, perhaps the candles,
and possibly the paid nurse. Yet there were many possibilities
for adaptation and improvisation. The 'month' could be

shortened in duration; in place of a separate room the bed itself could serve as the lying-in space; the mother could lie in at the house of a more wealthy relative (perhaps her own mother) or friend.[69] Each of these practices is documented; and in fact there is every reason to think that the ceremony of childbirth was effectively universal amongst married mothers. One oblique indication of this is the fact that wealthy mothers made an expensive display of their lying-in chamber: the mere fact of lying-in did not demonstrate their social status, and that status accordingly had to be shown by other means.[70] Again, we shall subsequently see that churching was observed by almost all mothers, and that the interval between birth and churching was generally about 4 weeks. The 'monthly nurses' of the nineteenth century worked amongst the poor as well as the rich.[71] Glimpses of the lives of the poor in the seventeenth and eighteenth centuries are rare indeed, but we know that Mary Toft – undoubtedly extremely poor – had a nurse during her lying-in before her famous superfetation of rabbits in 1726. (Mary was, incidentally, churched a fortnight after her initial delivery, a miscarriage.[72]) The parish overseers of the poor could subsidize the drinking associated with childbirth, supplying 'a pint of liquor for Anne Barne's lying-in'.[73] For the penurious 1790s, we have more systematic evidence in the form of agricultural labourers' budgets collected by middle-class observers sympathetic to the plight of the poor. The Anglican minister David Davies reckoned the expenses of lying-in at 20 shillings, assumed that this happened once in 2 years, and so concluded that 10 shillings per year was required. Out of a total family budget of £7 per year this was a very large sum.[74] The lying-in expenses included the midwife's fee, 'attendance of a nurse for a few days', 'a bottle of gin or brandy always had upon this occasion', and 'half a bushel of malt brewed, and hops'. The fact that these expenses were standard amongst the poorest families in a time of extreme hardship strongly suggests that the lying-in ritual was universally observed.[75]

What did *men* make of this exclusively female ritual? As usual, we have only fragmentary indications. Diarists referred rather casually and patchily to birth and lying-in. Thus, Ralph Josselin, perhaps the most meticulous recorder of such mundane matters, mentioned some of the stages of lying-in after some of his wife's ten deliveries, but never wrote down the whole story for any single confinement, only ever identified one of the

gossips by name, never named the midwife or recorded her fee
(unlike his contemporary Daniel Fleming) – and never made
any comment on the customs of lying-in.[76] Medical writers of the
seventeenth century were similarly laconic; they seem in general
to have accepted and endorsed the practices of women. A case
in point is Percival Willughby.[77] He believed that the chamber
should be dark and warm: '[As] for the labouring woman's
chamber, let it be made dark, having a glimmering light, or
candle-light, placed partly behind the woman, or on one side,
and a moderate warming fire in it.' The numbers of women, he
went on, should not be excessive: 'and let it not be filled with
much company, or many women; five or six women assisting will
be sufficient.' Thus, Willughby simply assumed that the birth
would be a collective female affair; male advice could aspire
only to regulating the numbers. Similarly, though he criticized
midwives at great length and regarded the midwife's practical
tasks as slight, he believed that midwives were the appropriate
practitioners to manage childbirth, and disapproved of 'men-
midwives' – that is, of men replacing the female midwife. As for
the timing of 'upsitting', Willughby agreed with James
Wolveridge that this should be *later* than the customary 3 or 4
days after birth.[78] Other matters such as caudle, swaddling, the
further stages of lying-in, or the duration of the whole process,
Willughby did not discuss at all. Here (and in other medical
treatises of the period) we seem to find an attitude of passive
acceptance.[79]

However, there are also some signs of male hostility. The
Puritans of the early seventeenth century criticized churching
along with other ecclesiastical ceremonies: as we shall see a little
later, some male Puritan attacks on churching extended to the
whole process of lying-in. After the Restoration, we find William
Sermon constructing the fantasy that lying-in was not observed
by American wives, and suggesting that English women should
similarly return to their wifely duties immediately after birth.[80]
The Woman's Advocate of 1683 attributes to a husband some
aversion to women's sociability during lying-in, and then
defends the women in the following terms:

> for gossips to meet . . . at a lying-in, and not to talk, you
> may as well dam up the arches of London Bridge, as stop
> their mouths at such a time. 'Tis a time of freedom, when
> women . . . have a privilege to talk petty treason.[81]

In the eighteenth century, as a result of the new 'man-midwifery', male medical practitioners began to criticize many aspects of the ceremony of childbirth: swaddling, the enclosed room, eventually even the presence of gossips.[82] We know that these criticisms were supported by some husbands; nevertheless much of the childbirth ritual remained intact well into the nineteenth century. William Cobbett, in his *Advice to Young Men* of 1830, implied that young husbands resented the duty of having to fetch gossips and midwife at the onset of labour. Characteristically, Cobbett went on to say that they should learn to accept that duty.[83] Here we have a few hints that men's acceptance of the ritual practices of women could be tinged with a certain resentment. It is perhaps significant that these criticisms tended to be voiced indirectly. Cobbett, writing in 1830, followed the same convention as the anonymous male author of *The Woman's Advocate* a century and a half before him: attributing to husbands a critical attitude, and then arguing against that attitude. It is as if the ceremony of childbirth were so well established in custom as to be almost beyond the reach of explicit criticism in print.

Both of these male responses – passive acceptance and muffled resentment – serve to underline the universality and hegemony of the ritual. Herein lies a significant irony for the historian: for these responses, while attesting to the normative power of the ceremony of childbirth, also had the effect that only scattered and fragmentary documentary traces were left. There is no single document, so far as I am aware, which describes the process in full: a reconstruction such as I have attempted here has to be based on assembling disparate details from a wide range of sources. And it is striking that even texts relatively rich in such details – such as Josselin's diary and Willughby's midwifery treatise – omit many aspects of the ritual. Thus, our sources systematically conceal from us the central importance of the ceremony of childbirth in the lives of seventeenth-century women.

The meaning of the ritual

The early-modern ceremony of childbirth followed a coherent and consistent structure: it comprised an ordered pattern of actions governed by a discernible set of rules. But where did these rules arise? How had the ritual come into being, and why was it maintained? What were its origins, and what was its meaning? In turning to these questions, we enter a territory in which the historian has almost no documentary evidence; in which his or her interpretations therefore stand naked. When it was a matter of reconstructing the ritual (the task of the previous section), our evidence was fragmentary; here at the level of investigating its meaning, we pass from fragments to documentary silence. Though the documents are silent, however, the historian will speak; and in fact, three distinct interpretations of the ceremony of childbirth can be found in the literature.

One interpretation (to which I formerly adhered) assimilates this specific ritual to the general pattern of 'rites of passage', classically delineated by Arnold van Gennep.[84] According to this reading, certain critical life-events – such as birth, puberty, death – are always, in every society, surrounded by ritual procedures. The existence of the ritual is unsurprising: it stemmed simply from 'ancient folk tradition'.[85] It was necessary for such an 'event of nature' to be 'immersed in culture', since this 'made the birth a social and human act'.[86] Thus, the meaning of the various specific activities was that these comprised the necessary stages of rites of passage in general. All such rites, according to van Gennep, entailed three stages: separation, transition, reincorporation. The early-modern ceremony of childbirth conformed to this pattern, with the demarcation of the lying-in room achieving separation, the 'month' of isolation accomplishing transition, and the final churching ceremony making for reincorporation. Thus, this specific historical ritual bears out van Gennep's anthropological argument, even though van Gennep himself had not applied that argument in this particular direction.

A second interpretation (that of Keith Thomas) offers a more specific reading. Here the focus is upon popular attitudes: the customs of lying-in and churching, it is argued, flowed from these attitudes, so that the attitudes themselves can in turn be read off from the popular customs. Specifically, the meaning of lying-in and churching was that these reflected concepts of women's inferiority and impurity:[87]

medieval churchmen had ... devoted a good deal of energy to refuting such popular superstitions as the belief

that it was improper for the mother to emerge from her
house ... before she had been purified ... The church
... was reluctant to countenance any prescribed interval
after birth before [churching] could take place ... But *for
people at large churching was indubitably a ritual of purification
closely linked to its Jewish predecessor* (emphasis added).

Thus, lying-in satisfied a popular demand for the ritual purification of women after childbirth. The 'origin' of the ritual of
churching was 'the primitive view of woman as shameful and
unclean'. This in turn was an aspect of a seventeenth-century
'universal belief in [women's] inferior capacity', a belief which
determined the subordinate place of women in the social order.
Consequently, Puritans' criticisms of the churching ritual 'had
done something to raise women's status'.[88]

The weakness of these two interpretations is that they have
little or no explanatory force. We may grant, for the sake of
argument, that a 'rite of passage' was involved; but why did the
rite take the particular form it did? Alternatively, we may accept
that a popular belief in women's 'impurity' was at work; but this
will not explain the complex structure of customs outlined in
the previous section. Above all, neither of these interpretations
can come to grips with the two central facts about the ceremony
of childbirth – namely, the fact that this ritual was exclusively
female and the fact that it was *collective*. These basic features of
the ritual have no significance within the 'rites of passage'
framework; and they can be taken to contradict the 'impurity'
reading, since the women who thronged around the mother
during and after the delivery did not behave as if *they* felt her to
be impure. Thus, while Thomas and I have both managed to
bring to light some valuable information about the
management of childbirth, the particular readings which we
have given to this material do not stand up to critical
assessment.

The third interpretation, which has a very different thrust,
was offered by Natalie Zemon Davis in the course of her essay
'Women on top'.[89] Davis's material came chiefly from
continental Europe in the early-modern period, but much of
her argument applies also to England, including her brief and
telling observations on the ritual of childbirth. The essay as a
whole was concerned with a popular tradition, displayed in
stories, paintings, and carnivals, in which women were depicted

in roles of dominance over men. Exploring the complex meanings and uses of this imagery, Davis asked what the 'woman-on-top' image might have meant to 'the majority of unexceptional women living within their families'. She pointed out that the subjection of wives to husbands, prescribed within marriage, was not always obeyed, and speculated that 'the ambiguous woman-on-top of the world of play made the unruly option a more conceivable one within the family'. And in the course of this argument, Davis wrote: 'In actual marriage, subjection . . . might be reversed temporarily during the lying-in period, when the new mother could boss her husband around with impunity.' In a note to this passage, Davis acknowledged the contribution to this argument of three other scholars, all women, and added: 'Italian birth-salvers (that is, trays used to bring women drinks during labour and the lying-in) dating from the fifteenth and sixteenth centuries were decorated with classical and Biblical scenes showing women dominating men.'

Davis was suggesting, then, that the process of lying-in accomplished a reversal of the normal power-relations between wife and husband; that the mother's lying-in month was indeed 'her month'; that the ceremony of childbirth placed the woman 'on top' amidst *all* families. Here we have a very different interpretation from the two readings of the ritual discussed above. Those readings portrayed women as essentially obedient to the ritual; Davis's reading depicts the ritual itself as reflecting the interests of women. As I shall now argue, it is this interpretation which offers the key to the meaning of the ceremony of childbirth.

Since the ceremony of childbirth withdrew the mother from the world of men, and placed her within the world of women, its significance will emerge only if we attend to the general context of relations between the sexes in seventeenth-century England. Those relations were patriarchal: that is, men had power over women. A central aspect of male power, one which operated in daily life and which was also used as a significant ideological resource,[90] was the authority of the husband over the wife. As we saw earlier, marriage was a contract of inequality: the wife vowed to 'obey and serve' her husband.[91] More specifically, the common law conferred on the husband an absolute property in the wife's worldly goods; in her physical labour and its fruits; and last but not least, in her sexuality.[92] Thus, if conjugal relationships went to law – as they sometimes did – the husband's ownership was endorsed and his power over his wife reinforced. This structural inequality of conjugal life did not preclude loving relationships between husband and wife, any more than the authority of parents over children today precludes love between the generations within the family. On the contrary, love and power were closely related, a fact made explicit in images of God: God *was* both Power and Love – that is, power and love attained a relationship of identity at the apex of the natural order. The male ideal of conjugal relations involved female submission to male power, enabling that power to be wielded with gentleness and consideration. Thus, in the event of a personal contest between husband and wife, the husband would behave as Samuel Pepys did on such an occasion: he first 'desired' Elizabeth, 'and then commanded her', to do his bidding.[93] Husbands had a rich range of resources to deploy: their very abstention from the iron fist of patriarchy was itself an instrument of power, a kindness which should command acceptance of their wishes.[94]

The effect of the lying-in month was to withdraw from the husband two of the customary fruits of marriage: his wife's physical labour and her sexual services. From the woman's point of view this made possible a period of rest and recovery. Her physical labour, both inside and outside the house, was replaced by that of the monthly nurse: the payment made to the nurse was effectively a subsidy to the wife on the part of the husband. Thus, the ceremony of childbirth inverted the normal pattern of conjugal relations: the wife's bodily energies and sexuality now, for the space of 'the month', belonged to her; what marriage had taken away from her, the ceremony of childbirth temporarily restored. This makes intelligible the fact that the ritual was a collective female event. The presence of other women may have served to police the lying-in – to ensure that the husband respected the norms. More generally, the immersion of the mother in a female collectivity elegantly inverted the central feature of patriarchy, namely its basis in individual male property.

All this goes to support Davis's interpretation of the ceremony of childbirth. The strength of that interpretation is that it enables us to situate the management of childbirth within the context of women's actual lives: lives of hard physical labour, performed under a rubric of love and an ethos of service, on behalf of an individual male master, the husband.

The ritual of childbirth was constructed and maintained by women *because it was in the interests of women*; and it represented a successful form of women's *resistance* to patriarchal authority.

The churching of women

If the main lines of the ceremony of childbirth were constructed by women in this way, what are we to make of the ecclesiastical ritual which marked the completion of lying-in – the occasional service of churching?: for the churching service has every appearance of having emanated from the world of men. It was an ecclesiastical ceremony; it had been described in the Middle Ages as a ritual of 'purification'; after the English Reformation, it still involved various features which in the eyes of the Puritans bore the same stigma of defilement-by-birth; it required the mother to pay money to the priest and to the parish clerk.[95] At first glance, then, churching seems an alien and male imposition on what was otherwise a female ritual. However, a more careful investigation suggests the very opposite, as we shall now see.

Perhaps the first thing to note about churching is that this was a highly *popular* service. Even in strongly Puritan London parishes, it was followed by over 90 per cent of mothers in the early seventeenth century, probably about 4 weeks after the birth.[96] Such precise evidence is difficult to find for the eighteenth century, but we know that it was specifically the need for churchings and baptisms which was given as the reason for establishing a sub-parochial chapel at Brentwood hamlet in 1715.[97] Again, in the nineteenth century, when the irreligion of the working class was the central lament of the Anglican Church, churching apparently remained just as popular as ever.[98] As late as the 1950s, it was still being practised by forty-one out of forty-five married women in Bethnal Green, interviewed by Michael Young and Peter Willmott.[99] To bring the picture almost up to the present, however anecdotally, let me report two stories.[100] One came from a large British hospital in the late 1970s; here an Anglican minister visited the maternity ward, offering to church the mothers *in situ*, and all the women but one took up his offer. (Not all these women were Anglicans.) The second anecdote comes from a married woman friend of mine who hails from an Anglican family. She is not a church-goer, and when she had her two children (in the 1970s) she was not churched. However, after the second delivery she had a particular experience which, with hindsight, she regards as relevant to the question of churching. For perhaps 5 weeks after the birth, she felt emotionally confused – not 'postnatally depressed', simply overwhelmed by the range and intensity of the feelings she was experiencing. Once she had recovered her equilibrium, she had a strong desire *to go and give thanks to somebody for her recovery*. Interestingly, she did not at the time connect this with churching, even though she had been brought up an Anglican and had even attended at least one churching. Instead, she simply experienced this as a spontaneous and rather inchoate wish, one which she did not know how to satisfy and therefore never did satisfy.

I have already introduced, surreptitiously, a second point: that if churching was (and perhaps still is) popular, its popularity was specifically amongst *women*. This can be illustrated by what Young and Willmott reported from Bethnal Green.[101] One woman's explanation (amongst several) will suffice as an example: '*It's the Mums*. It's not that I actually believe in it, but I'd get an uneasy feeling if I didn't do it. You don't like to break tradition.' (emphasis added) The attitude of husbands, by contrast, was hostile. Mr Jeffreys sneered (after his wife had said, 'It's your religion, isn't it? I mean you've got to do it') – 'Your Mum's done it – you do it. They're all the same.' We are beginning to glimpse that attitudes to churching are gendered; and so it was in the late sixteenth century. As is well known, churching was vigorously opposed by the Puritans; and in the case of Henry Barrow, his denunciation of churching extended to an ironic critique of the whole lying-in process:[102]

After they have been safely delivered of childbirth, and have lain in, and been shut up, their month of days accomplished; then are they to repair to church and to kneel down in some place nigh to the communion table (not to speak how she cometh wimpled and muffled, accompanied with her wives, and dare not look upon the sun nor sky . . .) unto whom (thus placed in the church) comes Sir Priest . . . [etc.] . . . And then, she having offered her accustomed offerings unto him for his labour, God speed her well, she is a woman on foot again, as holy as ever she was; she may now put off her veiling kerchief, and

look her husband and neighbours in the face again . . .
What can be a more apish imitation, or rather a more
reviving of the Jewish purification than this?

Such were the words of a Puritan *man*. Puritan women, on the
other hand seem to have satirized the ecclesiastical ritual as to
its form, while adhering to the lying-in period and using the act
of coming to church as a means of publicly announcing its
completion. Thus, in 1578 Katherine Whithed, according to the
churchwardens of Danbury,[103]

> came into the church, with a kerchief over her head, to
> give thanks for her childbearing, at the sermon time,
> [and] whilst [the minister] was at the sermon, she with a
> loud voice demanded of him if he were ready to do his
> duty she was ready to do hers; whereby she troubled him
> in his sermon and caused the people to make a laughter.

Similarly, in 1597 Jane Minors of Barking not only kept her
child unbaptized for a month after birth, but also[104]

> very unwomanlike, came to be churched at the end of the
> said month, together with her child to be baptised, and
> feasted at a tavern 4 or 5 hours in the forenoon; and [in
> the] afternoon came to the church . . . to be seen . . .
> [and] went out of the church, unchurched, unto the
> tavern again. And when she was spoken unto by the clerk
> to return to church again and to give God thanks after her
> delivery, she answered it was a ceremony.

Or again Mrs Pinson of Wolverhampton, at some point in the
1630s, went with her husband[105]

> and her midwife, and other women . . . to be churched,
> but being demanded by the priest why she did not wear a
> veil, she answered she would not; and being told by the
> priest that he was commanded by the ordinary not to
> church any but such as came thither reverently and lowly
> in their veils, she in the church, after prayers ended,
> scornfully pulled off her hat and put a table napkin on her
> head, and put on her hat again, and so departed from the
> church.

In two of these three cases (the first and third), the husband was described as being involved in the wife's defiance; in the case of Jane Minors, the husband was not mentioned. What is common to all these cases is that the women in question *wanted to be churched*; and where there are further details, we find that the lying-in month had been observed and that the midwife and other women attended the mother on the way to the church.

The key to Puritan responses, I suggest, is provided by the defiant words of Richard Morley of Grantham, who in February 1589 was reported as saying that[106] 'the churching of women is a beggarly ceremony, and that all those which do use it do in some respect forsake Christ, and *if he could have persuaded his wife she should never have given thanks*' (emphasis added).

All the available evidence in fact suggests that while both men and women amongst the Puritans criticized the *form* of churching, it was men and men only who criticized the *fact* of it. We have here, couched in different language and centring on different issues, the same gender-division of responses that appeared, over three centuries later, in Bethnal Green. As far as the Puritans go, we might say that one *man's* 'purification' was another *woman's* popular ritual. Here lies a crucial point: that popular attitudes to an ecclesiastical ritual were and are by no means a simple matter.[107] We certainly cannot read off women's attitudes to churching from male denunciations of the practice, nor from the words of the ceremony itself. It was perfectly possible for a woman to regard the ecclesiastical rite as a piece of meaningless nonsense, while also wanting very badly to go through that rite. After all, the officiating clergyman was only one of the people present: the church ritual involved the presence of the congregation, and it may well have been this which mattered.[108] In short, observance of churching could mean many different things. The ritual for the mother herself was what she and her gossips made of it.

However, this point can be pressed a little further. It is not just that women accepted the churching ritual and made of it what they wished; more than this, there were many aspects of that ritual which in fact had probably been created by women in the first place. So far as can be ascertained, the various surrounding customs were precisely *customs*; they derived their force not from canon law but from popular usage. It was thus that the woman was accompanied by her 'wives', including the midwife; thus that the period of a month was followed; it may have been for this reason that an 'uprising seat' was placed in some churches; even the veil itself was possibly of popular rather than ecclesiastical origin.[109] (The question of the veil came to law in 'Shipden's case' of 1622: it was decreed that the wearing of the veil was compulsory, but only on the grounds 'that it was the ancient usage of the church of England'.[110]) Seen through male Puritan eyes, these various trappings were all Popish or Jewish. However, the eye which sees in order to denounce is no key to the origins. In particular, the regular presence in the churching procession of the company of women links the ecclesiastical ritual firmly with the lay ceremony of childbirth – hence the popularity of churching. Women liked it because it was a women's ritual.

Let us take one final step further down this interpretative road, and ask a question: how and why did churching enter the rites of the Christian Church in the first place? Works of Church history answer this chiefly by reference to the fact that Jesus's mother was purified (a nice paradox, this) after his birth. Textual warrant does not however constitute efficient cause; and churching was in fact introduced into medieval Christian practice, without any apparent apostolic or patristic basis. Why was it introduced at all, and indeed when was it introduced? These questions require an expert answer, which I cannot attempt. However, the suggestion can be made, for the medievalists to refine or refute, that the purification of women was an ecclesiastical response to some *prior popular ritual*. If, as seems plausible, the ritual of lying-in was practised not just in England but all over Europe, and dates from the Middle Ages or earlier, then there is every reason to suppose that the lying-in interval was concluded by some collective rite, some act of 'reincorporation' (in the terminology of van Gennep). It would not be surprising to find the Church responding to this by offering its own ritual, Christian instead of pagan, and absorbing some elements of the pagan ritual in the process. Moreover, we should expect such a process to have been fraught with struggle and contest; such contest might well produce documentation; and thus it may become possible to test this hypothesis. Certainly, the origins of churching would be well worth investigating, in view of its long-lived later popularity amongst the women of England.

Churching enjoyed this popularity, I suggest, because it legitimated the wider ceremony of childbirth. The concept of the lying-in month achieved an elegant fusion between Biblical precedent (the Jewish ritual of purification) and the material needs of women (for rest and recovery after childbirth). That fusion broke down, of course, in the Reformation, and the consequent struggles over churching enable us to see what women's priorities were: they wanted churching, but not the veil; lying- in, but not purification. Once we focus in this way on the gender specificity of Puritan responses to churching, it becomes clear that the history of churching provides strong support for Natalie Zemon Davis's interpretation of lying-in: that the ceremony of childbirth placed 'the woman on top'.

Conclusion

It is likely that not only the general structure of the childbirth ritual, but also its specific details, will turn out to be intelligible in terms of the material lives of women. If we view the procedures of the ritual through modern medical concepts, those procedures are likely to appear irrational and even dangerous; thus, bed-rest for a week is now supposed to be attended with risks to the mother's health. Once situated in the context of women's lives, however, those same procedures will emerge in a very different light. One case in point is the swaddling of the child. Swaddling is precisely a child-care practice which women would favour, for it does no harm to children but confers an immense benefit upon mothers – since its central effect is to send the child to sleep. Moreover, swaddling is much more acceptable to children if they have been accustomed to it from the moment of birth.[111] This is exactly the way in which women actually implemented swaddling in early-modern England. Here we see that an immense rationality underlay swaddling, a rationality which inhered in the needs of *both* the mother *and* the child. Along these lines, I suggest, we may later be able to explain the other features of the ceremony of childbirth – just as François Loux has disclosed the rationality of many French peasant customs of child-care.[112] Those customs, Loux has found, were denounced as 'irrational' by nineteenth-century observers who came from a different social milieu and deployed different criteria of welfare. In fact, it is not a question of the rational versus the irrational; rather, it is a question of *whose* rationality will prevail.

Such is the burden of Loux's findings; and I suggest that the same will apply to all the details of the ceremony of childbirth when these have been adequately reconstructed and contextualized. The darkened room, the caudle, the presiding midwife, the timing of 'upsitting' and of the subsequent stages of lying-in – all these invite explanation in terms of the material needs of women.

It would be valuable to compare the early-modern English ceremony of childbirth with the childbirth rituals of other societies, and to subject these, too, to a political reading. There are some indications of national differences with early-modern Europe; and there is a large and open question as to how the early-modern English ritual was transformed, by the mid-twentieth century, into the hospitalized ritual of today. So far as I am aware, very little research has been undertaken in this area by historians.[113] The discipline which has focused on ritual in great detail is of course anthropology; and from this quarter there derives some qualified and indirect support for the reading of ritual I have developed in this chapter. In a recent study, Karen and Jeffery Paige have interpreted 'reproductive rituals' as 'a continuation of politics by another means'.[114] On their analysis, every such ritual results from an underlying conflict, and is a way of expressing that conflict while also containing it within manageable bounds. In interpreting ritual as the result of political conflict, this approach is similar to the interpretation offered here. However, the meaning assigned to politics differs radically between the present reading of early-modern English childbirth, on the one hand, and the Paiges' comparative analysis of ethnographic material on the other. On their reading, reproductive politics reduces to competition *between men* over the limited available 'resources' of women and children. Here all agency is seen as residing in men; women are passive, the objects and not the subjects of reproductive rituals. In the words of Paige and Paige,[115] 'men are the most important political actors in preindustrial societies'. Correspondingly, the underlying conflicts are individual ones: they partake of the social only in so far as this individuation is universal. Preindustrial 'man' thus acquires a somewhat Benthamite character. By contrast, taking my lead from Natalie Zemon Davis, I have interpreted the politics of ritual as a matter of contest *between the sexes*, stressing the active agency of women. As a result, the underlying conflict appears as a social one, with the conjugal power of the individual husband representing simply the particular instantiation of a set of structural relations. No doubt there is much room here for further exploration. On the one hand, the interpretation of tribal 'reproductive rituals' needs to take account of the agency of women. On the other hand, much could doubtless be learnt about historical ritual by placing this in a comparative setting, drawing upon the very rich ethnographic literature which Paige and Paige have surveyed and analysed.

The historiographic context of the present argument is of course the increasing impact on early-modern history of women scholars, who are bringing into focus a variety of themes which male historians have tended to neglect, to marginalize, or to misunderstand. Many studies in this tradition have influenced this essay. Valerie Fildes and the late Dorothy McLaren, for instance, have demonstrated both the coherence and the demographic impact of the activities of women as mothers in the past.[116] Again, Jean Donnison and Audrey Eccles have enabled us to see the historical importance of midwives, opening up a different perspective from that of traditional medical history.[117] Natalie Zemon Davis and her colleagues initiated the interpretation of lying-in as resistance. Several women scholars have produced important critiques of the 'history-of-the-family' tradition.[118] More generally, Linda Gordon and Sally Alexander have called for a historiography of gender-*relations*, and for a focus upon women as active agents, as subjects rather than passive objects of historical processes.[119] This opens up a very large agenda for historians of the early-modern period. It is true that for this period, direct documentation of the lives of women is relatively sparse and diffuse. Nevertheless, as Sara Mendelson and Patricia Crawford have demonstrated, there is available a considerable corpus of both manuscript and printed material from the pens of seventeenth-century women: and this testimony is only beginning to be exploited.[120] Moreover, the indirect imprint of women can be found across a vast range of historical documents,[121] particularly if we attend to the *genesis* of our sources,[122] remembering in doing so that relations of gender were constitutive of the social order.

These considerations must prompt us to ask whether women's resistance to patriarchal power, so effectively organized in the ceremony of childbirth, was manifested in other ways and in other areas. In fact there is every reason to believe that this resistance was widespread in early-modern England; that women mounted a *counter-power* against male control, long before the advent of an organized feminist movement and literature. Patriarchy evolved in a series of *contests*: there were innumerable individual struggles like those of Elizabeth Pepys, and collective struggles like those of the London women petitioners of the 1640s and 1650s.[123] The 'woman on top' tradition, demonstrated by Davis, not only nourished but also reflected these struggles. This phenomenon of women's resistance to patriarchal power is immensely important in at least two ways: first, as a striking instance of women's agency; second, because this resistance and the responses it provoked effect for us a real-life analytical dissection of patriarchal power, permitting us to investigate the structuring of gender relations.[124] Intense interest therefore attaches to the project of systematically reconstructing the struggles of women against familial and civic forms of male power. Historians are only beginning to recapture these episodes: as yet it is too early to attempt either a typology of their occasions, or a chronological analysis of the unfolding of patriarchy within the early-modern period. Nevertheless two basic points are already clear. First, the struggles of women were far more effective when collective support could be mobilized. The individual wife could seldom triumph over her husband, since the husband held the final sanction of the law; but collective action could wrest back for women certain rights and victories. Second, such collective action could often transcend divisions of social class and of marital status. The propertied widow could make common cause with married women; married women could support the unmarried bastard-bearer; respectable wives and poor women could join together in political action.[125]

What made such solidarity possible was the fact that women of many different stations in life shared certain central experiences, such as the pains of childbearing, the inequality of marriage, or at least the expectation or memory of these. But what gave force to these shared experiences was something else: a collective culture of women. A network of so-called 'gossip' bound together the women of each locality in a web of relationships which partly mirrored the male hierarchy (squire, tenant farmer, husbandman, landless labourer), yet partly cut across that hierarchy.[126] Wider networks, made possible by the continual migration which characterized English populations, conferred a national character upon many aspects of this culture. Gender roles were socially constructed, and the collective culture of women played an important part in this process.[127] Until the mid-eighteenth century, this culture was probably more important, for most women, than the culture of social class; and it was to this shared women's culture that the ceremony of childbirth belonged.

Indeed, it is tempting to suggest that the childbirth ritual not only reflected women's general culture, but also played an important part in the construction and maintenance of that culture. Childbirth was sufficiently frequent, and lying-in sufficiently protracted, that a typical English village would have had at least one mother 'in the straw' at most times of the year. Thus, childbirth provided frequent and more or less continuous opportunities for women to get together; and these opportunities were probably unique in the separateness from men which they made possible. Perhaps, then, the expanding meanings of 'gossip' – childbirth witness, female friend, getting together of women, hostility to men – reflect an underlying social reality, a range of women's activities in which childbirth was as central in real life as it seems to have been in the history of this word. If so, we may wonder whether the role of midwives was restricted to childbirth and associated healing activities. Perhaps the midwife's authority in childbirth was but one aspect of some wider role she played in maintaining the collective culture of women.[128] At all events, these possibilities offer us a rich and interesting field for further investigation.

Acknowledgements

The research for this chapter has been supported by the generosity of the Wellcome Trust. The staff of Cambridge University Library and of the Lichfield Joint Record Office have extended invaluable facilities. Linda Pollock has very kindly made available a wealth of material from family papers – far more than I have had space to cite here. For detailed advice I wish to thank Anna Abulafia, Timothy Ashplant, Jeremy Boulton, David Cressy, Andrew Cunningham, Anna Davin,

Valerie Fildes, John Henderson, Ann Hess, Gill Hudson, Henry Krips, Valerie Krips, Philippa Levine, Susan Magarey, Jane Morgan, John Morrill, Roy Porter, Wilf Prest, Miri Rubin, Simon Schaffer, Shulamith Shahar, Hendrik van der Weef, and Mike Woodhouse, Finally, I am particularly grateful to Rosalind Bayham and to Hugh McLeod for their indispensable help in the development of the argument.

Notes

1. P. Laslett, *The World We Have Lost* (London, 1965); *The World We Have Lost Further Explored* (London, 1983). Throughout this chapter, dates are given according to New Style year, and spelling and punctuation are modernized.

2. C. Wilson, 'The proximate determinants of marital fertility in England 1600–1799', in L. Bonfield, R. M. Smith, and K. Wrightson (eds), *The World We Have Gained: Histories of Population and Social Structure* (Oxford, 1986), 203–30.

3. R. A. Houlbrooke, *The English Family 1450–1700* (London, 1984), 72–3, 83–4; A. Macfarlane, *Marriage and Love in England: Modes of Reproduction 1300–1840* (Oxford, 1986), 267–8, 276–7.

4. M. Chaytor, 'Household and kinship: Ryton in the 16th and 17th centuries', *Hist. Workshop J.*, 10 (1980), 25–60, p. 48; K. Wrightson, 'The nadir of English illegitimacy in the seventeenth century', in P. Laslett, K. Oosterveen, and R. M. Smith (eds), *Bastardy and Its Comparative History*, (London, 1980), 176–91, p. 179.

5. R. W. Malcolmson, 'Infanticide in the eighteenth century', in J. S. Cockburn (ed.), *Crime in England, 1550–1800* (London, 1977), 187–209.

6. H. Fielding, *The History of Tom Jones, a Foundling* (London, 1749); W. E. Tate, *The Parish Chest: A Study of the Records of Parochial Administration in England* (Cambridge, 1969), 61–2; R. K. McClure, *Coram's Children: The London Foundling Hospital in the Eighteenth Century* (New Haven, 1981), 8–9.

7. See A. Wilson 'Illegitimacy and its implications in mid-eighteenth century London: the evidence of the Foundling Hospital', *Cont. & Change*, 4 (1989), 103–64.

8. J. H. Baker, *An Introduction to English Legal History* (2nd edn, London, 1979), 391–407. For an overview of women's position, see P. Crawford, 'From the woman's view: pre-industrial England, 1500–1750', in Crawford (ed.), *Exploring Women's Past* (2nd edn, Sydney, 1984), 49–85.

9. Examples of the former genre include H. R. Spencer, *The History of British Midwifery from 1650 to 1800* (London, 1927); H. Thoms, *Our Obstetric Heritage: The Story of Safe Childbirth* (Handen, Conn., 1960); W. Radcliffe, *Milestones in Midwifery* (Bristol, 1967). Childbirth received 6 pages in R. Trumbach, *The Rise of the*

Egalitarian Family: Aristocratic Kinship and Domestic Relations in Eighteenth-century England (New York, 1978), 180–5; but a page or less in M. D. George, *London Life in the Eighteenth Century* (first pub. 1925; Harmondsworth, 1966), 60–61; G. M. Trevelyan, *English Social History* (London, 1944), 65, 345; L. Stone, *The Family, Sex and Marriage in England 1500–1800* (London, 1977); R. Porter, *English Society in the Eighteenth Century* (Harmondsworth, 1982), 41, 294; Houlbrooke, *The English Family*, 129–30.

10. J. Donnison, *Midwives and Medical Men: A History of Inter-professional Rivalries and Women's Rights* (London, 1977); A. Eccles, *Obstetrics and Gynaecology in Tudor and Stuart England* (London, 1982).

11. The specific 'paths' by which male practitioners were called to childbirth in seventeenth- and eighteenth-century England are outlined in A. Wilson, 'William Hunter and the varieties of man-midwifery', in W. F. Bynum and R. Porter (eds), *William Hunter and the 18th-century Medical World* (Cambridge 1985), 343–70, esp. 349–57, 365–9.

12. P. Willughby, *Observations in Midwifery*, ed. H. Blenkinsop (Warwick, 1863; repr. ed. J. L. Thornton, Wakefield, 1972), 184, 197; Trumbach, *The Rise of the Egalitarian Family*, 181.

13. *OED* (12 vols, Oxford 1933), under 'nidget', verb (2). Ralph Josselin directly mentioned his own activity in summoning the women for only two (the third and eighth) of his wife's ten deliveries; however, in a further case (the fourth birth) a chance indirect reference makes it clear that this was his customary role. This is an excellent example of the very patchy nature of our evidence. See A. Macfarlane (ed.), *The Diary of Ralph Josselin* (London, 1976), 50, 415, 118.

14. L. Sterne, *The Life and Opinions of Tristram Shandy, Gentleman* (9 vols, York and London, 1760–7). In fact, it is by no means clear how the father-to-be passed the time. The most explicit indications I have encountered both come from America: Samuel Sewall, in 1677, was sitting with his father 'in the great hall' when he heard the cry of the newborn child; William Byrd, in 1709, having sent for the midwife at about 9 o'clock, did not wait up but went to bed an hour later. See L. Pollock (ed.), *A Lasting Relationship: Parents and Children Over Three Centuries* (London, 1987), 33, 35.

15. Macfarlane, *Diary of Ralph Josselin*, 415.

16. Ibid., 615. See also Willughby, *Observations*, 186, 205, 215–16 (mother); 218 (husband's mother); 235 (sister); 238 (kinswoman).

17. See M. Macdonald, *Mystical Bedlam: Madness, Anxiety and Healing in Seventeenth-century England* (Cambridge, 1981), 109; cf. K. Thomas, *Religion and the Decline of Magic: Studies in Popular Beliefs in Sixteenth- and Seventeenth-century England* (first pub. 1971; Harmondsworth, 1978), 665.

18. *OED*, 'gossip', noun (1a, 1c, 2a, 2b), verb (1,2); and 'gossiping', noun (1,2).

19. N. Culpeper, *A Directory for Midwives* (first edn 1651; London, 1675), 119.

20. *OED*, 'grace', noun (21b).

21. Macfarlane, *Diary of Ralph Josselin*, 165.

22. CUL, Ely diocesan records, B/9/1 (25 September 1662).

23. W. Harvey, *Exercitationes de generatione animalium* (London, 1651), trans. G. Whitteridge (*Disputations Touching the Generation of Animals*, Oxford, 1981), 404.

24. Willughby, *Observations*, 11, 31–6, 233–4.

25. LJRO, Lichfield diocesan records, B/V/4, bundle for Staffs., 1667–8.

26. *OED*, 'midwife'.

27. Willughby, *Observations*, 142–5, 226.

28. J. Lane, 'The administration of an eighteenth century Warwickshire parish: Butlers Marston', *Dugdale Soc. Occ. Pap.*, 21 (1973), 20; Donnison, *Midwives and Medical Men*, 9–10, 208 (note 66); Trumbach, *The Rise of the Egalitarian Family*, 181; J. H. Aveling, *English Midwives: Their History and Prospects* (1872; London, 1967), 31.

29. J. R. Magrath (ed.), *The Flemings in Oxford* (3 vols, Oxford, 1904–24), vol. 1, 451 and *passim*.

30. R. C. Matthews and W. Latham (eds), *The Dairy of Samuel Pepys* (11 vols, London, 1970–83) quoted (with further examples) in Donnison, *Midwives and Medical Men*, 10.

31. Willughby, *Observations*, 4, 25, 158–60; Eccles, *Obstetrics and Gynaecology*, 87–8; H. Bracken, *The Midwife's Companion* (Lancaster, 1737), 105, 207.

32. C. White, *A Treatise on the Management of Pregnant and Lying-in Women* (London, 1772), 4–5, 248–9; Willughby, *Observations*, 65; J. Cooke, *Mellificium Chirurgiae, or the Marrow of Chirurgery* (London, 1648), 257; M. Thale (ed.), *The Autobiography of Francis Place* (Cambridge, 1972), 184.

33. *OED*, 'caudle' (noun, verb).

34. Ibid.

35. A. Clark (ed.), *The Life and Times of Anthony Wood, Antiquary, of Oxford, 1632–1695, Described by Himself* (5 vols, Oxford, 1891–1900), vol. 1, 138–41.

36. J. H. Aveling, *The Chamberlens and the Midwifery Forceps: Memorials of the Family and an Essay on the Invention of the Instrument* (London, 1882), 37; Donnison, *Midwives and Medical Men*, 8–9; Willughby, *Observations*, 72, 126.

37. Willughby, *Observations*, 6–7, 19, 73–4. The quote which follows is from ibid., 32.

38. Ibid., 8, 71, 73–4; Cooke, *Mellificium Chirurgiae*, 1685 edn, 255; W. Smellie, *A Treatise on the Theory and Practice of Midwifery* (3 vols, London, 1752–64), vol. 1, 199.

39. Willughby, *Observations*, 328–9.

40. Eccles, *Obstetrics and Gynaecology*, 92–3, 107, 125–30; Willughby, *Observations*, 43–51, esp. 45; Wilson, 'William Hunter', 344–5.

41. Willughby, *Observations*, 40, 66, 82 (note also the revival of the mother: ibid., 49, 234, 256); Donnison, *Midwives and Medical Men*, 50–1; Macfarlane, *Diary of Ralph Josselin*, 415.

42. J. Sharp, *The Midwives Book* (London, 1671), 372–4; J. Maubray, *The Female Physician* (London, 1724), 327; Bracken, *The Midwife's Companion*, 207–8.

43. See *OED*, 'bed' (noun, 2b, 6c); 'bring' (8c); 'cry' (verb, 21c); 'crying' (noun, 2); 'straw' (noun, 2b); 'month' (3f, 6).

44. LPL, Shrewsbury and Talbot papers, MS 3205, f. 151 (Anne, Countess of Arundel to George, Earl of Shrewsbury, August 1608, undated but after 21 August). I owe this example to Linda Pollock. See also Willughby, *Observations*, 211–13; Cooke, *Melleficium Chirurgiae*, 1685 edn, 167.

45. Sharp, *The Midwives Book*, 229; C. E. Fox, 'Pregnancy, childbirth and early infancy in Anglo-American culture: 1675–1800', unpub. Ph. D. thesis, University of Pennsylvania, 1966, 187–91.

46. See notes 44, above, and 47, below; Fox, 'Pregnancy', 203; Macfarlane, *Diary of Ralph Josselin*, 465–6, 415–19.

47. Trumbach, *The Rise of the Egalitarian Family*, 184; *OED*, 'upsitting' (1).

48. Macfarlane, *Diary of Ralph Josselin*, 167; Fox, 'Pregnancy', 204–5.

49. Trumbach, *The Rise of the Egalitarian Family*, 184–5. But compare S. Richardson, *Pamela; or, Virtue Rewarded* (first pub. 1740; ed. P. Sabor, Harmondsworth, 1980), 500–1: 'I had intended to make her a visit, as soon as her month was up.'

50. Matthews and Latham, *Diary of Samuel Pepys*, vol. 8, 177, 200 (courtesy Linda Pollock).

51. Aveling, *The Chamberlens*, 141; R. Barret, *A Companion for Midwives, Childbearing Women, and Nurses* (London, 1699); R. Gough, *The History of Myddle* ed. D. Hey, (Harmondsworth, 1981), 207.

52. *OED*, 'monthly' (4); for the quotation from Penelope Mordaunt see Pollock (ed.), *A Lasting Relationship*, 28.

53. Macfarlane, *Diary of Ralph Josselin*, 503; and see note 46, above.

54. M. Spufford, *Contrasting Communities: English Villagers in the Sixteenth and Seventeenth Centuries* (Cambridge, 1974), 254–5.

55. Sharp, *The Midwives Book*, 211–12; Blundell quoted in Trumbach, *The Rise of the Egalitarian Family*, 178.

56. The quoted phrases are from Macfarlane, *Diary of Ralph Josselin*, 118. Only for another four deliveries did Josselin record the date of his wife's first attendance at church after delivery; these were at intervals of 32, 36, 38, and 45 days after the birth, which suggests that the present case (36 days) was typical. See ibid., 165–9, 415–19, 465–6, 502–3.

57. F. Procter and W. H. Frere, *A New History of the Book of Common Prayer, with a Rationale of its Offices* (London, 1905), 638–9.

58. W. P. M. Kennedy, *Elizabethan Episcopal Administration* (3 vols, London, 1924), vol. 3, 149–50; P. Cunnington and C. Lucas, *Costume for Births, Marriages and Deaths* (London, 1972), 18.

59. 'In Herefordshire it was not considered "correct" for the husband to appear in church on the day of his wife's churching, at all events in the same pew with her.' J. E. Vaux, *Church Folk-lore*

(2nd edn, London 1902), 112. Contrast the case from the 1630s in note 105, below.

60. W. M. Campion and W. J. Beaumont (eds), *The Prayer Book Interleaved with Historical Illustrations* (10th edn, London, 1880), 219.

61. Ibid., *Notes and Queries*, 9th series, 2 (1898), 5, 212, 255; *OED*, 'uprising' (noun, 2c). (The 116th Psalm was slightly edited in its churching version, to render it specifically female in reference.)

62. Tate, *The Parish Chest*, 131.

63. Thomas, *Religion and the Decline of Magic*, 40–1.

64. See the case of Jane Minors, cited in note 104, below.

65. Matthews and Latham, *Diary of Samuel Pepys*, vol. 8, 201 (courtesy Linda Pollock; cf. note 50 above). See also Macfarlane, *Diary of Ralph Josselin*, 12, 327, 415, 503.

66. Campion and Beaumont, *The Prayer Book Interleaved*, 219; *OED*, 'chrisom' (2, 4); Tate, *The Parish Chest*, 59–60; Thomas, *Religion and the Decline of Magic*, 41, 63, 86.

67. Tate, *The Parish Chest*, 104. For tips to the nurse and midwife at baptism, see also Donnison, *Midwives and Medical Men*, 10, 29.

68. A significant exception to the all-female birth ritual was the specific case of Royal births, where male witnesses were always present. This was presumably because of the dynastic importance of the delivery, famously illustrated by the Whigs' promotion of the 'warming-pan' story concerning Mary of Modena's delivery in 1687.

69. The shortened 'month' is discussed in note 96, below. For the use of the bed as a lying-in space, see White, *Management of Pregnant and Lying-in Women* (2nd edn, 1777), Appendix, 58. Deliveries (and therefore lying-in) away from home are found, for instance, in Willughby, *Observations*, 120, and Laslett et al. (eds), *Bastardy*, 145.

70. See M. St Clare Byrne (ed.), *The Lisle Letters* (6 vols, Chicago, 1981), vol.1, 517; vol.3, 526; vol.4, 119,122; J. J. Cartwright (ed.), *Wentworth Papers 1705–39* (London, 1883), 325; C. E. Doble et al. (eds), *Remarks and Collections of Thomas Hearne* (11 vols, Oxford, 1885–1921), 6, 261.

71. Donnison, *Midwives and Medical Men*, 52–4 (though see also ibid., 110, 113).

72. N. St André, *A Short Narrative of an Extraordinary Delivery of Rabbits* (London, 1726), 25, 36. Mary Toft's experience and its wider significance have been explored by G. Hudson, 'The politics of credulity – the Mary Toft case', unpub. M.Phil. thesis, University of Cambridge, 1986.

73. A Warne, *Church and Society in Eighteenth-century Devon* (Newton Abbot, 1969), 156, quoting from accounts of overseers of the poor for either Kenton or West Alvington, n.d.

74. D. Davies, *The Case of the Labourers in Husbandry Stated and Considered* (London, 1795), 16.

75. Additional, indirect evidence to the same effect comes from the age profile of foundling children, which shows a marked bulge at ages of 30–39 days. The only plausible explanation for this pattern

is that it reflects the 'uprising' of mothers – in which case the children brought to the Foundling Hospital at younger ages (the great majority) would have been taken there not by the mothers but by someone else. See Wilson, 'Illegitimacy and its implications', section VI and Figure 3.

76. Macfarlane, *Diary of Ralph Josselin*, 12, 14–15, 50, 111–119, 165–9, 257–9, 324–7, 415–19, 465–6, 502–3. For Fleming see note 29, above.

77. Willughby, *Observations*, 305; see also ibid., 38.

78. Willughby, *Observations*, 213.

79. See also Cooke, *Melleficium Chirurgiae*, 1648 edn, 247–57; 1685 edn, 165–78; cf. John Locke's advice to Henry Fletcher, in Pollock (ed.), *A Lasting Relationship*, 33–4.

80. See A. Fraser, *The Weaker Vessel: Woman's Lot in Seventeen Century England* (2nd edn, London, 1985), 511–12.

81. Quoted in M. Roberts, '"Words they are women, and deeds they are men": images of work and gender in early modern England', in L. Charles and L. Duffin (eds), *Women and Work in Pre-industrial England* (London, 1985), 154–5.

82. This will be further explored in A. Wilson, *A Safe Deliverance: Ritual and Conflict in English Childbirth, 1660–1750* (Cambridge, forthcoming).

83. W. Cobbett, *Advice to Young Men* (repr. Oxford, 1980), 203 (Letter IV, 'Advice to a husband', para. 211).

84. A. van Gennep, *The Rites of Passage*, trans. M. B. Vizedom and G. L. Caffee (London, 1960; French original pub. 1906), 10–11, 46.

85. J. H. Miller, '"Temple and sewer": childbirth, prudery and Victoria Regina', in A. Wohl (ed.), *The Victorian Family: Structure and Stresses* (London, 1978), 27.

86. A. Wilson, 'Participant or patient? Seventeenth century childbirth from the mother's point of view', in R. Porter (ed.), *Patients and Practitioners: Lay Perceptions of Medicine in Pre-industrial Society* (Cambridge, 1985), 135.

87. Thomas, *Religion and the Decline of Magic*, 42–3 (cf. note 101, below.)

88. K. Thomas, 'Women and the Civil War sects', *P&P*, 13 (1958), 43.

89. N.Z. Davis, 'Women on top', in her *Society and Culture in Early-modern France* (London, 1975), 124–51. The quoted passages are from 145, 313.

90. For the deploying of conjugal power as an ideological resource, see P. Higgins, 'The reactions of women, with special reference to the women petitioners', in B. Manning (ed.), *Politics, Religion and the English Civil War* (London, 1973), 179–222, esp. 179–82, 203, 211–13; S. M. Okin, 'Women and the making of the sentimental family', *Phil. Pub. Aff.*, 11 (1982), 65–88; S.D. Amussen, 'Gender, family and the social order, 1560–1725', in J. Stevenson and A. Fletcher (eds), *Order and Disorder in Early Modern England* (Cambridge, 1985), 196–217, esp. 197–205.

91. Campion and Beaumont, *The Prayer Book Interleaved*, 203–7.

92. See Baker, *An Introduction to English Legal History,* Crawford, 'From the woman's view' (note 8, above); K. Thomas, 'The double standard', *J. Hist. Ideas,* 20 (1959), 195–216, esp. 210–16.

93. The particular issue was that Elizabeth had written a memoir which, in Samuel's own words, was 'so piquant, and wrote in English and most of it true, of the retiredness of her life and how unpleasant it was, that being . . . in danger of being . . . read by others, I was vexed at it and desired her and then commanded her to tear it.' Matthews and Latham, *Diary of Samuel Pepys,* vol.4, 9, quoted in S. H. Mendelson, 'Stuart women's diaries and occasional memoirs', in M. Prior, (ed.), *Women in English Society 1500–1800* (London, 1985), 184.

94. This point has been elegantly developed by K. Hodgkin, 'The diary of Lady Anne Clifford: a study of class and gender in the seventeenth century', *Hist. Workshop J.,* 19 (1985), 148–61, esp. 150–1, 153–4.

95. C. Hill, *Economic Problems of the Church from Archbishop Whitgift to the Long Parliament* (Oxford, 1956), 168. The parish Poor Law officers might pay on the mother's behalf: Tate, *The Parish Chest,* 206. In Wakefield, Yorkshire, the custom had obtained that *every* householder with children would pay the vicar 10d at any churching. This was successfully challenged in law in 1558: see R. Burn, *Ecclesiastical Law* (2 vols, London, 1763), vol.1, 229–30.

96. See J. Boulton, *Neighbourhood and Society: A London Suburb in the Seventeenth Century* (Cambridge, 1987), 276–9. Most mothers were churched 14–27 days after the child's baptism, that is, probably 25–31 days after the birth. However, some were churched at longer intervals after the baptism, and a few (23 out of 671 churchings) within 0–13 days of the baptism. (These numbers pertain to a total of 732 baptisms, including seven where the mother is known to have died in childbirth.)

97. E. Gibson, *Codex Juris Ecclesiasticae Anglicani* (2nd edn, 2 vols, Oxford, 1761), vol. 2, 1468–9.

98. J. Cox, *The English Churches in a Secular Society: Lambeth, 1870–1930* (Oxford, 1982), 88–9, writes that 'it was to the parish church that working-class mothers regularly went for churching', citing Booth's survey material from St Mary, Lambeth, and St Philip's, Kennington. Hugh McLeod (pers. comm. 1985) has kindly passed on to me some more precise figures, from the same source, pertaining to East End parishes in the 1890s: 'The vicar of St Barnabas, Bethnal Green, said that he had conducted 150 baptisms and 200 churchings in the previous year . . . The vicar of St Paul, Virginia Row, said he had done 119 baptisms and 119 churchings.' Thus, churching was as popular as, or more popular than, baptism.

99. M. Young and P. Willmott, *Family and Kinship in East London* (3rd edn, Harmondsworth, 1986), 57.

100. The first anecdote I owe to Hugh McLeod (per. comm. 1984); my second informant wishes to remain anonymous.

101. Young and Willmott, *Family and Kinship,* 57. (It is worth noting that the authors' gloss – 'The idea still lingers on that

childbirth has in some way made the mother unclean' – has no
support within the interview material they quote.)

102. Quoted in Thomas, *Religion and the Decline of Magic*, 68–9.

103. W. H. Hale, *A Series of Precedents and Proceedings in Criminal
Causes, Extending from the Year 1475 to 1640, Extracted from Act-books of
Ecclesiastical Courts in the Diocese of London* (London, 1847), 506; F. G.
Emmison, *Elizabethan Life: Morals and the Church Courts, Mainly from
Essex Archidiaconal Records* (Chelmsford, 1973), 160.

104. Hale, *Precedents and Proceedings*, 634; Emmison, *Elizabethan
Life*, 159.

105. J. Bruce (ed.), *Calendar of State Papers, Domestic Series, of the
Reign of Charles I, 1637–8* (London, 1869), 382. For a further
example from the 1630s, in similar vein, see Spufford, *Contrasting
Communities*, 236.

106. C. W. Foster, *The State of the Church in the Reigns of Elizabeth
and James I as Illustrated by Documents Relating to the Diocese of Lincoln*
(Horncastle, Lincs, 1926), 1, p.xxxix. See also Emmison, *Elizabethan
Life*, 160: in 1586 Edmund Fanning was accused of having been 'a
hindrance to his wife in giving thanks'.

107. Compare A. Wilson, 'Inferring attitudes from behavior',
Hist. Meth., 14 (1981), 143–4. Nowadays I am inclined to doubt the
assumption that there exists a generalized 'popular attitude', either
in the past or in the present, which could meaningfully be
reconstructed.

108. After the suppression of the Book of Common Prayer, and
the substituting of the Directory for Public Worship, in 1645,
churching was sometimes performed at home: see, for instance, E. S.
De Beer (ed.), *The Diary of John Evelyn* (London, 1959), 325, 333.
The Directory did not include any churching service; however,
under the discretion permitted to ministers, it was entirely possible
for churching to continue in the traditional way. See J. W. Packer,
*The Transformation of Anglicanism 1643–1660, with Special Reference to
Henry Hammond* (Manchester, 1969), 13, 140.

109. Thomas, *Religion and the Decline of Magic*, 42–3; T. Comber,
The Occasional Offices Explained (London, 1679), 510.

110. Burn, *Ecclesiastical Law*, vol. 1, 229; *Second Report of the
Commissioners Appointed to Inquire into the Rubric, Orders, and Directions
for Regulating the Course and Conduct of Public Worship, etc.* (London,
1868), Appendix, 165.

111. E. L. Lipton, A. Steinschrader, and J. B. Richmond,
'Swaddling, a child care practice: historical, cultural and
experimental observations', *Paediatrics*, Suppl., 35 (1965), 519–67.

112. F. Loux, *Le Jeune Enfant et son Corps dans la Médecine
Traditionelle* (Paris, 1978).

113. The presence of the husband during the birth is attested for
Germany and for some parts of France. See L. Heister, *A General
System of Surgery in Three Parts*, transl. anon., Innys et al., (London,
1743), 207; E. Shorter, *A History of Women's Bodies* (London, 1982),
55; Loux, *Le Jeune Enfant*, 100–2. (Yet Mireille Laget suggests that the
French father was absent, though represented symbolically in some

localities by his shirt or hat: *Naissances: l'Accouchement avant l'Âge de la clinique* (Paris, 1982), 135–7.) On the modern hospital ritual see P. Lomas, 'An interpretation of modern obstetric practice', in S. Kitzinger and J. Davis (eds), *The Place of Birth* (Oxford, 1978), 174–84. The process of historical transformation has been explored for the case of North America by J. W. Leavitt, *Brought to Bed, Birthing Women and Their Physicians in America 1750–1950* (Oxford, 1987). A wealth of comparative material is available in G. J. Witkowski, *Histoire des Accouchements Chez Tous les Peuples* (Paris, 1887).

114. K. E. Paige and J. M. Paige, *The Politics of Reproductive Ritual* (Berkeley, 1981), 43.

115. Ibid., 54. In sharp contrast, Diane Bell has recently stressed that Australian aboriginal women's rituals are constructed and chosen by the women themselves: *Daughters of the Dreaming* (Melbourne, 1983). I am grateful to Gill Hudson for this reference. For an open-ended exploration, written by women anthropologists and nurses, see M. A. Kay (ed.), *Anthropology of Human Birth* (Philadelphia, 1982). This collection contains some twenty new ethnographic reports, produced under the guidance of the editor, and also includes an invaluable critique of earlier approaches: C. McClain, 'Toward a comparative framework for the study of childbirth: a review of the literature', ibid., 25–59.

116. V. Fildes, *Breasts, Bottles and Babies: A History of Infant Feeding* (Edinburgh, 1986); D. McLaren, 'Marital fertility and lactation 1570–1720' in Prior (ed.), *Women in English Society*, 22–53; and their other studies listed in the bibliography to this volume.

117. Donnison, *Midwives and Medical Men*; Eccles, *Obstetrics and Gynaecology* (note 10, above).

118. S. M. Okin, 'Patriarchy and married women's property in England: questions on some current views', *Eighteenth-Cent. Stud.*, 17 (1983), 121–38; R. Mitchison, 'Man and wife', *Lond. Rev. Books*, 22 May 1986, 9–10; L. Pollock, '"An action like a stratagem": courtship and marriage from the Middle Ages to the twentieth century', *Hist. J.*, 30 (1987) 483–98.

119. S. Alexander, 'Women, class and sexual differences in the 1830s and 1840s: some reflections on the writing of a feminist history', *Hist. Workshop J.*, 17 (1984), 125–49; L. Gordon, 'What's new in women's history', in T. de Lauretis, (ed.), *Feminist Studies/Critical Studies* (Bloomington, 1986), 20–30.

120. Mendelson, 'Stuart women's diaries'; P. Crawford, 'Women's published writings 1600–1700', in Prior (ed.), *Women in English Society*, 211–82 (both including invaluable lists of such sources).

121. For example, Okin in 'Women and the making of the sentimental family' has shown that conjugal relations were treated, in distinctive ways, by all major classical political theorists. Again, Estelle Cohen has demonstrated that gender relations strongly impinged upon learned theories of generation – and has found a tradition of contest within this literature. See her 'Medical debates

on women's "nature" in England around 1700', *Bull. Soc. Soc. Hist. Med.*, 39 (1986), 7–11.

122. See T. G. Ashplant and A. Wilson, 'Present-centred history and the problem of historical knowledge', *Hist. J.*, 31 (1988).

123. The term 'counter-power' has been used with similar meaning, though in the different context of factory struggles, by Michelle Perrot, in a conversation with Jean-Pierre Barou and Michel Foucault. See M. Foucault, *Power/Knowledge: Selected Interviews and Other Writings 1972–1977*, ed. C. Gordon (Brighton, 1980), 163. For Elizabeth Pepys's resistance see note 93, above; other examples can be found in, for instance, Crawford's essay (note 8, above); Hodgkin's study (note 94, above); P. Mack, 'Women as prophets during the English Civil War', *Fem. Stud.*, 8 (1982), 19–45. Compare Macfarlane's perceptive summary: 'The kind of tension of identity and opposition that one finds in any system of hierarchy . . . was central to the marriage relationship as well' (*Marriage and Love*, 290). For some examples of collective struggles see Higgins, 'The reactions of women'; Clark (ed.), *The Life and Times of Anthony Wood*, vol. 1, 250–1; BL, Sloane MS 529, fols 1–19 (paginated 1–35), 'Domini Willoughbaei Derbiensis de puerperio tractatus', 14,22 (cf. Willughby, *Observations*, 99–101, 125.

124. On such a methodological strategy, compare Foucault: 'I would like to suggest another way to go further towards a new economy of power relations . . . . It consists of taking the forms of resistance against different forms of power as a starting point . . . . To use another metaphor, it consists of using this resistance as a chemical catalyst so as to bring to light power relations, locate their position, find out their point of application and the methods used' ('Afterword', 210–11, in H. L. Dreyfus and P. Rabinow, *Michel Foucault: Beyond Structuralism and Hermeneutics* (2nd edn, Chicago, 1983). The scope for a 'dissection' of patriarchal power is well illustrated by Middleton's pioneering exploration of this theme (based on a different methodological strategy) for the medieval period. See C. Middleton, 'Peasants, patriarchy, and the feudal mode of production in England: a Marxist appraisal', *Soc. Rev.*, 29 (1981), 105–35, 137–54.

125. I hope to explore these themes in a future paper, provisionally entitled 'Patriarchal power and women's resistance in early-modern England'.

126. See Chaytor, 'Household and kinship', esp. 48–9.

127. S. D. Amussen, 'Féminin/masculin: le genre dans l'Angleterre de lépoque moderne', *Annales ESC*, 40 (1985), 269–87; and *idem*, 'Gender, family and the social order'.

128. Ann Hess has suggested such a role for midwives in New England, drawing on court depositions: 'The New England midwife: women's work and culture in seventeenth-century America and England', unpub. dissertation, Yale University, 1987.

4

Puritan attitudes towards childhood discipline, 1560–1634

Robert V. Schnucker

> It may well be said that the whole Puritan movement has
> its roots in the family and that we cannot even begin to
> understand it if we leave the family out of the account.[1]

So wrote Levin L. Schücking in 1929. Since then a goodly
number of scholars have investigated early-modern families,
including the families of English Puritans. Lawrence Stone's *The
Family, Sex, and Marriage in England 1500–1800*, Steven
Ozment's *When Fathers Ruled*, Ralph Houlbrooke's *The English
Family 1450–1700*, and most recently, John Morgan's *Godly
Learning*,[2] have pointed to the idea that both Protestants and
Catholics hoped there would be an interpenetration of faith
and conduct within the family that would permeate the essence
of each family member and then extend through their actions
into their public and private worlds all to the glory of God.

The English Puritans prior to 1640 were no exception to this
hope. In fact the Puritans wrote twice as many books as any
other group providing directions for the raising of children so
the hope could be accomplished.[3] By 1635, they had written
close to two dozen such books plus pamphlets, treatises, and
sermons touching on child rearing. The first book in English
dealing with childhood discipline was a translation of Jacques
LeGrand's *Boke of Good Manners* published by Caxton. Other
volumes appeared over the years with Coverdale's translation of
Bullinger's *Christen State of Matrimonye* in 1541 as the most
complete and detailed book until Becon published his works in
the 1560s. Becon, Cranmer's chaplain, expanded some of
Bullinger's ideas in the *New Catechism* and again in *Boke of
Matrimonye*. Becon was carefully read and often followed by

many in the new movement of the 1560s derisively called puritanism. The general reliance of Becon upon Bullinger, and subsequent reliance of other Puritan writers upon those two, contributes to a consistency of point of view;[4] but at the same time, later writers considered new issues and presented considerably more detail supporting their arguments than did Bullinger or Becon.

Almost from the beginning, the Puritans expressed a deep concern for and interest in the Christian family. Whether or not they were innovative in their description of family life – what they called domestical duties – is arguable. They might have been descriptive in what they wrote and not prescriptive; and it must be admitted that there are many parallels between their ideas and those expressed by other Christian writers in the sixteenth century.

Table 4.1 Attitudes to childhood discipline, 1560–1634

No.	Attitude identified	Attitude code
1.	The end of correction was to ensure salvation.	A
2.	God will punish parents if they allow children to be disobedient.	B
3.	Parents were not to give unlawful commands to children.	C
4.	Children were to honour and obey their parents.	D
5.	To disobey parents was to go against God's will.	E
6.	Children were to demonstrate outward signs of honour to their parents.	F
7.	Discipline was to begin early.	G
8.	Parents were to command respect from children by godly example.	H
9.	Parents were not to be too familiar with children.	I
10.	Correction was to be made for some good end – and not arbitrarily.	J
11.	Correction was to be made in wisdom.	K
12.	Correction was to be made according to child's capabilities and nature of fault.	L
13.	Correction was to be done in moderation.	M
14.	Correction not to be done when parents angered.	N
15.	Correction not to be in bitterness or with cruelty.	O
16.	Correction to be given after children aware of fault.	P
17.	First correction to be verbal.	Q
18.	Physical correction to be last resort.	R
19.	Child to be struck on 'sides'.	S
20.	Children must submit to parental correction.	T

Sources: See Appendix

Figure 4.1 Attitudinal frequencies for discipline, 1560–1634

Attitude Code	1 1560	2 1562	3 1578	4 1581	5 1582	6 1583	7 1591	8 1597	9 1598	10 1603	11 1609	12 1609	13 1611	14 1612	15 1612	16 1612	17 1617	18 1620	19 1622	20 1622	21 1627	22 1633	Total	Frequency of attitudes %	Frequency of sources w/disc. attitudes %
A				1			1		1														3	2.2	13.6
B	1	1																					2	1.5	9.0
C	1	1	1			1			1	1													6	4.5	27.2
D	1	1	1	1				1	1	1	1	1	1	1			1	1	1	1	1	1	17	12.7	77.2
E				1				1															2	1.5	9.0
F	1				1				1	1				1				1	1	1			8	6.0	36.3
G		1			1				1	1				1							1		6	4.5	27.2
H	1	1			1	1			1	1				1		1	1			1	1		11	8.2	50.0
I										1	1		1	1									4	3.0	18.1
J									1	1				1			1		1		1		6	4.5	27.2
K			1	1											1	1	1				1		6	4.5	27.2
L	1	1							1	1	1		1					1	1		1		8	6.0	36.3
M	1	1	1	1					1		1			1	1	1		1	1	1	1	1	14	10.4	63.6
N				1							1		1		1				1				5	3.7	22.7
O			1							1											1		3	2.2	13.6
P	1	1										1						1		1			5	3.7	22.7
Q	1	1							1	1	1	1	1		1					1	1		10	7.5	45.4
R		1	1						1	1	1		1		1		1			1		1	10	7.5	45.4
S		1		1						1											1		3	2.2	13.6
T					1				1	1			1	1								1	5	3.7	22.7
Totals	7	8	4	7	4	1	1	3	10	12	7	4	5	8	4	4	6	4	5	11	9	10	134	100.0	

Sources: See Appendix

Figure 4.2 Percentage frequency of attitudes to discipline (solid line) and sources containing attitudes to discipline (dotted line) in 25-year periods, 1560–1634

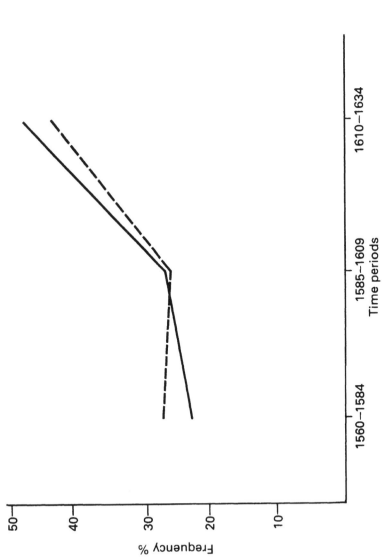

Frequency %

1560–1584   1585–1609   1610–1634
                   Time periods

Sources: See Appendix

The purpose of this study is not to explore the innovativeness of the Puritans but to examine the internal consistency of their attitudes to one aspect of the all-important family, their attitudes toward childhood discipline. The time span covered by this study is from 1560–1635. The twenty-two sources examined include the genre termed domestical duty books plus commentaries on appropriate passages of the Bible that relate to childhood discipline, sermons, and catechisms, all written by Puritans. The technique used in examining the sources is word-content analysis with the sources grouped into three consecutive 25-year periods. Twenty basic attitudes involving childhood discipline were identified (see Table 4.1). The distribution of these twenty attitudes over 75 years was plotted. Then the percentage of the frequency with which each appeared, and the percentage of the frequency with which they appeared in the sources, were charted in order to identify variations (see Figures 4.1 and 4.2). These data were then analysed using the Chi-square test to determine the statistical significance of the findings.

A number of problems confront scholars attempting to study families of the past.[5] A constant criticism is that there is no provable causal connection between the attitudes expressed in the writings and the actual practice of those who were in the same group which produced the writings. Did the Puritan families of the 75-year span of this study follow the formulae and theories put forth by their leaders? Is it not reasonable to assume that the followers accommodated the ideas that appeared in print or were given in sermons, and modified their behaviour according to their own circumstances and situations? Certainly, eye-witness accounts and the revelations of diaries might provide a glimpse of any causal relationship between theory and practice – but only a fleeting glimpse since the number of accounts and diaries that survives is meagre.

In order to work around the problem of causal connection between theory and action, some scholars have become innovative. Some have used family account books as a means of understanding family life. Robert Jütte's 'Household and family life in late sixteenth century Cologne: The Weinsburg family' is an example of an innovative approach.[6] Stephen Ozment's *When Fathers Ruled, Family Life in Reformation Europe* is an example of overgeneralizing from one diary that did survive. Others have used almost every arrow in the quiver of historical demography to reveal something about family and society in early-modern Europe. Lawrence Stone is one of the masters of such efforts and he is closely followed by Sheldon Watts, who has provided an excellent overview for Europe as Stone has provided a detailed view of England.[7] It could be that the motivations that drove family life in early-modern Europe will never be known. All we have are intriguing probes that fuel our efforts to create possible explanations. To put the problem into twentieth-century US terms: How influential is Dr Spock's book for the raising of children in the last half of the current century?

Content analysis used in this study is but another attempt, certainly not perfect, to come to an understanding of a past attitude of the family and in particular here, to understand childhood discipline. Before stating the results of the Chi-square test, some of the Puritan attitudes about childhood discipline need to be given.

The Puritan view of the family was 'pot-bound' in the Bible. The Old Testament passage always cited to support the importance of the family was the fifth commandment: 'Honour your father and mother.' With the father mentioned first, together with the fact that God was envisioned as the Heavenly Father, all Puritan writers insisted that the family was to be a hierarchy with the human father over all others within the household.[8] Religious and political parallels were used to reinforce this 'truth.' Just as the magistrate presided over the state, and God as the Father was over his earthly children, so the family father presided over his wife, their children, the servants, and the other relatives and people who might reside in their household. As the Heavenly Father is 'The' source of all authority and of all religious belief, so should the human father function as the source of all authority and religious instruction within the family. The father was God's representative in the home and as such was to provide the example for religious instruction. All of the Puritan writers in this study emphasized this basic belief throughout the entire time span of the study.

The New Testament sources used to support the idea of the pre-eminence of the father in the family usually came from the writings of Paul where he exhorted children to obey their parents and fathers not to provoke their children into disobedience. The Paulline passages were used equally throughout the 75-year span of this study along with the fifth commandment.

The mother's place was always one of subordination to the father; but she was second in command over the entire household.[9] The subordination of the wife to the husband taught the children their first lesson of discipline: obedience. Various reasons were cited for the mother's subordination ranging from the fact that the father was named first in the fifth commandment and by Paul, to the theological justification that it was Eve who really caused the fall, and with her status of being created second rather than first, the mother's proper place was that of subordination to the father. However, when the father was absent, the mother's role had the full authority of the father. Thus, as the Bible revealed, the father was first and the mother second. The children, as seen by the Puritans and many others of that time, were tertiary in the hierarchy and were in addition sinful.

The sinfulness of children coloured the Puritan approach to childhood discipline. As they saw it children were not neutral beings who became evil for some reason; they began life as sinful. Discipline was thus needed to prevent the child from falling further into the grasp of sin. Although the Catholic Church had argued that children were not capable of mortal sin until the age of 7, some of the Puritans argued that original sin manifested itself while the children were at their mothers' breasts. It was thus necessary to give the child discipline and to teach it obedience early in order to prevent sin's domination in the child's life.[10] Over a quarter of the Puritan writings emphasized the necessity for an early beginning in discipline and by early was meant prior to the age of 7.[11] The use of correction and discipline as a means of helping a child attain salvation received the most emphasis in the first 25 years of this study and then it decreased. A concomitant decrease is also found in the assertion that parents who did not discipline their children were evil. Although both ideas will be found in the third 25-year span of this study, the two ideas were not as frequent in their appearance, nor stated with the same intensity as earlier.

Although some of the Puritans suggested women discipline the females in the household and men the males,[12] it was the universal view that parents must support each other in whatever discipline was meted out,[13] and that parents supply in their own behaviour the model that the children should follow.[14] Throughout the 75-year span of this study, the variation in these two attitudes was between 2 and 3 per cent, thus showing a high degree of consistency.

One term not found during the first 25 years of Puritan writing is 'cockering',[15] which can probably best be translated into the modern term of 'coddling'. By the last 25-year period, almost all of the writers warned about coddling children. Why this was the case is difficult to determine. Earlier writers had warned about the danger of a lack of discipline and it could be that the later writers were following the same path but simply used a term more appropriate for their own day. There is also the possibility that the grandchildren of the first believers were not following in the same pattern as the grandparents and a call to earlier ideals was given.

When a child was to be corrected, it was to be for a good reason: as the Puritans put it, there was to be a 'need' for correction. Further, the correction had to be appropriate to the infraction. Capricious correction was inconsistent with the example of God the Father. This 'need' for correction was not found in the early Puritan writing but by the last 25-year span, two-thirds of the writers mentioned the need for a reason for correction.[16] Implied in the 'need' was the belief that the correction must not only fit the infraction but also the characteristics of the child. That meant age, sex, temperament, and physical and moral development of the child had to be taken into account before discipline could be given.[17]

Wisdom was also required of the parent prior to discipline. The parent was to have reflected about the nature of the infraction, the capacity of the child, and then to have prayed for proper guidance. By the second 25-year span, the use of wisdom in discipline had been included in a quarter of the sources and continued so during the third 25-year span.

'Birtch breaketh no bones', wrote Robert Cleaver in his *A Godly Forme of Household Government*.[18] In the 1630s William Gouge wrote that parents who were churlish in their discipline, or violent, would bring about the same in their own children, and the result would be a denial of the function of discipline, which was to lead the wayward back to the straight and narrow path of morality.[19] The rejection of severity of punishment is the most common attitude found throughout the 75-year span of this study. Almost all of the writers cautioned against the overbearing and physically violent parent. The middle course was to be preferred, for too much indulgence could spawn more sin while too much severity would provide an occasion for wrath and anger on the part of the child, a result that Paul had warned against in the New Testament.[20]

Certainly, a corollary to the middle approach to discipline was the Puritan admonition never to correct a child while the parent was angry or provoked. Ephesians 6:4 was always the New Testament passage cited: 'And you father, provoke not your children to wrath.' In commenting on this, Robert Cleaver, reflecting all of the Puritan writers in this study, wrote, 'for he that commeth to reforme with anger shall hardly keep a measure in rebuking or chastising'.[21] Later, Dod and Cleaver wrote a commentary on the Ten Commandments, and in dealing with the Fifth Commandment, they wrote that discipline be 'not in bitterness to ease oneself with the paine of the child, which is too barbarous crueltie'.[22] When the parent was to discipline a child, it was to be done with wisdom, prayer, reflection, and moderation, and never in anger or with provocation.

To increase the effectiveness of discipline, the Puritans insisted that the one about to be disciplined be aware of the reason for the discipline. The assumption was that the child, in swearing, lying, stealing, or whatever, had not only sinned against his or her father and mother but more importantly, against God, 'The' Father. Once the child understood the gravity of the infraction, the discipline to be given could be done to the glory of God. In his *A New Catechism*, Becon wrote, 'first of all, before they punish their children which have offended, they lay the fault openly before them, declare unto them how greatly they have offended and broken God's commandment and exhort them from thence forth to do better'.[23] Becon advised children to realize that the words of reproof and physical punishment they received from their parents came from the desire 'not of their destruction but their salvation'.[24] Thus, the punishment was not only to fit the crime but should also bring about the child's conversion to a better life. This attitude was a theme found 100 per cent of the time throughout the 75-year span of this study.[25]

The exact nature of the discipline is not difficult to imagine. It came in two forms, verbal and physical. The less serious infractions merited verbal reproof, and the Puritans were aware that too much talking would make a child immune to effective reform. Idle threats could lead to total immunity. Thus, almost

all of the Puritan writers cautioned parents about indiscrim-
inate use of verbal reproof.[26] However, when spoken chastise-
ment did not bring about reform, then physical punishment
could be used. Almost all (90 per cent) of the sources
throughout the 75 years supported this idea.[27] It would seem
that the Puritan approach was: It is better to be whipped than
damned but a greater virtue to be persuaded verbally to reform
than to be whipped. The Puritans were careful in designating
where the child was to be whipped. A parent was never to strike
the head for fear of permanently hurting the child. The preferred place was 'the sides' which in our terminology would be
the buttocks, the fleshiest parts.[28] One Puritan writer, Batty,
even argued that God created human beings with buttocks
specifically to receive the blows of correction without serious
bodily injury.[29]

Thus far it would seem that the Puritan approach to
disciplining children is not too far removed from many modern
theories. Parents were to be the authority in the family; they
were to set the examples for their children; parents were not to
spoil their children nor correct them for no apparent reason;
discipline should be done with common sense, wisdom, by
assessing the nature of the infraction, the capability of the child,
and then carrying out the discipline when in a calm state of
mind after explaining to the child why the correction was to be
done. The parent was to use verbal reproof first and physical
punishment only as a last resort. The Puritan difference from
the modern world is found in their religious orientation to
discipline – discipline is to bring the child back to the straight
and narrow path of righteousness and should lead the child to
salvation. Children submit to discipline and parents mete it out
since this is part of a heavenly hierarchical scheme revealed in
the Bible.

In examining Puritan ideas on disciplining children,
attitudes were found early in the Puritan movement that were
sustained throughout the time-span studies. Some attitudes that
appeared early were not as prevalent later, and others appeared
later that were not present earlier. The purpose of this
investigation was to determine the consistency of Puritan
attitudes on childhood discipline during the first 75 years of
English Puritanism. The question now is, were the changes
found significant, thus showing inconsistency? A Chi-square test
on the data from the content analysis gave a figure of 1·3405.

This is not statistically significant as p<0·05. Thus, it can be concluded that Puritan attitudes towards childhood discipline did not significantly change, but remained consistent during the 75 years studied.

Appendix

Works analysed for content on attitudes to child discipline 1560–1634 in chronological order (source code number given in brackets)

(1) Becon, T. *A New Catechism Set Forth Dialogue Wise in Familiar Talk Between the Father and the Son*, ed. J. Ayre (Cambridge, 1844; first pub. 1560).

(2) Becon, T. *Boke of Matrimonye*, in *Workes* (London, 1562), vol. 1.

(3) Stockwood, J. *A Sermon Preached at Paules Crosse on Barthelmew Day, Being the 24th of August, 1578 Wherein . . . is . . . Prooved, that it is the Part of All These that are Fathers, Householders, and Cholemaister to Instruct All Those under Their Government, in the Word and Knowledge of the Lorde.* (London, 1578).

(4) Batty, B. *The Christian Mans Closet Wherein is Contained a Large Discourse of the Godly Training up of Children: as Also of Those Duties that Children Owe unto Their Parents*, trans. W. Loroth (London, 1581).

(5) Browne, R. *A Booke which Sheweth the Life and Manners of All True Christians and howe Vnlike They are vnto Turkes and Papistes, and Heathen Folk* (Middelburgh, 1582).

(6) Jones, R. *A Briefe and Necessarie Catechisme . . . for the Benefit of all Householders, Their Children and Familie. With a Short Instruction for All that Doo Receiue the Holy Communion* (London, 1583).

(7) Smith, H. *A Preparative to Marriage*, in *The Sermons of Master Henry Smith Gathered into One Volume* (London, 1591).

(8) Dering, E. *A Bryefe and Necessary Catechisme in Maister Derings Works More at Large than Ever Hath Heare-to-fore Been Printed* (London, 1597).

(9) Cleaver, R. *A Godly Form of Householde Government: for the Ordring of Private Families, According to the Directions of Gods Word* (London, 1598).

(10) Dod, J. and Cleaver, R. *A Treatise or Exposition upon the Ten Commandments, Grounded upon the Scriptures Canonicall* (London, 1603).

(11) Dillingham, F. *Christian Oeconomie, or Houshold Government, that is, the Dueties of Husbands and Wives and Children, Masters and Servants* (London, 1609).

(12) Perkins, W. *Christian Oeconomie: or, A Short Survey of the Right Manner of Errecting and Ordering a Family, According to the Scriptures*, trans. T. Pickering (London, 1609).

(13) Greenham, R. *Short Form of Catechising* (London, 1611).

(14) Hieron, S. *A Help unto Devotion: Containing Certain Moulds or Forms of Prayer* (4th edn, London, 1612).

(15) Greenham, R. *Godly Instructions for the Due Examination and Direction of All Men in the Workes of the Reverend Richard Greenham, Collected into One Volume* (London, 1612).

(16) Greenham, R, *Of Domesticall Duties Eight Treatises. I. An Exposition of that Part of Scripture out of which Domesticall Duties are Raised. II. A Right Conunction of Man and Wife. 2. Common-mutuall Duties Betwixt Man and Wife. III. Particular Duties of Wives. IV. Particular Duties of Husbands. V. Duties of Children, VI. Duties of Parents. VII. Duties of Servants. VIII. Duties of Masters* (London, 1622).

(17) Whately, W. *A Bride-bush or a Wedding Sermon: Compendiously Describing the Duties of Married Persons: by Performing Whereof, Marriage Shall Be to Them a Great Helpe, which now Finde It a Little Hell* (London, 1617).

(18) Gataker, T. *Marriage Duties Briefly Couched Togither: Out of Colossians, 3.18,19* (London, 1620).

(19) Whately, W. *A Pithie, Short and Methodicall Opening of the Ten Commandments* (London, 1622).

(20) Gouge, W. *Of Domesticall Duties Eight Treatises. I. An Exposition of that Part of Scripture Out of which Domesticall Duties are Raised. II. A Right Conunction of Man and Wife. 2. Common-mutuall Duties Betwixt Man and Wife. III. Particular Duties of Wives. IV. Particular Duties of Husbands. V. Duties of Children. VI. Duties of Parents. VII. Duties of Servants. VIII. Duties of Masters* (London, 1622).

(21) Carter, T. *Caters Christian Common Wealth; or Domesticall Dutyes Deciphered* (London, 1627).

(22) Griffith, M. *Bethel: or a Forme for Families* (London, 1633).

Notes

(For full details of the works analysed see Appendix.)

1. L. L. Schücking, *The Puritan Family*, trans. B. Battershaw from 1929 German edn (New York, 1970), 56.

2. L. Stone, *The Family, Sex, and Marriage in England 1500–1800* (New York, 1977); S. Ozment, *When Fathers Ruled, Family Life in Reformation Europe* (Cambridge, Mass., 1983); R. A. Houlbrooke, *The English Family 1450–1700* (London, 1984); J. Morgan, *Godly Learning, Puritan Attitudes Towards Reason, Learning and Education 1560–1640* (New York, 1986).

3. Stone, *Family, Sex, and Marriage*, 175. Stone cites here an unpublished paper by J. C. Somerville.

4. R. C. (Robert Cleaver?), *A Godly Form of Householde Gouernment* of 1598 has sections in it lifted from Henry Smith's earlier work, *A Preparative to Marriage* of 1591. Often, domestic-duty books used the same illustration. In Cleaver's book cited below, p. 201, an illustration is used that is found on p. 125 of Perkin's *Christian Oeconomie*; the same illustration is found in Griffith's *Bethel*, 289, and again in the anonymous *A Curtaine Lecture* (1637), 170, and finally in one of John Donne's sermons where he attributes it to St Jerome.

5. L. A. Pollock, *Forgotten Children, Parent–Child Relations from 1500–1900* (New York, 1983). The first two chapters of this book present a fine discussion of problems faced in dealing with the history of childhood.

6. R. Jütte, 'Household and family life in late sixteenth century Cologne: the Weinsburg family', *Sixteenth Cent. J.*, 17 (1986), 165ff.

7. S. J. Watts, *A Social History of Western Europe, 1450–1720: Tensions and Solidarities Among Rural People* (London, 1984). See R. Manning's review of this important book in *Sixteenth Cent. J.*, 17 (1986), 353.

8. R. Browne, *A Booke Which Sheweth the Life*, 127ff; R. Jones, *A Briefe and Necessarie Catechisme*, Biii v ff. J. Dod and R. Cleaver, *A Treatise upon the Ten Commandments*, 2 r; Perkins, *Christian Oeconomie*, 698 ff; F. Dillingham, *Christian Oeconomie*, 26 v; Whately, *A Bride-bush*, 16 ff.

9. Batty, *The Christian Mans Closet*, 3 b; Becon, *Boke of Matrimonye* DCLxxvi r; Whately, *A Bride-bush*, 16f; Carter, *Carters Christian Commonwealth*, 173ff.

10. Dering, *A Bryefe and Necessary Catechisme*, 14.

11. Becon, *Boke of Matrimonye*, DCLxxi v; Dod and Cleaver, *A Treatise upon the Ten Commandments*, 8 v; Carter, *Carters Christian Commonwealth*, 123; Cleaver, *A Godly Form of Householde Gouernment*, 255; Greenham, *Of the Good Education*, 278; Hieron, *A Help unto Devotion*, 399.

12. Smith, *A Preparative to Marriage*, 57.

13. Whately, *Bride-bush*, 17–18.

14. All the writers supported this. Batty, *The Christian Mans Closet*, 26; Browne, *A Booke which Sheweth the Life*, 128; Smith, *A Preparative to Marriage*, AV r; Cleaver, *A Godly Form of Householde Gouernment*, 242; Hieron, *A Help unto Devotion*, 399; R. Greenham, *Of the Good Education*, in *Workes* (3rd edn, London 1601), 278; Whately, *Bride-bush*, 19; Griffith, *Bethel*, 365. These are but some of the examples that can be cited.

15. Cleaver, *Godly Form of Householde Gouernment*, 295; Batty, *The Christian Mans Closet*, 29.

16. Dillingham, *Christian Oeconomie*, 40 v; Whately, *Bride-bush*, 18; Griffith, *Bethel*, 365ff; Gouge, *Domesticall Dueties*, 555.

17. Becon, *A New Catechisme*, 354; Batty, *The Christian Mans Closet*, 24b; Cleaver, *A Godly Form of Householde Gouernment*, 42ff; Perkins, *Christian Oeconomie*, 699; Hieron, *A Help unto Devotion*, 405; Whately, *A Piethie, Short and Methodicall Opening of the Ten Commandments* 113; Gouge, *Domesticall Dueties*, 536ff; Griffith, *Bethel*, 406; Carter, *Carters Christian Commonwealth*, 132.

18. Cleaver, *A Godly Form of Householde Gouernment*, 246.

19. Gouge, *Domesticall Dueties*, 155–6.

20. Hieron, *A Help unto Devotion*, 394–400; Becon, *A New Catechism*, 54; Batty, *The Christian Mans Closet*, 14; Cleaver, *A Godly Form of Householde Gouernment*, 259; Stockwood, *A Sermon Preached at Paules Cross*, 89–90; Dod and Cleaver, *A Treatise upon the Ten Commandments*, 8 r; Perkins, *Christian Oeconomie*, 694; Dillingham, *Christian Oeconomie*, 35 r; Hieron, *A Help unto Devotion*, 405; Greenham, *Of the Good Education*, 666; Whately, *Bride-bush*, 18; Gouge, *Domesticall Dueties*, 556ff; Carter, *Carters Christian Commonwealth*, 132; Griffith, *Bethel*, 408.

21. Cleaver, *A Godly Form of Householde Gouernment*, 49. cf. Batty, *The Christian Mans Closet*, 14, 26; Dod and Cleaver, *A Treatise on the Ten Commandments*, 8 r; Dillingham, *Christian Oeconomie* 39 r; Whately, *Bride-bush*, 22.

22. Dod and Cleaver, *A Treatise on the Ten Commandments*, 8 rff.

23. Becon, *A New Catechism*, 354.

24. Ibid.

25. Batty, *The Christian Mans Closet*, 22; Cleaver, *A Godly Form of Householde Gouernment*, 43; Gouge, *Domesticall Dueties*, 553; Griffith, *Bethel*, 407.

26. Becon, *Boke of Matrimonye*, DCLxxvii v; Cleaver, *A Godly Form of Householde Gouernment*, 50; Gouge, *Domesticall Dueties*, 550; Carter, *Carters Christian Commonwealth*, 134.

27. Becon, *New Catechism*, 354; Stockwood, *A Sermon Preached at Paules Cross*, 89–90; Batty, *The Christian Mans Closet*, 15b; Cleaver, *A Godly Form of Householde Gouernment*, 42; Perkins, *Christian Oeconomie*, 694; Dillingham, *Christian Oeconomie*, 30 v; Greenham, *Of the Good Education*, 652; Gouge, *Domesticall Dueties*, 552ff; Griffith, *Bethel*, 406.

28. Becon, *Boke of Matrimonye*, DCLXXIIII v; Batty, *The Christian Mans Closet*, 26ff; Gouge, *Domesticall Dueties*, 556; Carter, *Carters Christian Commonwealth*, 122ff.

29. Batty, *The Christian Mans Closet*, 26ff.

5

Wet nursing and child care in Aldenham, Hertfordshire, 1595–1726: some evidence on the circumstances and effects of seventeenth-century child rearing practices

Fiona Newall

This chapter examines the situation of families involved in wet nursing and the care of children in the parish of Aldenham, 1595–1726.[1] Aldenham lies astride Watling Street, some 15 miles north-west of London. In the sixteenth and seventeenth centuries, the parish economy was based on the production of grain, and later livestock, for London markets. During this period a society of yeoman farmers and labourers with small holdings was being replaced by larger-scale commercial farming and landless labourers.[2] The parish made generous provision for its poor and needy through poor-law reliefs and private charities. Prominent among the latter was the London Brewers' Company.

Families living in Aldenham in the period 1560–1812 have been reconstituted from the parish registers.[3] In addition, socio-economic information on the families has been derived from taxation and other listings, and a particularly useful set of poor-law accounts which span the whole period of the reconstitution after 1628. These extra sources allow more detailed analysis of the demography of the reconstituted families than is often possible, and have allowed the accuracy of the linkage for many families to be confirmed.

English and European child care practices

Literary evidence and demographic studies provide insight into child rearing practices in the seventeenth and early-eighteenth centuries. Throughout the pre-industrial period England is known to have had low, but not artificially controlled, marital

fertility rates. As part of his analysis of fertility in sixteen reconstituted parishes, Wilson ascribes the low fertility to the fact that
'mothers in England probably suckled their infants for between
15 and 18 months . . . this action led to a suppression of
ovulation and a lengthening of birth intervals by about a year.'[4]
This factor has also been observed in other parishes, particularly by McLaren in Buckinghamshire and Somerset.[5]

For England, further evidence of breastfeeding comes from
written sources such as diaries, medical texts, and, circumstant-
ially, from parish registration. Other researchers have analysed
data on the effects of breastfeeding for a range of historical
European communities.[6] Wilson's study of sixteen pre-
industrial English parishes found that birth intervals in these
were comparable to those in continental areas which
traditionally breastfed their infants, such as Ostfriesland and
Waldeck in Germany, and Crulai and Tourouvre-le-Perche in
France. In areas with a long-standing antagonism towards
breastfeeding, such as Bavaria in Germany or Oschelbronn and
Blankenberge in Flanders, the intergenesic intervals are much
shorter.[7] These findings are supported by McLaren and by
Finlay's appraisal of the demography of London, in which high
fertility in wealthy parishes is explained by the custom of
sending children out to wet nurses soon after birth, completely
eliminating the ovulation-inhibiting influence of lactation on
their mothers.[8]

Although breastfeeding was clearly an important feature of
early-modern English society, Wilson does not believe that the
practice of wet nursing was widespread among the populations
of his sixteen parishes. These include Aldenham, and he notes
the burials of nurse children recorded throughout the seventeenth and early-eighteenth centuries in the parish registers.
However, Wilson's fertility index suggests that, overall, there
was a lower than average incidence of breastfeeding in
Aldenham. His results are open to discussion, but it is not
proposed to take the arguments further here.[9]

Child care in Aldenham

The main sources used in this study of the families caring for
children in Aldenham are the poor-law entries, including
payments to families who fostered parish children, and the

burial register entries for the 255 nurse children who are known to have died in the parish between 1595 and 1726. These sources, used in conjunction with the reconstitution, allow the identification of three groups of families involved in child care:

(1) *Nursing families*: the families of those named as nurses in the burial entries of children.

(2) *Fostering families*: the families identified in the poor-law accounts as caring for orphans and children of very poor or disadvantaged families, including some cases of nursing.

(3) *Families with children in care*: the families identified in the poor-law accounts as having children cared for by other parish families, whether or not the fostering families have been traced.

All the identified families are included in the analysis, regardless of the quality of the reconstitution linkages. A number of the families would not normally be included in such demographic analyses, because either only a few events are recorded in the Aldenham registers, or there are doubts about the accuracy of the reconstitution. The observation rules usually applied in demographic analysis are also relaxed. Thus, in discussing infant mortality, the requirement for a later event than the last childbirth is not used, whilst in family size and fertility analysis, the marriage date is not considered essential. As a result, the findings can only be treated as cautious estimates, or pointers to trends.[10] Nevertheless, they may add to the picture of wet nursing and child care in pre-industrial England which is currently being constructed by other scholars.

Nursing of children in Aldenham

The number of burials of nurse children recorded in the Aldenham registers reaches a peak in the half-century before 1726. Registers only record nurse children who are buried in the parish. There is no way of identifying children who survived the period of nursing or who were returned to parents in another parish to die or for burial, and it cannot be estimated how many children were cared for by each identified nurse, or how many nurses never lost a child.[11]

The burial entries give no indication of the ages of the children buried. In the registers for 1635–6 and 1718–26, nurse children are invariably described as 'infants'. In accordance with other studies, this terminology is assumed to refer to un-weaned children, at a time when weaning often coincided with teething.[12]

The recorded burials of nurse children end abruptly in 1726. This sudden end has been observed in other Hertfordshire parishes, and coincides with the changing medical and social opinion which encouraged women to suckle their own children, for the health of both parties, or to have them dry nursed at home. As a result, fashionable use of wet nurses began to decline. In addition, parishes in London opened workhouses in this period and many of these no longer sent their infants out to nurse in the surrounding country but fed them within the workhouse.[13]

Table 5.1 Decadal totals of nurse child burials recorded in the Aldenham burial registers, with indications of the number of years in which various diseases were noted in the registers, and the periods during which the original registers are missing

Decade	Nurse child burials	Years with burial register records of:			Years with copies of registers
		smallpox	plague	others	
1595–1600	5				
1601–1610	6	1	4	1 (unhealthy)	
1611–1620				1 (typhus/dysentry)	
1621–1630	11	2	1	1 (pest)	
1631–1640	23		1	3 (fever and spotted fever)	
1641–1650	22	1	2	5	
1651–1660	23	2			
1661–1670	20	4	1		
1671–1680	16	2			3
1681–1690	11	2			10
1691–1700	36	1			10
1701–1710	44	1			10
1711–1720	28	1			2
1721–1726	6	2		1 (fever)	

Source. Information extracted from entries in W. Brigg (ed.) *The Parish Registers of Aldenham, Hertfordshire, 1559–1812* (2 vols, St Albans, 1902, 1910).

The distribution of nurse child burials over time is shown in Table 5.1. Known outbreaks of disease are also indicated, from annotations to burial entries. Although the original burial registers for the years 1678–1712 are missing, a copy and the Bishop's Transcripts survive. The entries in the latter are very brief and infuriatingly unhelpful, not least because of the number of children buried during the period covered (1705–12). However, the entries in the copies are good, and there are few gaps in the record.

Although in many nurse child burials it is not possible to identify the nurse, women in ninety-five reconstituted families can be recognized as the nurses named in the burial entries. These families are associated with 143 nurse child burials, although it is likely that other children were also nursed by them.

There is an unexplained increase in the number of nurse child burials in the eighteenth century and also, despite the poor quality of the transcript entries, an increase in the number of identified fatalities per named nurse. A number of Hertfordshire parishes are known to have been involved in contract nursing for institutions in the eighteenth century, but there is no evidence for this in Aldenham, and the rise predates the foundation of the London Foundling Hospital (1739).[14] Other possible reasons include the increased use of dry nursing (artificial feeding) and multiple nursing. These ideas may be supported by the common terminology in the eighteenth-century burial entries, which refers to nurse children buried from an individual's 'nursery'. The named person may be a widow, or the husband of the nurse. There is some evidence that widows may be able to maintain lactation for many years in response to demand, but it is also possible that the term 'nursery' indicates multiple nursing, possibly involving other wet nurses or artificial feeding. This is supported by evidence from certain London parishes that, in some instances, several children were sent out to each country nurse.[15]

Other forms of child care in Aldenham

Apart from nursing, some Aldenham families were involved in fostering orphans and the children of local paupers. Entries in the poor-law accounts often include sufficient detail to trace both natural and foster parents, and thirty-three fostering families have been identified among the reconstituted population. These received substantial payments (up to 8 shillings per 4 weeks) from the parish poor-law relief fund for each child in care.[16] Thirty-six of the families whose children were in care have also been identified. Some families had all their children in care, whilst others needed foster parents for only some of their children or only for a short period.

Many of the families involved in child care are interrelated, both within and between generations, but only fourteen families are identified as participating in more than one form of care. These are all nursing families, of which four had children in care after the death of one or both parents, and ten fostered parish children.

Demographic characteristics of families involved in child care

As already noted, the demographic characteristics of families involved in child care are analysed without reference to the standard observation rules normally applied to reconstituted populations since the samples are small, and the aim is to compare groups rather than to find the absolute levels for any statistic.

Birth intervals

The mean birth intervals for the reconstituted Aldenham population, and the comparative figures for the groups of families involved in child care, and shown in Table 5.2. Only families which had children in care have birth intervals shorter than the parish mean. Among the nursing families, the average length of the interval during which a nurse child is buried is almost 9 months longer than the parish mean for each parity.

These calculations exclude the interval between marriage and the first registered baptism, in order to exclude any bias resulting from estimation of marriage dates. However, the data probably contain other inaccuracies. Some couples certainly used more than one church for the registration of vital events, and a few were nonconformists, who made erratic use of parish registration. It is also likely that a number of families left the parish before the end of their reproductive spans. The effect of this on their nursing careers cannot be guessed, but later births and nurse child fatalities in these families would be lost to the analysis. All these problems would result in longer mean birth intervals, and it is thus highly significant that the families with children in care have a short mean birth interval.

Table 5.2 Parity-specific mean birth intervals in years for Aldenham and for the three care groups

			Parity		
	1–2	*2–3*	*3–4*	*4+*	*1+*
Aldenham population	2·3 (714)	2·5 (618)	2·6 (505)	2·5 (936)	2·5 (2773)
Nursing families	2·3 (86)	2·8 (80)	2·9 (69)	2·9 (55)	2·7 (290)
Fostering families	2·5 (27)	2·9 (24)	3·7 (22)	1·9 (15)	2·8 (88)
Children in care	2·0 (30)	2·4 (28)	2·9 (22)	2·5 (17)	2·4 (97)
Interval containing burial	2·9 (7)	3·8 (16)	2·9 (13)	3·0 (26)	3·2 (63)

Source: Newall, 'Socio-economic influences', Table 6.10

Note: Figures in brackets are the number of observations used in the calculations. In the first column, only families with known marriage dates are included.

Infant mortality

Mortality statistics are likely to be affected more than birth intervals by inaccuracies in the data. The usual rules for infant mortality calculations state that families should be in observation for at least a year after the birth or baptism of each child included in the analysis. In this study, the data are not sufficiently consistent to determine whether all families were still in the parish a year after the last baptism. When families left the area within a year, there is potential underestimation of the number of deaths recorded among infants. In Table 5.3, the recorded number of children dying within the first year of life is compared with the Cambridge Group summary statistics for the reconstituted parish population, which has observation rules applied.

Nursing families have a much lower infant mortality than the full reconstituted population, whilst families with children in care have a higher rate. A third of families with children in care have neither parent alive when the children enter care; a further fifteen (including the three illegitimate families) had only one parent alive. This suggests that high infant mortality is associated with high adult mortality.

Table 5.3 Gross infant and parental death rates for the three care groups (no observation rules applied)

	No. of families	Infant deaths	IMR	Father dies	Both die
Nursing families	95	49	102·1	6	0
Fostering families	33	20	131·6	7	0
Children in care	36	24	141·2	17	11

Source: Newall, 'Socio-economic influences', Table 6.11

Note: IMR (infant mortality rate) is the death rate per thousand live births of infants in the first year of life. Parental deaths relate to the date of the first record of nursing or care for the family. The infant mortality of the reconstituted population of Aldenham, with observation rules applied, is 121·8 live births (1600–1799)

Nurse child burials often occur after the last known baptism in a nursing family, a factor also noted by McLaren and Fildes in studies of other English parishes in this period.[17] In Aldenham this may be a result of incomplete data, but other possible explanations include the continuation of lactation in response to demand well beyond the normal period, possibly as a contraceptive measure. It is also feasible that later nurse child deaths represent attempts to dry nurse when the nurse's milk ran out.[18] Another possibility is that nurse children buried from widows' establishments had been placed specifically for weaning.[19] Children still with nurses at weaning, or placed with weaning nurses, are at risk of nutrition-related diseases, and of becoming part of the annual mortality from childhood epidemic and endemic diseases.[20]

The long birth intervals and low infant mortality of the nursing families are typical of a group which breastfeeds its own children, but the mortality is very low for a group which divides its feeding resources between its own and other peoples' infants. It is for instance contrary to findings in France, where the financial incentives of wet nursing often resulted in the accidental sacrifice of the nurses' own children.[21]

If the low mortality of Aldenham nurses' children is not a result of data inaccuracy, then one explanation may be that nurse children were only taken when a stillbirth or neonatal death occurred. In such instances, the mother would have milk to give without depriving her own children. The prolonged mean birth interval within which nurse children are buried would thus result from a combination of an aborted pregnancy and lactation amenorrhoea in the period of wet nursing. In such a case, the taking of nurse children may represent a deliberate move to avert the rapid resumption of ovulation, or to alleviate the physical or emotional problems consequent to the loss of a child. A second explanation is suggested by evidence from neighbouring Hertfordshire parishes in the mideighteenth century, where wet nurses did not usually accept a child for nursing until her own last-born infant was, on average, 10 months old. At this age the nurse's own child would be less likely to succumb from lack of breast milk than a very young infant.[22] It is quite possible that this was also the pattern followed by the nursing families of Aldenham.

Family size

Because the data on families is incomplete in a number of cases, completed family sizes cannot be accurately calculated. Some families for which no starting date (marriage) is known will have no record of low-parity births, whilst other families, for which residence in the parish cannot be proved, may have higher parity omissions. The mean of the known number of child births for each group of families is shown in Table 5.4

Table 5.4 Estimated completed size of families in the three care groups

	Usable families	*Mean no. children*
Nursing families	90	5.3
Fostering families	28	5.4
Children in care	33	5.1

Source Newall, 'Socio-economic influences', Table 6.11.

Note: Five nursing and five fostering families have insufficient detail for use in these calculations. Three families having children in care had only one illegitimate child each and are not included in the data.

There is reason to believe that, whatever the errors in these data, the relationships between groups are realistic. In particular, the observed characteristics of the families with children in care suggest that these would indeed have a smaller mean family size than the norm. As noted above, a third of the identified children in care are known to have been orphans, and an even higher proportion had only one surviving parent. The loss of one or both parents would obviously prevent the family achieving its full potential size. The families with children in care also have the shortest birth intervals. This is related to high mortality and small achieved family size, since the termination of breastfeeding consequent on the death of an infant encourages rapid conception. In addition, repeated pregnancies weaken the mother, and increase the chance of her dying before the end of her childbearing years. If the birth sequence is interrupted before the mother's age and parity introduce a significant sterility factor, the mean birth interval for all parities will be relatively short.[23]

Socio-economic characteristics of families involved in child care

As stated earlier, the Aldenham reconstitution includes taxation and poor-law listings as well as parish registration. These sources give indications of the socio-economic status of some families, and allow consideration of the circumstances of the three groups.

Families with children in care

Of the families which have children in care, 53 per cent were in receipt of poor-law reliefs other than those related to the children's needs. This group appears to be poor and crisis-prone, although the direction of causality between these characteristics and high infant and adult mortality rates cannot be established. The four known occupations of men in this group are all in the agricultural sector. Poor agricultural societies are associated with conservative habits, including the reliance on folklore and old wives' tales, despite the observable ill-effects of many traditional practices.[24]

Incidentally, the possibility that infant mortality was increased by very young children being in care is countered by the fact that, in all three cases where the youngest legitimate child was aged less than one year at the start of care, the infant survives.

The peak incidence of traced cases of children in care corresponds to periods in which the burial registers note plague and epidemic disease. It is clear from poor relief payments made during family illnesses, plus the burial records for parents and other children, that these periodic outbreaks of disease hit this group of families particularly hard. One explanation of this high adult and infant mortality, and thus of the need for children to be put into care, is that crisis mortality is concentrated in these poor families.

Families fostering parish children

The socio-economic evidence for families fostering children places this group between that having children in care and that involved in nursing. The group comprises a number of widowed people, many of whom had been part of nursing families, who are in need of periodic parish support. However, these families seem to be less crisis-prone than those for whose children they care.

Children fostered by parish families often became apprentices of the same families in later years, still at the parish expense, and the apprenticeship agreements are an important source of information on the occupations of fostering families. The nine known occupations in this group are all unskilled, but the families sometimes had sufficient property to be called upon to contribute to the parish poor-law funds.

Nursing families

The nursing families are the most prosperous of the three groups. Many contribute to the parish poor-law funds, and nine families had members holding parish offices (overseer, constable, parish clerk, and so on). Among the occupation records are a number of small farmers and skilled men. As in the other groups of families, relief payments are more common than the parish norm, but most payments are made to family members in old age.

Discussion

Although there is only limited socio-economic evidence for the three groups of families, it can be used to suggest some possible reasons for the observed variations in demographic characteristics of the families.

Families of children in care are the poorest and, apparently, the least skilled. It is likely that some, if not all, the women in these families had to assist in supporting the family by working alongside their husbands during harvesting and at other times of increased labour demand. Even if infants were taken into the fields at such times, they would have poor supervision and irregular feeding, and the risk of disease and malnutrition must have increased. The condition of the women, weakened by poverty and manual labour, might further increase the risk of fatalities, either during childbirth or under the stress of child rearing.[25]

In comparison with the poorest group, the nursing families are quite wealthy, and might have less need for the wife to work outside the home. Nursing might be seen as a simple way in which wives could supplement the family income, whilst controlling their own fertility. The male occupations, in farming and the skilled trades, would have involved some links with London, and with local towns such as St Albans, where members of the urban élite requiring wet nurses were to be found.

Families fostering parish children are of intermediate social status, and have middle-order birth intervals and infant mortality rates. The reproductive history is rarely curtailed by parental mortality, which is reflected in a higher mean family size than for the other groups of families. A quarter of the fostering families were also named as nurses in nurse child burials, and it is likely that birth spacing was affected by the use of breastfeeding and wet nursing to control conception. It is possible that families identified as foster parents nursed until widowhood or nursing fatalities made them ineligible as wet nurses, and then turned to fostering. However, the socio-economic evidence suggests that the families identified as both nurses and foster parents differed from those identified only as nurses. Although the fostering group was less frequently in receipt of poor-law payments than the group with children in care, it was also less often assessed for payment of the poor rate than the group identified only as wet nurses. Possibly the poor-law overseers used respectable but impoverished families, which would have to be relieved anyway, to nurse or foster the orphans, bastards, and pauper children for whom the parish was responsible.[26]

A final point concerns the increased numbers, and the concentration in fewer families, of nurslings and children in care in the early-eighteenth century, before the sudden decline of the 1720s. As already noted, the apparent termination of private nursing in Aldenham after 1726 coincides with changing fashion, and the increasing role of maternal breastfeeding and dry nursing amongst the upper and middle classes of society. At about this date, the fostering of parish children becomes concentrated in a smaller number of families, which suggests a greater degree of organization by the parish, the logical next stage of which was the founding of a workhouse in the 1730s. This in turn produced a marked decline in the incidence of parish-paid fostering.

The changing patterns in Aldenham child care correspond to evidence for other parishes around London, discussed by Fildes and McLaren, using evidence from burial and baptism registers, poor-law accounts, the private diaries of the nobility and bourgeoisie, medical writings, and case histories. These studies show that, until the second quarter of the eighteenth century, the practice of wet nursing was widespread around London.[27]

French studies, as quoted above, show that it was normal for all ranks of society, and institutions such as orphanages, to employ wet nurses, and that the practice commonly led to high infant mortality.[28] However, the evidence from Aldenham, together with that of other wet nursing parishes, suggests that the less-intensive English wet nursing industry did not result in a comparable 'massacre of the innocents'.

Notes

1. This chapter is based on a seminar given to the Cambridge Group for the History of Population and Social Structure, 28

November 1983, and on part of my Ph.D. thesis: F. A. C. Newall, 'Socio-economic influences in the demography of Aldenham: an exploration of the techniques and application of family reconstitution', unpub. Ph.D. thesis, University of Cambridge, 1985. The co-operation and assistance of local historian Mr W. Newman Brown, who is responsible for the painstaking work of reconstitution, and the linkage of additional material to Aldenham families as part of his long-term interest in the parish history, is gratefully acknowledged.

2. Ibid. ch. 4.

3. The method of family reconstitution was developed in France by L. Henry and others. The rules are set down in, for example, M. Fleury and L. Henry, *Nouveau manuel de dépouillement et l'exploitation de l'état civil ancien* (Paris, 1965). For the application of family reconstitution to English parish registers, see E. A. Wrigley, 'Family reconstitution', in E. A. Wrigley (ed.), *An Introduction to English Historical Demography, from the Sixteenth to the Nineteenth Century* (London, 1966), 96–195. The reconstitution of the Aldenham population is of a high quality.

4. C. C. Wilson, 'Marital fertility in pre-industrial England, 1550–1840', unpub. Ph.D. Thesis, University of Cambridge, 1982.

5. D. McLaren, 'Nature's contraceptive: wet nursing and prolonged lactation, the case of Chesham, Buckinghamshire, 1578–1601', *Med. Hist.* 23 (1979), 426–41; D. McLaren, 'Marital fertility and lactation 1570–1720', in M. Prior (ed.), *Women in English Society 1500–1800* (London, 1985), 22–53.

6. Their findings contradict those of some modern clinical studies which suggest that breastfeeding has no effect on fertility. The latter experimenters have probably found no effect because modern mothers in industrialized societies tend to feed at regular intervals, whilst the hormonal stimulation which suppresses ovulation is related to a natural demand-feeding regime. The historical evidence comes from, for example, J. Knodel, 'Two and a half centuries of demographic history in a Bavarian village', *Popul. Stud.*, 24 (1970); E. van de Walle and S. H. Preston, 'Mortalité et l'enfance au XIX siècle à Paris et dans le Départment de la Seine', *Population*, (1974). Modern evidence is reviewed in for example, G. S. Masnick, 'The demographic view of breastfeeding: a critical review', *Hum. Biol.*, 51 (1979), 109–25. The relationship between breastfeeding and ovulation is discussed in the context of wet nursing by C. Corsini, 'La fecondité naturelle de la femme mariée. Le cas des nourrices', paper from Dipartemento Statistico, University of Florence, 1973, 4–5. A list of the literature on lactation and ovulation is given in McLaren, 'Marital fertility', 47–9.

7. Wilson, 'Marital fertility'. Wilson's references are to J. Knodel, 'Demographic transitions in German villages', paper presented to the Summary Conference on European Fertility, Princeton, 1979; and L. H. Leridon, *Human Fertility: The Basic Components* (Chicago, 1977).

8. R. A. P. Finlay, 'Population and fertility in London, 1580–1650', *J. Fam. Hist.*, 4 (1979), 26–38; R. A. P. Finlay, *Population and Metropolis. The Demography of London 1580–1650* (Cambridge, 1981), 29–30. See also V. A. Fildes, *Breasts, Bottles and Babies: A History of Infant Feeding* (Edinburgh, 1986), 107–9.

9. For discussion of Aldenham fertility, see Newall, 'Socio-economic influences', 160–79.

10. For elaboration of the observation rules used for calculation of mortality and fertility statistics from reconstituted populations, see E. Gautier and L. Henry, 'La population de Crulai, Paroisse Normande', *INED Travaux et Documents*, 33 (1958), ch. 8; L. Henry *Techniques d'Analyse en Démographie Historique* (Paris, 1980); E. A. Wrigley, 'Mortality in pre-industrial England: the example of Colyton, Devon, over three centuries', *Daedalus*, 97 (1968), 550. The alternatives to marriage date for start of observation are discussed in Newall, 'Socio-economic influences', 170–3.

11. The mortality of English nurse children is discussed in Finlay, *Population and Metropolis*, 97–100, and in V. Fildes, *Wet Nursing: A History from Antiquity to the Present* (Oxford, 1988), ch. 11. Evidence from French parishes indicates a death rate of 60–90 per cent for nurslings in their first year: Finlay, *Population and Metropolis*, 98. Other evidence is presented by, for example, A. Chamoux, 'L'enfance abandonée à Reims à la fin du XVIIIe siècle', *Ann. Démog. Hist.* (Paris, 1973), 272–85.

12. The definition of infancy is discussed in V. A. Fildes, 'Weaning the Elizabethan child', *Nurs. Times*, 76 (1980), 1357–9, 1402–3.

13. Fildes, *Breasts, Bottles and Babies*, 262–98. See also V. Fildes, 'The wet nursing of London's children 1538–1800', in W. F. Bynum (ed.) *Living and Dying in London 1500–1900* (London, forthcoming).

14. Fildes, *Breasts, Bottles and Babies*, 277–9. Information for other Hertfordshire parishes comes from V. A. Fildes (personal communication), discussion with W. Newman Brown, and F. Dulley, 'Nurse-children: a forgotten cottage industry', *Herts Count.*, 37 (1982), 14–15.

15. For further explanation of these features, as they relate to the history of wet nursing, see, for example, Fildes, *Breasts, Bottles and Babies*, 152–63; Fildes, 'The wet nursing of London's children'; R. Etienne, 'La conscience médicale antique et la vie des enfants', *Ann. Démog. Hist.*,(Paris, 1973).

16. This sum compares with the seventeenth-century labourer's wage of about 2 shillings per week (8s per 4 weeks), and with the 10–12 shillings a week (40–48s per 4 weeks) paid to craftsmen in Hertfordshire: H. A. Doubleday (ed.), *The Victoria History of the Counties of England: A History of Hertfordshire* (4 vols. 1971), vol. 2, 226. See Fildes, *Breasts, Bottles and Babies*, 283, for amounts paid to parish nurses in other parishes in this period. It is not always possible to discover how many children were cared for by a family, as the rate is not always broken down and names of children are not given in detail.

17. McLaren, 'Nature's contraceptive', 433; Fildes, 'Wet nursing of London's children'.

18. The details of feeding practices, the quality of milk, and the ethics of nursing and nurses are discussed at length in Fildes, *Breasts, Bottles and Babies*.

19. Ibid., 379, notes this custom. For France, the apparent nursing of children by widows and the use of weaning nurses are discussed in R. Berthieu, 'Les nourrissons à Cormeilles-en-Parisis 1640–1789', *Ann. Démog. Hist.* (Paris, 1975), 259–90, p. 262.

20. In France, children were sent to nurses for many years, and swell the mortality figures of provincial towns. See ibid., 263–5; P. Gaillano, 'La mortalité infantile (indigènes et nourrissons) dans la banlieue sud de Paris à la fin du XVIIIe siècle (1774–1794)', *Ann. Démog. Hist.* (Paris, 1966), 139–77.

21. For instance, in France, ibid., 156–8; C. Rollet, 'Allaitement, mise en nourrice, et la mortalité infantile en France à la fin du XIXe siècle', *Population*, 6 (1978); A. Bideau, 'L'envoi des jeunes en nourrice: l'exemple d'une petite ville: Thoissey-en-Dombes 1740–1840', in J. Dupâquier (ed.), *Sur la Population Française au XVIIIe et au XIXe Siècles: Homage à Marcel Reinhard* (Paris, 1973).

22. Fildes, *Wet Nursing*, ch. 11.

23. For a discussion on the effects of infant mortality on birth intervals and vice versa, see D. McLaren, 'Fertility, infant mortality and breastfeeding in the seventeenth century', *Med. Hist.*, 22 (1978), 378–96; McLaren, 'Nature's contraceptive'. The importance of the length of post-partum amenorrhoea is also discussed in C. Wilson, 'Marital fertility and intermediate fertility variables: some results from European historical populations', paper from Katholieke Universiteit Leuven Centrum voor Economische Studien, 1980.

24. Perhaps the most detrimental of the traditional medical advice given to mothers was that the first milk (colostrum) should be discarded as unfit for the newborn child. When taken to extremes by village midwives and superstitious parents, this practice led to the starvation of infants who refused to suck when eventually offered sustenance. Discussion of this and other traditions can be found in Fildes, *Breasts, Bottles and Babies*, 81–97. See also A. Wilson, 'Ignorant midwives – a rejoinder to David Harley', *Bull. Soc. Soc. Hist. Med.*, 32 (1983), 46–9. Continental studies show the resistance to change of agricultural societies – for example, G. Brostrom, A. Brandstrom, and L. A. Persson, 'The impact of breastfeeding patterns on infant mortality in a nineteenth-century Swedish parish', *Demographic Database Newsletter*, vol. 1, Umea University, Sweden, n.d.

25. The neglect of children by working mothers and the early weaning which is often consequent on female employment are discussed, in relation to the growth of the lower classes in nineteenth-century Britain, by McLaren, 'Nature's contraceptive', 439–41; Fildes, *Wet Nursing*, ch. 12.

26. The employment of widowed nurses by the Aldenham parish authorities can be illustrated by the case of Widow Hagood, who has been identified in six nurse child burials, before and after her

husband's death. After the last of these burials, the parish paid her for 'keeping children' for a further 10 years, until 1715.

27. See for instance, McLaren, 'Nature's contraceptive', 431; McLaren, 'Marital fertility', 29–32; Fildes, *Breasts, Bottles and Babies*, 153–6; Fildes, 'Wet nursing of London's children'.

28. A. Bideau, 'La Mortalité des enfants dans la Chatellenie de Thoissey-en-Dombes: essai de pathologie historique', in *Démographie Urbaine XVe–XIXe Siècles* (Lyons, 1977), 111–41.

6

Maternal feelings re-assessed: child abandonment and neglect in London and Westminster, 1550–1800

Valerie Fildes

Hard is my lot in deep distress
To have no help where most should find.
Sure nature meant her sacred laws
Should men as strong as women bind.
Regardless he, unable I,
To keep this image of my heart,
'Tis Vile to Murder! hard to Starve
And death almost to me to part!
If Fortune should her favours give
That I in better plight might live
I'd try to have my Boy again
And train him up the best of men.
                    (Note attached to a London foundling, 1759.)

In continental Europe and its colonies most large towns had at least one foundling hospital which accepted and cared for children, of all ages, who had been abandoned by their parent(s). It has been argued that the constant presence of these foundlings in pre-industrial European societies is evidence of maternal neglect, or indifference to the fate, of their offspring who would be left to the mercy of callous and uncaring nurses.[1] However, a closer look at the problem of abandonment in England shows that this was not necessarily true. It may appear so if seen only from the perspective of the child, but looked at from the mother's point of view it may also have involved a heart-rending decision to relinquish a wanted and beloved child.

In order to look at both the mother's and the child's experience of abandonment, this chapter reports the preliminary findings of a study of some of the children abandoned in the cities of London and Westminster between c.1550 and c.1800. After making an estimate of the extent of abandonment over this period, it will examine the age and sex of the foundlings, the season and place in which they were left, and then look at some of the reasons why mothers surrendered their children to the uncertain fate of a parish or institution. It will define who was responsible for the overseeing and direct care of found-lings, and end by discussing the foster mothers who nursed these children, and other parish infants, and the allegations of poor mothering, neglect, and abuse frequently made against these women.

Although many European institutions have records dating back to the medieval period, making possible relatively detailed studies of the extent of, and reasons for, abandonment and the method of caring for foundlings,[2] England had no comparable institution until the London Foundling Hospital was founded in 1739.[3] This makes it difficult to find sufficient information to estimate the extent of child abandonment in pre-industrial England. However, since the responsibility for the care of aban-doned children lay with the parishes in which they were found, the principal sources used are the records of London and Westminster parishes, particularly baptism and burial registers, churchwardens' accounts, vestry minutes, nursing lists, and parish books.[4] In addition, details of foundlings entered in the court minutes and admission registers of Christ's Hospital between 1554 and 1599 are used to study the sixteenth century,[5] for which parish records are frequently scanty or non-existent. Archives of the London Foundling Hospital are also employed but, as for most of the eighteenth century this institution had a restricted intake, parish records tend to give a more representative picture of abandonment in the capital.[6]

The extent of abandonment

The population of London greatly increased over the period 1550–1800.[7] Although the number of foundlings baptized in London parishes appears to increase over time, and the comments of concerned contemporaries also indicate that the incidence of abandonment was correspondingly greater in the late-seventeenth century, this could be merely a reflection of the general increase of the population. To obtain some concrete measure of the scale of abandonment, seven parishes which have good records from the 1590s to the 1750s were selected for detailed study. These were of varying size and included two wealthy parishes, two that were relatively poor, and three of medium prosperity.[8] These were not selected because they recorded more or less foundlings but had been identified in a previous study of wet nursing in London and were principally chosen because of their relatively unbroken series of baptism registers.

The baptisms of foundlings were counted and expressed as a percentage of all baptisms in the parish in 10-year periods. The decades showing the highest number of foundlings varied from parish to parish but, as Figure 6.1 and Table 6.1 show, increasing numbers of abandoned children were baptized over time and this was not merely a reflection of the increasing general population.

Table 6.1 Foundling baptisms as a percentage of total baptisms in seven London parishes, 1590s–1750s

Parish	SCS	SDB	SDE	SLJ	SMA	SMC	SPC	Total
No. foundling baptisms	135	141	276	182	103	147	162	1,146
No. total baptisms	2,278	3,720	8,835	5,710	3,080	3,918	4,409	31,950
Decade	%	%	%	%	%	%	%	%
1590s	1·4	1·5	1·3	0·8	0·5	0	0·7	0·8
1600s	1·1	0	1·1	1·6	3·2	0·9	2·4	1·4
1610s	0	1·0	0·8	1·5	1·2	0·6	2·5	1·1
1620s	0·6	2·7	1·4	2·5	2·0	1·8	1·4	1·7
1630s	4·8	1·3	1·4	2·6	2·5	2·6	4·0	2·4
1640s	4·2	2·9	0·6	0·9	1·6	1·2	4·6	1·9
1650s	6·8	4·1	0·4	5·7	3·3	5·4	3·6	3·6
1660s	5·3	6·7	2·0	3·8	7·1	4·4	3·3	4·1
1670s	16·7	2·2	3·1	4·8	4·4	8·2	3·5	5·3
1680s	10·9	5·3	3·8	4·8	4·4	3·5	1·1	4·3
1690s	9·1	7·4	5·6	6·3	7·8	8·4	5·3	6·6
1700s	6·3	4·6	6·8	[0]	4·5	5·6	3·9	[4·4]
1710s	6·3	8·4	8·3	3·1	4·8	1·8	9·7	6·2
1720s	7·0	3·5	5·4	4·7	6·5	8·2	9·4	6·1
1730s	8·3	5·6	4·8	1·2	0·7	8·4	6·0	4·4
1740s	8·1	2·1	3·0	4·7	1·6	7·5	0·9	3·5
1750s	3·3	[4·4]	[2·1]	2·7	[2·1]	[14·6]	0·6	[2·8]
1590s–1750s	5·9	3·8	3·1	3·2	3·3	3·8	3·7	3·6

Sources: Baptism registers of SCS, SDB, SDE, SLJ, SMA, SMC, SPC (see Appendix).

[ ] indicates that the registers are known or suspected to be incomplete.

Figure 6.1 Foundling baptisms as a percentage of total baptisms in seven London parishes, 1590s–1750s

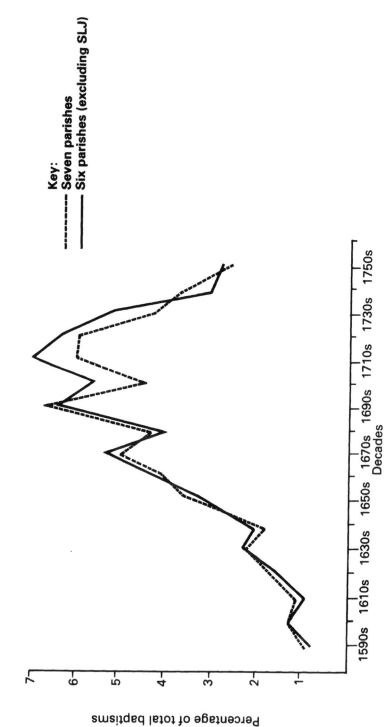

Key:
- - - - - **Seven parishes**
——— **Six parishes (excluding SLJ)**

Sources : Baptism registers of SCS, SDB, SDE, SLJ, SMA, SMC, SPC (see Appendix)

The incidence in just seven out of the ninety-seven parishes in London can be used only as an indicator of trends in abandonment, but the increase in the percentage of foundlings baptized coincided both with the first proposal to build a foundling hospital in London (1687)[9] and with suggestions for the building of parish workhouses in which foundlings and other poor children could be cared for.[10] Similarly the increase in foundling baptisms was associated with problems with the many nurses who cared for them, as will be described below. Taken together, these facts suggest that the increase shown in the seven parishes reflects the situation in other city parishes.

The London Bills of Mortality can be used to gain some idea of actual numbers of foundlings in the capital. No accurate series of Bills survive for the 1590s, 1600s, 1640s, and 1650s, but Wrigley and Schofield give corrected figures for the remaining decades.[11] Using these, and the percentage of foundling baptisms from the seven parishes, the figures in Table 6.2 are obtained. These show that, by the later seventeenth century, approximately 1,000 foundlings a year were possibly abandoned on the streets of London. This tallies with contemporary reports of the many infants found on the streets, stalls, and dunghills of the capital.[12] The apparent decline in the numbers of foundlings during the eighteenth century was mainly related to the building of workhouses and will be discussed further below.

Table 6.2 Decadal totals of baptisms in the London Bills of Mortality and estimated decadal totals of foundling baptisms, 1610s–1750s

Decade	Corrected total baptisms	*Foundling baptisms %*	*No. of foundlings*
1610s	86,405	1·1	951
1620s	97,517	1·7	1,658
1630s	121,121	2·4	2,907
1660s	115,339	4·1	4,729
1670s	133,335	5·3	7,067
1680s	155,660	4·3	6,693
1690s	164,641	6·6	10,866
1700s	164,474	[4·4]	[7,237]
1710s	183,918	6·2	11,403
1720s	205,037	6·1	12,507
1730s	197,042	4·4	8,670
1740s	172,952	3·5	6,053
1750s	174,666	[2·8]	[4,891]

Sources: For corrected total baptisms see E. A. Wrigley and R. S. Schofield, *The Population History of England 1541–1871. A Reconstruction* (London, 1981), pp. 79, 81; for percentage of foundling baptisms see Table 6.1.

[ ] indicates that the figures for foundling baptisms are known or suspected to be incomplete.

In fact, foundling baptisms and burials were grossly under-recorded over the whole period but particularly from the 1680s onwards. In this study the only baptisms included were those where the child was stated to be a foundling, a 'dropt' infant, or left in the parish by unknown parents. Where newborn infants were said to have been born or left in the 'privie' or similar public places, and/or said to be the bastard of a known woman, these were not included in the total since they were more likely to be cases of intended infanticide than abandonment. Similarly, where burial registers recorded dead children found in the parish, sometimes in a coffin, these were not classified as foundlings unless they were clearly abandoned children who had died before being discovered. Thus, for example, an infant in a basket on a stall, or at the door of a parishioner, or the church itself, was probably a foundling and counted as such. However, dead children were sometimes left in the churchyard because the parents could not afford burial fees; others were murdered and left by their attackers.[13] These were not counted as foundlings.

Aside from these criteria, the degree of underrecording of foundlings can be shown by comparing foundling baptisms with foundling burials in a parish. The number of foundlings buried as a percentage of all burials is always much lower than that of baptisms because of the practice of sending foundling infants into the country or into other London parishes to be nursed. The burials of these children were then recorded in the burial registers of the parish in which they died and not in the parish from which they came.[14] Even when foundlings do appear in the burial register of the parish in which they were abandoned, in every parish studied to date a proportion are not the same children as those who appear in the baptism register. In some parishes the burials of foundlings are recorded some years before entries of baptism of foundlings begin to appear.[15]

A study of the foundlings baptized and buried in the Temple Church in the eighteenth century shows that over 20 per cent of the foundlings buried do not appear in the baptism register. Children found abandoned at the Temple were always given the surname 'Temple', always called a foundling, and the place (i.e. the Inner Temple, or the Middle Temple) in which they were abandoned was always named. In addition, it is clear from the records that from each part of the Temple only one foundling at a time was given a particular Christian name and this was not given to another foundling until the former owner of that name was dead. This makes it possible to assess the degree of under-recording of baptisms (see Table 6.3).[16]

Table 6.3 Baptisms and burials of foundlings at the Temple, 1700–1799, showing underrecording of foundling baptisms

Decade	No. of foundlings baptized	No. of foundlings buried but not baptized	Revised total of foundlings	Foundlings as % of total baptisms (n=1,116)
1700s	[4]	3	[7]	[9]
1710s	[1]	2	[3]	[7]
1720s	29	2	31	26
1730s	32	6	38	34
1740s	45	10	55	31
1750s	37	8	45	24
1760s	49	3	52	27
1770s	49	6	55	40
1780s	[14]	3	[17]	[35]
1790s	[4]	2	[6]	[38]
1700s–1790s	264	45	309	28

Sources: Baptism and burial registers of the Temple Church (see Appendix).

[ ] indicates that the registers are known or suspected to be incomplete.

Further evidence of underrecording can be found by tracing London infants who have been buried in country and other city parishes to the parish in which they were abandoned. Because each parish used a specific surname or sometimes a selection of surnames when they baptized foundlings, these children can be readily identified when they occur in other parishes.[17] Even when the nursing parish records not only this identifying name, but also confirms it by entering the fact in the burial register, for many of these foundlings no baptism is recorded in the parish in which they were discovered and whose officials have been paying for their care.[18]

Underrecording can also be suspected when, for a period of time, foundlings are not recorded at all. In St Lawrence Jewry, one of the seven parishes, no foundling baptisms are listed in the 1700s, a decade in which foundlings are baptized in every other London parish so far examined, and evidence from burial registers shows that children from this parish were being nursed and buried both in the parish and in the country.[19] This artificially lowers the total percentage of baptisms in the 1700s.

When St Lawrence Jewry is excluded from the seven sample parishes, the effect of the probably 'artificial' fall in this decade can be seen in Figure 6.1.

It is possible that, where a large number of foundlings are baptized in a particular parish in a certain period of time, this could represent accurate registration of foundling baptisms as compared to underrecording in other periods. However, all the parishes so far examined demonstrate that underrecording was a constant factor over the whole time-span.

A study of the foundlings admitted to Christ's Hospital between 1557 and 1599 shows similar underrecording in parish records for the sixteenth century. Christ's Hospital was founded in 1552, primarily as an educational institution for the poor and orphaned children of the City of London. In its first 50 years it accepted children of all ages and some children abandoned in city parishes were also accepted.[20] Approximately 10 per cent of admissions between 1557 and 1599 were foundlings who came from 93 out of the 114 parishes of London and the Liberties.[21] When an attempt was made to trace the baptismal records of these foundlings in the parishes where they were abandoned, very few were recorded in the baptism register. For many parishes baptism registers do not survive for the sixteenth century, but even those with good and apparently complete registers in this period record very few foundlings. Where the baptism of an infant admitted to Christ's Hospital is listed it is frequently recorded as just a few days prior to admission, but some are recorded as being baptized in the parish of abandonment *after* they have been admitted to the hospital.[22] It is probable that this occurred because parish clerks made a note of the foundling's baptism and then did not record it, or recorded it wrongly, when writing up the register proper. This practice also led to the discrepancies between information and dates in the parish registers and the transcripts of them which were sent annually to the bishop. Some rough copies of registers and parish memoranda books survive which show that the parish clerk made a rough list of entries which were later copied out neatly in the register proper.[23]

It seems more likely that the register of admissions to Christ's Hospital recorded the correct date of admission since children were listed in chronological order of admission, with their age, parish of origin, and the date when they were sent to nurse. From this register a sample of 312 foundlings has been extracted for study. To make it suitable for more detailed examination, only those foundlings with a specific age have been included. Some entries which state only 'a young sucking infant' have been omitted. Similarly, older children said to be found on the streets are not included because many of these were not foundlings. The officials of the hospital 'rounded up' children out on the streets of London, some of whom were between 10 and 14 years old. These 'street children' were not necessarily abandoned.[24] Many were orphans or migrants to London and some had parents living. Only children said to be foundlings or to have been 'left' at a certain place are included in the sample of 312.

This group of children is of value in assessing the degree of abandonment in sixteenth-century London because it shows that infants were not only abandoned in the wealthy parishes of the capital as is sometimes stated.[25] Although some parishes may have had more foundlings to cope with than others, every London parish had to deal with the problem of abandoned children during all or part of the period 1550–1800.

This sample of foundlings does not include all of London's abandoned children. As the years passed, Christ's Hospital had far more applications for entry than it could cope with. By the 1580s, parishes petitioning the governors to accept their poor children were frequently turned down. Not only were foundlings refused entry but many deserving parish children who were motherless or orphans had to be refused purely because of the pressure of numbers already admitted. By 1624, the governors ruled that only children of 4 years and over were to be admitted and the hospital became primarily an educational establishment with restricted entry.[26]

The sample of 312 Christ's Hospital foundlings, together with the 1,146 in the seven parishes and the 264 at the Temple, provide a basis for a more detailed study of child abandonment in London. In addition, records from other city and Westminster parishes are used to illustrate some of the aspects discussed below.

Age when abandoned

It is not possible to discover the age of all, or even most, foundlings because baptism and burial registers do not routinely record the age of such children. It is possible to discover whether a foundling was an infant or an older child by seeing what clothing was provided for it by the parish, whether a wet nurse was employed, and if, and when, the child went to school and/or was apprenticed.[27] However, for the exact age it is necessary to examine the information stated by the officials writing in the registers.

Christ's Hospital recorded the age of virtually all admissions so that the ages of the 312 hospital foundlings are known. There is the problem that, where the precise age of the child was not known from an attached note, the age was probably estimated either by the official or the woman who initially cared for it. This may account for the peaks which occur at 6 months, 9 months, and 1 year. Nevertheless many foundlings did have notes attached to their clothing which stated their age. This fact is often noted in parish registers, although many of the notes themselves have not survived.[28] In addition to the Christ's Hospital children, a sample of foundlings whose age is stated have been found from eighteen parishes (see Table 6.4). Although the numbers are small, particularly for the early-seventeenth century, they do indicate that children were not generally abandoned at, or soon after, birth, especially in the sixteenth and seventeenth centuries.

In all periods, the majority of foundlings were under 1 year old when discovered, most being under 6 months. An example of the age at which children were abandoned in one parish over a 20-year period is the relatively poor riverside parish of St Dunstan in the East. Between February 1699 and February 1720, ninety-four foundlings were baptized in this parish, forming 7.7 per cent of all baptisms in that period. For seventy-eight (83 per cent) of these the age of the child is stated. Their age when abandoned ranged from newborn to 6 years with a median of 2 months. Only twenty (26 per cent) were under 4 weeks of age and, as in the Christ's Hospital and parish samples, there is a peak at 1 and 2 months of age. Only fourteen (18 per cent) were over 4 months of age.[29] Because of the small numbers the figures must be treated with caution, but the evidence of these samples indicates that children were abandoned at a slightly younger age as the number of foundlings increased in the late-seventeenth and early-eighteenth centuries. The finding that only a relatively small proportion of abandoned infants were under 4 weeks of age is probably related to the fact that women did not normally leave their place of confinement until about 1 month after childbirth.[30] Consequently, a mother would be unable to relinquish her child before this time unless another individual (such as a friend, relative, or midwife) undertook to abandon it for her.

Table 6.4 The age of foundlings when abandoned, 1550s–1790s

Date	Source	No. of foundlings	Age range	Median age all foundlings (months)	Median age of foundlings aged 0–2 yrs (months)
1550–99	Christ's Hospital	312	2 days – 9 yrs	6	3 (n=266)
1600–49	4 London parishes	12	newborn – 2 yrs	6	6 (n=12)
1650–99	10 London Parishes	35	newborn – 5 yrs	6	3 (n=31)
1700–49	9 London parishes	118	newborn – 6 yrs	2	2 (n=116)
1750–99	6 London parishes	7	3 wks – 3 yrs	5	5 (n=6)
1760–99	2 Westminster parishes	23	2 wks – 1 yr[a]	3	3 (n=23)[a]

Sources: Christ's *Hospital Admissions Register 1554–1599* (London, 1937); Baptism registers of CCN, SCS, SDB, SDE, SGP, SHB, SLJ, SMA, SMB, SMC, SMO, SMOut, SMQ, SMW, SNA, SPC, STA, SVFL; SCD 'Register of returns of infant poor'; SCD 'The Enfield book'; SMF 'Memoranda book' (see Appendix).

Note: a. This sample only includes foundlings aged 0–1 year when abandoned.

Seasonality of abandonment

There were marked seasonal differences in child abandonment in London. A larger proportion of children were abandoned in the winter months, November to April, than in the summer months, May to October. Although there may be other reasons for this, such as the need for warmer clothing and increased necessity for food and shelter during the winter months, the main factor in this seasonality is the well-identified seasonality of conceptions and baptisms. This has been noted for both urban and rural populations in pre-industrial England, although no causative explanation has yet been given.[31] To test this hypothesis, the sample of foundlings with a known age was used. When their age of abandonment is employed to discover their probable date of birth (which, in the sixteenth and seventeenth centuries at least, was only a few days prior to their baptism),[32] the resulting distribution follows that frequently found in the seasonality of baptisms, with a 'lag' which reflects the fact that children were not generally abandoned within a week of birth.

Sex of foundlings

In most periods the number of boys abandoned was considerably greater than the number of girls. In this study, some children were listed as having uncertain sex because they had names which could be male or female and, with the variable spelling in the registers, the sex is not always clear. The main names of this type were Francis/Frances and Christian. A further group of children were given the name of the place where they were discovered (for example, Mitre Square) and unless the sex of the child was also stated it is uncertain whether such foundlings were boys or girls. However, these children form a small minority in most periods (see Table 6.5)

Table 6.5 The sex of London foundlings, 1560s – 1790s

Date	Source	Number	*Male*	*Female*	Uncertain
			%	%	%
1560s–1590s	Christ's Hospital	295	51·9	41·7	6·4
1580s–1640s	21 London parishes	241	56·9	37·3	5·8
1590s–1640s	7 parish sample	190	50·0	45·8	4·2
1650s–1700s	7 parish sample	600	42·7	53·3	4·0
1710s–1750s	7 parish sample	356	52·8	44·1	3·1
1700s–1790s	Temple	264	56·8	42·8	0·4

Sources: Christ's Hospital Admissions Register 1554–1599 (London, 1937); Baptism registers of AHBS, AHHL, AHL, SCS, SDB, SDE, SDW, SGP, SHB, SLJ, SMA, SMAman, SMB, SMBass, SMC, SMMMS, SMO, SMW, SNA, SPC, SPSL, STA, SVFL, Temple (see Appendix).

The greater number of boys abandoned is partly related to the sex ratio at birth, more boys being born than girls.[33] However, this is clearly not the only factor because the preponderance of boy foundlings over girls is greater than can be accounted for by the sex ratio alone. Studies of foundlings in other parts of Europe in this period usually show that more girls were abandoned than boys[34] so that this study indicates that, with the exception of the period 1650s–1700s, London appears to have been markedly different from other European societies in this respect.

Place where abandoned

Almost all the foundlings, for whom the details are given, were abandoned in places where they were likely to be discovered. These were principally on stalls, in the entry of a dwelling (frequently of a relatively wealthy family), in the church, at the church door, or in the cloisters of a church, hospital, or the Temple.

In the sixteenth century infants were also left at Christ's Hospital. Of the 312 Christ's hospital foundlings, thirty-two (10 per cent) were abandoned within, or at the door of, the hospital. Other studies have shown that abandoned children were left in a prominent place where they were likely to be quickly taken up and cared for.[35] Thus, newborn babies left in the privie or in the street where the mother had given birth were not typically foundlings but, as stated above, were probably intended to die rather than be discovered and cared for by others. In some instances it is clear that infanticide was the intention of the mother. Thus, for example, the newborn infant left in the parish of St Helen Bishopsgate, in 1612:

> Sep.1. Job Rakt out of the Ashes [baptized] being borne uppon Monday being the last of August about viij of the clock in the mornyng was then presently layd uppon a donghill of seacole ashes in the lane going to Sr John Spencer's back gate . . . wch child so layd & covered over wth the same ashes was w^{thin} a hower after found out by Richard Atkinson, boxmaker, comyng thither to shovell by the same donghill into a wheele barrowe and by that tyme he had taken up twoo shovells of the same ashes he espied the child almost stifled therewth.[36]

This infant died and was buried the following day.

In other cases, one or both parents were known and the mother might be charged with infanticide. In St Botolph's without Aldgate in 1615, for example:

> Elizabeth Asher, the reputed daughter of Thomas Asher in Wollsack Alley in hounsdich the mother named Joane Tagge, servant to Thomas Newton a Broker in Hounsdich who like a murderous strumpet, cast hir said child into a privie, but by Gods grace it was heard to cry by the neighboures and saved a live and christned [10 May 1615], shee [the mother] was taken afterwarde and araigned but escaped death. The poore infant dyed within a fortnight after.[37]

Reasons for child abandonment

It has been stated that abandoning a child was an alternative to infanticide, and that foundlings, like most of the victims of infanticide, were bastards.[38] However, the findings of this study do not support this idea. Several studies of infanticide in pre-industrial England have shown that the mothers were frequently unmarried and tended to be servants who had to conceal the fact of their pregnancy and the birth of their baby in order to remain in employment and avoid the social stigma of bearing an illegitimate child.[39] In these cases of infanticide, therefore, the infant was usually newborn or only a few days old. Since the majority of foundlings in London were not usually newborn but aged 1 month or more, it seems unlikely that illegitimacy was the only, or even the major, reason for mothers abandoning their children, because they could not hide the existence of their base-born children if they had to feed and care for them for a period ranging from a few days to a year or more. If mothers cared for their infants, particularly if they breastfed them, for any length of time they would become very attached to them emotionally. The maternal–child bond is a biological phenomenon, is usually very strong, and even the small proportion of mothers who do not bond to their babies soon after birth become increasingly close to their infants as the days and weeks pass.[40] Breastfeeding encourages and strengthens maternal–infant bonding and, particularly in the sixteenth and seventeenth centuries, the majority of English infants were suckled by their mothers.[41]. Thus, by the age at which the majority of children were abandoned, the mother would have strong emotional feelings for her child. Leaving it to be found and brought up by strangers would be a wrench, and was unlikely to be resorted to unless circumstances were bad enough for the mother to have no alternative other than murdering or abandoning her offspring.

Apart from the fact that murdering an older baby is very different from killing a newborn infant to whom the mother has had no time to become attached, an additional point against intended infanticide is the fact that these mothers left their children in well-frequented places in which they would be quickly discovered and cared for. Also, where records exist, the children were often, although not always, well-dressed and relatively healthy when found.[42] Many had notes attached to their clothing which stated the child's name, age, and whether it had been baptized.[43] A proportion stated the reason why the parent (usually the mother) had resorted to abandonment. Notes found with foundlings in the Westminster parish of St Martin in the Fields in 1709 demonstrate three reasons why mothers were driven to the painful decision to desert their children. Although one may have been due to the child's illegitimacy, the other two were probably equally, or more, common reasons for relinquishing a child: widowhood during or soon after pregnancy and desertion by the husband, both resulting in the mother's poverty and inability to support the child.

The following letter was found with a child left at a gentleman's door between midnight and 1 o'clock, 29 June 1709:

> This child was borne the 11 of June 1708 of unhappy parents wich is not abell to privide for it: tharfore I humbelly beg of you Gentellman however hands this unfourtunat child shall fall into that you will take that care that will become a feallow crattear & if God makes me albell I will repaye the charge & redame the child with thanks to you for the care: her name is Jahn Bennett: shee is baptisead: pray God Almitey belas you the cind undourtakeour & this child: & pray belivef that it is extrame neseassty that makes me do this: & shall be your humbell thankfull sarvnt to my livess end.[44]

The second letter was found with a child who was left at a gentleman's gate on 7 October 1709. Notice that the letter was dated 30 September, indicating that the decision to abandon the infant had been taken at least a week before he was actually abandoned.

> London ye 30th September 1709
>
> I am not able to subsist any longer by reason of my husband being dead & the times is severe hard & having had much sickness this half year, yt I cannot keep the child any longer by reason of infirmitys of body & limbs, being lame & canot goe w'out helper, so ye see your speed & care is desired herein, either to find a carefull nurse to your own liking or to find a good nurse for ye child. In so doing you'l obliges Sir.[45]

The third letter was found with a child left in a basket at the door of a lady (claimed to be his grandmother) on 14 May 1709. She promptly delivered him to the parish Overseer of the Poor.

> Madame Elizabeth Plowden.
>
> I am render'd most miserable by your son Mr Charles Rumbold, who not only marryed me in [. . .] is worst of circumstances, but has left me with two children (this boy named Charles after his own name, and a girle who is with me) and is now gone for a soldier to the East Indies.
>
> I am not able to support myselfe, haveing neither money, any calling, or friends, much less am I able to support them, and I cannot see them starve, and I thank God that he has given me the grace to overcome the temptation I lay under to make away with them; and since I very well know, and am assured, that your first husband Henry Rumbold my husbands own father did leave both you and him a plentifull fortune (as may be seen by his will now in Doctor's Commons) and that you, I am inform'd, inheratted a good part of the fortune my husbands father left him, and that you would not [. . .] let have had the remainder, but that he was forc'd to putt the law in execution against you, I think it is but highly reasonable that you should either keep your grandson (this present child Charles Rumbold) or some way or other provide for him; and if it be consistent wth your natural affection

(which you ought to have) and your present manner of liveing to send him to the parish, you are the best judge of that.

This from
your daughter in law

May 1709   A. Rumbold.[46]

This last letter raises again the question of the greater numbers of male foundlings in most periods. Although she says that she cannot support herself or her two children, this mother chose to keep an older girl and to give up the infant boy. Possibly she thought the grandmother would be more inclined to provide for her son's heir. However, there are wider issues here. It may be that girls were perceived as being less trouble and less expensive to bring up than boys. Girls were also very useful as carers for younger children and for helping with household chores if mothers, particularly those without a husband, had to work either within or outside the home. However, it is also possible that some mothers, especially if they had several children, may have chosen to surrender a son because they believed that parish officials, like society in general, would invest more care and education in a boy than a girl, at a time when boys were regarded as being of greater value to society than girls.

Not all foundlings were left by the mother: some records specifically state that the child was abandoned by the father.[47] In these cases the reason may still have been poverty, even though both parents were living. This is given weight by the fact that the number of abandoned infants increased in periods of high prices and poor social conditions. Figure 6.2 shows how abandonment increased in line with bread prices in the late-seventeenth and early-eighteenth centuries. As Stephen Macfarlane has stated:

The political events surrounding the Revolution of 1688, followed by the outbreak of war against France the following spring, shook London's economy and ushered in nearly a decade of distress for the poor of the metropolis. Depressions in the City's cloth markets in 1689, 1693–4, and 1696–7; arrears in pay to seamen and their families; a major shortage of coal in 1691; high bread prices in 1693–4 and from 1696 to 1698; and shortages of

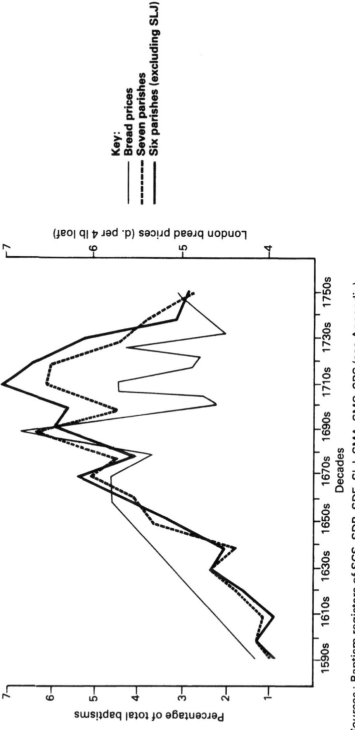

Figure 6.2 Foundling baptisms in seven parishes and bread prices in London, 1590s–1750s

London bread prices (d. per 4 lb loaf)

Percentage of total baptisms

Decades

1590s 1610s 1630s 1650s 1670s 1690s 1710s 1730s 1750s

Key:
— Bread prices
- - - Seven parishes
— Six parishes (excluding SLJ)

Sources: Baptism registers of SCS, SDB, SDE, SLJ, SMA, SMC, SPC (see Appendix)
For bread prices: A.L. Beier and R. Finlay (eds), *London 1500–1700. The Making of the Metropolis* (London 1986), p.173.

coin; all these contributed to unemployment among the London poor and strained the resources of many parishes in the City as well as in the suburbs.[48]

Given these economic conditions, and the increased incidence of abandonment during these difficult years, it seems probable that the foundlings of London and Westminster were not all bastards but that many were legitimate children whose parent(s) could not afford to feed another mouth. European studies of abandonment have demonstrated that poverty was a major reason for parents deserting their children, but in times of distress a greater proportion of older children were abandoned so that the average age of foundlings increased.[49] The preliminary findings of this study show that the opposite was true in London. In difficult years, when the number of foundlings increased, their median age decreased slightly. There is no obvious explanation for this difference although it could be related to the opening of workhouses in London to house older children in this same period.[50] A further observation of European practices is that, in times of hardship, more girls were abandoned than boys.[51] This also seems to have been the case in London from the 1650s to the 1700s (see Table 6.5).

It should be noted that if the mother of a foundling was traced she was subject to punishment, which could range from time spent in the pillory to a term in the house of correction. The following treatment meted out to such a woman in 1556 shows the attitude towards such 'unnatural' mothers in sixteenth-century London:

> Wheare by the Lord Maior and his bretherne Thaldermen it was adjudged that a woman named — Norton dwellinge in Southwerke for leavynge and forsaking of a childe in the streates shulde be whipped at Bridewell and from thence sent unto the govrnors of Christes hospitall for a further reformacion, whiche thinge beinge done she was sent unto the pillorye in Chepe wyth a paper on hir hed wherein was written in greate letters Whipped at Bridewell for leavynge and forsakinge hir childe in the streates, and from thense caryed into Southwerk and banished for hir offence out of the citie.[52]

Thus, not only did mothers have to make a positive decision to relinquish their children, for whom, in many cases, they had strong feelings, but ran the risk of ridicule and punishment of varying degrees of severity (although not execution as in the case of infanticide). If discovered, they were forced to take the child back even though they were unable to afford its keep. Some such mothers merely went to another parish and abandoned the child again.[53] However, there are also instances where the mother reclaimed her child. Sometimes this was after only a few days, as in St Christopher le Stocks in 1661: [20 March] 'Joanna Christopher a child layd to ye charge of ye parish [was baptised] & afterward fetched away Aprill ye 2nd 1662 by ye aforesd: childs mother who declared the name to bee Clara.'[54] Other mothers waited months or years before reclaiming their children, in some cases stealing them from their nurse.[55] These instances probably indicate that the woman had remarried or was in gainful employment and could afford to keep her child again. They also bear out the maternal feelings and promises expressed in many of the notes attached to foundlings, such as the one of June 1709 quoted above.

Responsibility for the care of foundlings

Responsibility for the care of foundlings lay with the parish in which they were discovered. Unless the mother was quickly found or the child was recognized as having been born in another parish, all the expense of nursing, schooling, and, ultimately, apprenticeship had to be borne by the parish in which the child was abandoned. On finding such a child, therefore, the parish officers set in train immediate and extensive enquiries to identify the mother and her parish. In some instances a woman parishioner might recognize the child, particularly if she was a midwife or engaged in parish nursing.[56] Whether or not they were successful, the persons who searched for the mother were paid for their trouble by the parish officers.[57] Many parishes also advertised a description of the child in the newspapers, sometimes successfully, as in St Mary Woolnoth in 1698:

23 October was taken up in the church, Jeremy Jenkins, son of Anne Sims, the wife of Jeffery Sims, living in Catt Alley, Long Lane, which was put in the Post Boy the friday following and taken away by the mother on satterday.[58]

If the parish, from which the foundling and/or its mother came, was discovered, the child was sent there so that the expense of its upbringing was met by its own parish. Because officials were anxious to avoid paying for children who were not settled in their parishes, this sometimes resulted in a foundling being passed from parish to parish as each denied responsibility for it.[59] In some cases two parishes might agree to pay for the child jointly, especially if it had been abandoned on the borders of adjoining parishes.[60]

All these arrangements took time, sometimes several weeks, and meanwhile the infant had to be cared for. When an abandoned child was found the most important person regarding its nursing and care was the sexton. Foundlings were normally baptized soon after their discovery and then were given to the sexton, his wife, or a (usually poor) woman to 'keep' until a nurse could be found. The sexton was then responsible for finding a wet nurse. Normally he travelled to the country parish in which other children from his parish were being nursed.[61] In the mid-seventeenth century, for example, St Christopher le Stocks sent all its foundlings and other poor infants to Leyton in Essex, about 6 miles from London. On arrival at the Green Man Inn in Leyton, the sexton enquired about a suitable woman and then went to her home or asked for the woman to be brought to the inn. Once a woman was found, the sexton either returned to London, collected the child, and carried it back to Leyton to meet the nurse; or he persuaded the nurse to return with him to London to collect the child and carry it back to her Leyton home. During this procedure parish money was used to pay the sexton for his trouble and the woman who 'kept' the foundling (usually for only a few days). The nurse, when found, was rewarded for her trouble, provided with refreshment and all her expenses incurred in transporting her and/or the infant from London to the country. Usually she was paid up to a month's wages when she accepted the child.[62] When a country nurse could not be found, or a suitable, willing woman was available in the area, the infant might be nursed within the city. Some officials in certain periods had a policy of bringing up most of their foundlings within their own, or another, city parish but this was not generally adopted because the death rate of such infants was acknowledged to be very much greater than if they were nursed in the country.[63]

Parish children were usually inspected at least once a year. Parish officials either went out to the country to see the children in the homes of their nurses, or they paid the nurse or her husband to bring the child to London for inspection. During the seventeenth century some officials visited their nurse children more frequently; three times a year was not unusual.[64]

In the sixteenth century, London parishes could avoid the expense of raising a foundling by sending it to Christ's Hospital, but, as described above, only a small proportion could be admitted because of the large numbers of children already on the roll. Christ's Hospital children were initially cared for in the same way as parish infants. They were sent out to be nursed in the country or sometimes within the city until old enough to be educated. To check on the care of its children, all Christ's Hospital nurses were obliged to take the children back to the hospital at Easter each year to be inspected.[65]

At this yearly visit the child would not always return to the same nurse or even the same parish. It was not unusual for infants to spend one year in one county, the second in a different county, and to be sent to yet another after its next annual return to the hospital. Some children were sent to the same or an adjoining parish so that some degree of continuity of care and/or contact was possible even if the nurse was not the same woman.[66] However, with some infants being moved yearly, sometimes up to 70 or 80 miles away from their nurses of the previous year, the psychological effect on the child must have been considerable. No evidence has been found in the hospital archives as to whether this annual change of nurses was a deliberate policy or purely depended upon the availability of nurses or the convenience of the official who made the decision. In either case, the child was the victim of the system. In many instances the foster mother must also have been adversely affected, especially if she had breastfed, and become close to, a young infant for a year or more and then had to give it up to an unknown woman many miles away. It is clear that these foster mothers often became very attached to the children for whom they cared: a proportion took their nurse child as their own child, discharging the Hospital of further expense.[67] Also, boys, in particular, were frequently apprenticed to the husband of one of the nurses who had helped to rear them.[68]

From the early-eighteenth century there was a change in the traditional system of infant care because parishes increasingly opened workhouses to accommodate their poor. In some of these the policy of sending infants out to nurse was changed to one of keeping all children within the workhouse to be nursed and cared for by its female inmates. Where this policy was instituted there was a high mortality, particularly among infants and young children who were not wet nursed but were fed by hand with unsuitable foods in insanitary conditions.[69]

The building of these workhouses had an effect on the apparent numbers of children abandoned. The fall in the frequency of foundling baptisms began and continued during the period when workhouses were being opened. Children were still abandoned, sometimes at the gate of the workhouse. However, workhouses frequently admitted poor women, both married and unmarried, during childbirth and for about 4 weeks afterwards. Previously, a proportion of these mothers might have abandoned their children, who would then have been baptized as foundlings. When the woman was delivered in the workhouse the name and parent(s) of the child was known, and, at its baptism, it would be registered with the name given by the mother rather than after the place or parish in which it was found. Some mothers ran away after their delivery leaving their babies to be cared for in the workhouse. Again, although these infants were abandoned they do not appear in the records as foundlings because the parent(s) were known.[70] Thus, the apparent fall in foundling baptisms in the early-eighteenth century may not reflect the true scale of abandonment.

In parishes which did not have a workhouse many foundlings continued to be baptized, especially in the parishes in the west of London and in Westminster, such as St Clement Dane and the Temple. Also, during this time, the movement to open the London Foundling Hospital was proceeding, and the fact that once it was opened in 1741 the number of infants whose mothers clamoured for their admission was always greater than the number who could be admitted[71] tends to show that the incidence of child abandonment was not necessarily falling in the eighteenth century.

Neglect and maltreatment of parish infants by their foster mothers

Different cultures regard aspects of child rearing in different ways. Whether or not a child is thought to be abused or neglected essentially depends on the society or culture in which it is living. Thus, what was regarded as acceptable or normal to sixteenth- and seventeenth-century English mothers might be seen as abnormal either by other countries in the same period or by English society in the twentieth century. However, studies of child abuse and neglect in many cultures show that certain children in all societies tend to be more subject to neglect than others, particularly those who are illegitimate, adopted, diseased, who appear different, either physically or mentally, or who otherwise do not easily 'fit in' to the environment in which they are living.[72] Thus, it might be expected that foundlings, as a group, who came from unknown parents and were cared for by paid foster mothers, were perhaps more vulnerable to neglect than other children in pre-industrial England. Superficial examination of the records by some writers, such as De Mause and Shorter, has tended to highlight the misdeeds of nurses involved in infant and child care.[73] Indeed, if certain sources are examined in isolation they do seem to show a plethora of evidence against these women.[74] However, other sources reveal relatively little abuse by parish nurses.[75] In any attempt to assess the scale of maltreatment, therefore, it is essential to look at a variety of the available sources, since different types of source material give a different point of view as well as additional information.

Medical, religious, and philanthropic writers of the period largely paint nurses as careless, murderous, systematically dosing their charges with opiates and alcohol, and depriving them of food.[76] The London Bills of Mortality had a separate category for children 'starved and overlaid at nurse'.[77] However, too much emphasis should not be placed on this fact alone since overlaying and starvation are two quite separate causes of death and the term was almost certainly used to accommodate all unexplained deaths of infants while at nurse. Compared with other causes of infant deaths in the Bills, the number of those starved or overlaid was minimal. Most babies were said to have died of 'convulsions' or 'teething', both of which were related to gastro-intestinal diseases (often due to an unsuitable diet) and illnesses accompanied by a high fever.[78]

Investigations into infanticide in England have identified 'infanticidal nurses': women who were paid by parents or guardians to take the baby to nurse on the understanding that it would not be seen again.[79] In 1645, for example, the Essex parents of a bastard travelled to London with their newborn infant. On arrival the man took the child, saying he was going to place it with a nurse in Thames Street, and the mother never saw it again.[80]

This child may have been 'overlaid' or abandoned in the streets. An example from the Court minutes of Christ's Hospital in 1556 shows that nurses may have preferred abandonment to direct murder:

> Jone Rice the wife of William Rice dwelling in Fleet Lane who received a woman child of one Robert Bannester gent dwelling at Cheltsey of whom she confessed that toward the keeping of the same she received 5s in money and afterwards turned and left the same child in the streets that before Easter next coming she shall bring forth the father of the said child or otherwise provide for it which is now in the charge of Robert Pennell in Secolane and hath been kept at the charges of this house this 2 years past or otherwise she to be openly punished and after to be banished the city with the said child.[81]

Undoubtedly some nurses did murder their charges. In 1621, the register of St Botolph without Aldgate records the burial of 'Paluda Foord a base-borne child nursed in the house of Thomas Overlin a Tyncker of Rosemarie Lane (where it was base-lie used, and starved)'.[82] In Berkshire in 1627 a nurse was charged with murdering a child she had taken to nurse. Her daughter testified that

> She did help her mother, Susan Hobbes, to kill the child [with a] whackinge staff or stick ... first buryed in a gravell pitt within a myle of Winsor and afterwardes the next day taken up and buryed in a churchyard ... the child's name was Elizabeth aged about 3 yeres ... they kept the child for half a year or there aboutes. It was such a trouble to them to carry about ... being a strong child byting and scratching [the accused].[83]

In 1697, the parish officers of St Gregory by St Pauls had to attend the inquest on one of their parish infants being nursed at Ware in Hertfordshire: 'Paid the expense of the Coroner's inquest of Harford about a parish child supposed to be starved att nurse att Ware, occasioned by the discourse of the people of ye towne.'[84] This statement indicates that suspected neglect or abuse by a nurse merited the disapproval of her neighbours.

In 1694, the Middlesex Justices issued an 'Order concerning the putting out to nurse of parish children. This matter is brought into notice owing to one Mary Compton having starved and murdered several infants placed into her care by public officers.'[85] Apparently, part of this problem was related to the fact that some parish officers put out their children for a lump sum so that nurses could profit substantially if the infant died, and the parish was spared further expense. The court ordered that payments must be only by the week or month, and parish officials were to make annual lists of their children and where they were at nurse. However, this was not enforced and there is little evidence that parishes complied with the order.[86]

Suspected abuses by parish officers in the Westminster parish of St Clement Dane had already led to an investigation by the Middlesex Justices in 1686. They reported

That we inspected the said books, and do find that in the year 1679 there were then at the charge of the parish 89 children, of which 16 were foundlings, all [named] Clements. And we find that there hath been added to the charge of the parish 110 in the following six years, in all 199, of which 51 are Clements, children laid in the streets. We find that of these, 55 hath been put forth to apprentice, and that there are now in being 32 of the said 55 only. And we find that there now remains of children at the charge of the parish, of which 13 are Clements, 58; and the apprentices living, of which 3 are Clements, 32; in all, 90. We find that the officers have expended for nursing these children in seven years last past, £1,943 9s; and for binding forth apprentices, £109 8s; in all, £2,052 17s. And we further find that they have given away, on extraordinary charges at their pleasure, some of which are for the children, £2,708 16s 5d.[87]

When Jonas Hanway investigated this parish in 1767 he drew attention to the Justices' figures relating to foundlings between 1679 and 1686:

> Note, that 51 of the 110 were foundlings, all Clements, laid in the parish in six years last, and so take the name of Clement from the parish, 51; were then there, 16; in all 67.
>
> Now, only 3 are bound out apprentices, and 13 are left of the number 16: and the 51, all Clements, are all lost and dead. Now, the parish books have been searched how many were christened of these foundlings or Clements, or buried, and very few appear upon the register. It is questionable if they ever were all there, though paid for. It is much that 51 should die out of 67 in seven years. The particular money paid for nursing of these children is £1,943 9s in seven years.[88]

In 1715, a parliamentary committee investigated the records of St Martin in the Fields, then considered one of the better parishes in regard to parish care. When the question of infant care was raised the committee found that the 'Book of burials being perused for the last three years [it was found] that the proportion of children far exceeds that of men and women, and, being examined touching the same . . . that with one year with another, there was about 1,200 christenings and that above 3/4 of those die every year'. The committee reported

> That a great many parish infants, and exposed bastard children, are inhumanly suffered to die by the barbarity of nurses, especially parish nurses, who are a sort of people void of commiseration, or religion hired by the churchwardens to take off a burden from the parish at the cheapest and easiest rates they can; and these know the manner of doing it effectively as by the burial books may evidently appear.[89]

One factor in such abuse was that, although many of the nurses of London foundlings were regularly supervised by parish officers in the late-sixteenth and most of the seventeenth century, by the last two decades of the seventeenth century the degree of supervision tended to be less. Officials did not always meet the women they were employing as nurses. Parish documents sometimes put a note against a nurse's name saying 'nurse — knows her.'[90] This lower level of supervision seems to have been connected with the increased incidence of abandonment in the capital. Possibly there were simply too many foundlings to police their care adequately.

The large numbers of London and Westminster foundlings recorded in the burial registers of country parishes around the capital may be another indication of poor nursing.[91] However, if over 1,000 infants a year were being sent out from London, at a time when up to half of the babies baptized did not survive till the age of 2,[92] these figures alone are not necessarily evidence of murderous nurses on a large scale. It must also be emphasized that the examples quoted above are the exception rather than the rule in all of the parishes (urban and country) studied to date. Cases of murder, physical abuse, and neglect of children under 4 years of age do not appear regularly in parish, hospital, and quarter sessions records. They have to be searched for at length.[93] Yet these unusual, isolated occurrences are the very examples selected by historians seeking to prove widespread cruelty and neglect by foster mothers.[94]

Parish nurses were usually poor women, often widowed mothers.[95] Fiona Newall has shown that, in Aldenham, they came from a lower socio-economic group than women who took in nurse children by private arrangement,[96] and they were also paid less, especially in the late-seventeenth and early-eighteenth century. They were not always paid regularly or at all; some had to go to court to claim the wages due to them.[97] For poor mothers, especially widows, it was often the only work available to them, and they depended on the goodwill of parish officials to send them infants to 'keep' or nurse. Most tended to take in relatively large numbers of parish children of varying ages at a time.[98] Some were aided in their dealings with London parishes by their husbands who transported children and organized their wives' occupation. Parish records show that where the husband was involved, the parish officer dealt directly with him.[99] Conditions in the homes of parish nurses were usually poor but in the country these were mitigated by the rural environment into which all children were said to venture. Conditions within London nurses' homes were apparently very poor and unrelieved by access to surrounding countryside. A contemporary view of nurses employed by the poor parish of St Botolph without Aldgate was given by the parish clerk in 1623:

a child 'yt was nursed in the house of one Edith Jones a poore widow of east Smithfeild, where it died . . . . There are verie few children prosper long in our parish, that are nursed in such places.' Six months later, another child at nurse in the parish died: 'hee that loveth his dogg would not put it in such a place to be brought upp'.[100]

Yet against this evidence is the survival rate of Christ's Hospital foundlings, some of whom were nursed within the city. Between 1563 and 1589 the fate of 119 foundlings is recorded: seventy-six nursed in the country lived for between 2 days and 23 years, with a mean of 6 years 4 months; forty-three nursed within the city lived for between 1 week and 15 years, with a mean of 6 years 3 months.[101]

Reliable survival rates of foundlings in London and Westminster parishes are almost impossible to find because, unless the precise parish in which they were buried is known, or there exist details of their eventual apprenticeship, many disappear from the records. Thus, in this study, foundling survival in the seventeenth century cannot be assessed.

Survival rates have been calculated for 151 of the Temple foundlings in the eighteenth century and, compared with the sixteenth-century children of Christ's Hospital, they are uniformly poor. Survival after baptism ranged from burial on the same day to $5^{1}/_{2}$ years, with a median of 10 weeks. Only thirty- six (23.8 per cent) survived longer than 6 months.[102] It is known that the Temple, from at least the 1730s, had a policy of keeping its foundlings within its boundaries and bringing them up by hand because it was cheaper than employing wet nurses.[103] The result was a high mortality (also noted in other city parishes which had this policy).[104] The month of burial of 183 foundlings between the 1730s and the 1780s confirms that artificial feeding must have been employed, with 34 per cent dying during the summer months, July to September, when diarrhoeal disease commonly affected and killed large numbers of infants who were handfed.[105] Also, during the eighteenth century a number of parishes which built workhouses instigated a policy of artificial feeding within the institution with the resulting mortality of 79–100 per cent of infants aged 0–3 years.[106]

It should be noted, therefore, that where a high mortality of infants cared for by parish nurses occurred it was not necessarily that all nurses set out to drug, starve, or murder their charges. Where the parish officers decreed handfeeding of infants under their care it was they who bore the greater responsibility. In the eighteenth century it was repeatedly shown that even the best dry nurses, living in the best conditions, and under the best medical supervision could not keep alive the majority of hand-fed infants, particularly in urban conditions.[107]

The philanthropist Jonas Hanway is frequently cited by writers seeking examples of bad or murderous parish nursing between the 1680s and the 1760s. Some of his descriptions of nurses are angry and evocative. Yet at the same time, the underlying criticism of parish officials, which pervades all his writings, is rarely noted. When he began his crusade against the poor standard of parish infant care in the 1760s, he was not concerned solely with exposing individual nurses. He used such examples to demonstrate that the parish officers did not care what happened to the foundling, and other, children for whom they were responsible.[108] His observations have been tested and confirmed by the research presented here and elsewhere.[109] Hanway was astute enough to apportion the true blame for so many infant deaths: not on the women involved in nursing, but on the men who employed, supervised, and, ultimately, exploited them.

Appendix

Parish records referred to in the text

AHBS: *All Hallows Bread Street*

W. B. Bannerman (ed.), *The Registers of All Hallows, Bread Street* (London, 1913).

AHHL: *All Hallows Honey Lane*

W. B. Bannerman (ed.), *The Registers of St Mary le Bowe, Cheapside, All Hallows, Honey Lane, and of St Pancras, Soper Lane, London, 1538–1837* (London, 1914).

AHL: *All Hallows the Less*

T. C. Dale (transcribed), 'All Hallows the Less, London. The register of baptisms 1558–1812' (1933), typescript, LSG, MX/R100.
T. C. Dale (transcribed), 'All Hallows the Less, register of burials 1558–1853' (1936), typescript, LSG, MX/R99.

CCN: *Christ Church Newgate*

W. A. Littlemore (ed.), *The Registers of Christ Church, Newgate, 1538 to 1754* (London, 1895).

SBA: *St Botolph without Aldgate*

'St Botolph Aldgate parish register 1558–99', GL, MSS 9220, 9221, 9223.
'Parish clerks' memoranda books 1583–1600', GL, MS 9234.

SBE: *St Bartholomew Exchange*

E. Freshfield (ed.), *The Vestry Minute Books of the Parish of St Bartholomew Exchange in the City of London 1567–1676* (London, 1890).

SCD: *St Clement Dane*

'Payment to . . . nurses for nursing children, 1719' WCA, B1233.
'Payments made for nursing of children, 1720', WCA, B1234.
'Register of returns of infant poor 1767–86', WCA, B1258.
'The Enfield book 1787–92', WCA, B1261.
'Clothing book and names of nurses and children 1799–1800', WCA, B1264.

SCS: *St Christopher le Stocks*

E. Freshfield (ed.), *The Register Booke of the Parish of St Christopher le Stocks, in the City of London* (3 vols, London, 1882).
E. Freshfield (ed.), *Accomptes of the Churchwardens of the Paryshe of St Christofer's in London, 1575 to 1662* (London, 1885).
E. Freshfield (ed.), *The Account Book of the Parish of St Christopher le Stocks in the City of London, 1662–1685* (London, 1895).

SDB: *St Dionis Backchurch*

J. L. Chester (ed.), *The Register Booke of Saynte De'nis Backchurch Parish 1538–1754* (3 vols, London, 1878).

SDE: *St Dunstan in the East*

A. W. Hughes Clarke (ed.), *The Register of St Dunstan in the East, London, 1558–1654* (London, 1939).
R. H. D'Elboux (ed.), *The Registers of St Dunstan in the East, London, 1653–1691* (London, 1955).
R. H. D'Elboux and W. Ward (eds), *The Registers of St Dunstan in the East, London, 1692–1766* (London, 1958).

SDW: *St Dunstan in the West*

R. E. C. Waters, *Parish Registers in England* (London, 1887), 39.

SGP: *St Gregory by St Pauls*

'Parish register of St Gregory by St Pauls', GL, MSS 10,233; 18,932.
'St Gregory by St Pauls churchwardens' accounts, 1673–1728', GL, MS 1337/1.

SHB: *St Helen Bishopsgate*

W. B. Bannerman (ed.), *The Registers of St Helens, Bishopsgate, London, 1575–1837* (London, 1904).

SLJ: *St Lawrence Jewry*

A. W. Hughes Clarke (ed.), *The Register of St Lawrence Jewry, London, 1538–1812* (2 vols, London, 1940–1).

SMA: *St Mary Aldermary*

J. L. Chester (ed.), *The Parish Registers of St Mary Aldermary, London, From 1558 to 1754* (London, 1880).

SMAman: *St Mary Aldermanbury*

W. B. Bannerman (ed.), *The Registers of St Mary the Virgin, Aldermanbury, London* (2 vols, London, 1931–2).

SMB: *St Mary le Bowe*

W. B. Bannerman (ed.), *The Registers of St Mary le Bowe, Cheapside, All Hallows, Honey Lane, and of St Pancras, Soper Lane, 1538–1837* (London, 1914).

SMBass: *St Michael Bassishaw*

A. W. Hughes Clarke (ed.), *The Register of St Michael Bassishaw, London, 1538–1892* (3 vols, London, 1942–4).

SMC: *St Michael Cornhill*

J. L. Chester (ed.), *The Parish Registers of St Michael, Cornhill, London 1546–1754* (London, 1882).
W. H. Overall (ed.), *The Accounts of the Churchwardens of the Parish of St Michael Cornhill in the City of London 1456 to 1608* (London, 1871).

SMF: *St Martin in the Fields*

'Examination book 1709', WCA, F5002.
'Memoranda book 1762–66', WCA, F4010.
'List of poor admitted to workhouse 1766–69', WCA, F4011.
'Annual lists of nurses and children 1789–1813', WCA, F4339.

SMMMS: *St Mary Magdalen Milk Street*

A. W. Hughes Clarke (ed.), *The Registers of St Mary Magdalen Milk Street 1558–1666* (London, 1942).

SMO: *St Martin Orgar*

A. W. Hughes Clarke (ed.), *The Register of St Clement Eastcheap and St Martin Orgar 1624–1812* (London, 1938).

SMOut: *St Martin Outwich*

W. B. Bannerman (ed.), *The Registers of St Martin Outwich, London, 1670–1873* (London, 1905).

SMQ: *St Michael le Quern*

W. A. Littledale (ed.), *The Registers of St Vedast, Foster Lane, and of St Michael le Quern, London, 1558–1837* (2 vols, London, 1902–3).

SMW: *St Mary Woolnoth*

J. M. S. Brooke and A. W. C. Hallen (eds), *The Transcript of the Registers of the United Parishes of S. Mary Woolnoth and S. Mary Woolchurch Haw in the City of London 1538 to 1760* (London, 1886).

SNA: *St Nicholas Acon*

W. Brigg (ed.), *The Register Book of the Parish of St Nicholas Acons, London, 1539–1812* (Leeds, 1890).

SPC: *St Peter Cornhill*

G. W. G. Leveson Gower (ed.), *A Register of All the Christninges, Burialles & Weddinges within the Parish of Saint Peeters upon Cornhill, 1538–1774* (2 vols, London, 1877–9).

SPSL: *St Pancras Soper Lane*

W. B. Bannerman (ed.), *The Registers of St Mary le Bowe, Cheapside, All Hallows, Honey Lane, and of St Pancras, Soper Lane, 1538–1837* (London, 1914).

STA: *St Thomas Apostle*

J. L. Chester (ed.), *The Parish Registers of St Thomas the Apostle, London, Containing the Marriages, Baptisms and Burials from 1558 to 1754* (London, 1881).

SVFL: *St Vedast Foster Lane*

W. A. Littledale (ed.), *The Registers of St Vedast, Foster Lane, and of St Michael le Querne, London, 1558–1837* (2 vols, London, 1902–3).

Temple

G. D. Squibb (ed.), *The Register of Temple Church, London. Baptisms 1629–1853* (London, 1979).
Register of Burials at the Temple Church 1628–1853 (London, 1905).

Acknowledgements

Research for this chapter was partially funded by the Leverhulme Trust and the British Academy. I am grateful for the interest and assistance of the staff of the following libraries and departments: British Library; Cambridge Group for the History of Population and Social Structure; Greater London Record Office; Guildhall Library; Hertfordshire County Record Office and Local Studies Library; Society of Genealogists; Wellcome Institute; Westminster City Archives; and the incumbents of the parishes whose records have been used in this study, and Christ's Hospital and the Thomas Coram Foundation for Children for access to the archives of Christ's Hospital and the London Foundling Hospital. I wish to thank Patricia Crawford for her constructive comments on the first draft of this chapter; also Jeremy Boulton, the late Amanda Copley, Roger Finlay, Richard Wall, and Adrian Wilson for help with the background history of London, foundlings, and the London Foundling Hospital.

Notes

To avoid lengthy repetition all references to London and Westminster parish records in the notes and tables are abbreviated. Full details are given in the Appendix. Dates throughout refer to the Old Style calendar: the year beginning 25 March.

1. L. De Mause (ed.), *The History of Childhood* (London, 1976); E. Shorter, *The Making of the Modern Family* (Glasgow, 1977), 170–203.

2. L. Lallemand, *Histoire des Enfants Abandonnés et Delaisses: Étude sur la Protection de l'Enfance aux Diverses Epoques de la Civilisation* (Paris, 1885); F. S. Hugel, *Die Findelhaüser und das Findelwesen Europa's* (Vienna, 1863); C. Delasselle, 'Abandoned children in eighteenth-century Paris', in E. Forster and P. M. Ranum (eds), *Deviants and the Abandoned in French Society* (Baltimore, 1978), 47–82; L. Martz *Poverty and Welfare in Hapsburg Spain. The Example of Toledo* (Cambridge, 1983), 224–36; R. C. Trexler, 'Infanticide in Florence: new sources and first results', *Hist. Childh. Quart.*, 1 (1973), 98–116; R. C. Trexler, 'The foundlings of Florence, 1395–1455', *Hist. Childh. Quart.*, 1 (1973), 259–84.

3. R. K. McClure, *Coram's Children. The London Foundling Hospital in the Eighteenth Century* (New Haven, 1981).

4. For details see Appendix.

5. *Christ's Hospital Admissions Register 1554–1599* (London, 1937). The original is in Guildhall Library, MS 12/818/1. This is the only surviving source for the sixteenth century which gives details about the children, their origin, and their nurses (the nurse books have not survived). The amount of detail contained in the register is very variable. In general, greater detail is given for the 1560s and 1570s; the quality of the recording deteriorates in the 1580s and is poor in the 1590s.

6. McClure, *Coram's Children*; for a detailed study of the infants admitted to the Foundling Hospital in the early years see A. Wilson, 'Illegitimacy and its implications in mid-eighteenth-century London: the evidence of the foundling Hospital', *Cont. & Change*, 4 (1989), 103–64.

7. R. Finlay, *Population and Metropolis. The Demography of London 1580–1650* (Cambridge, 1981); A. L. Beier and R. Finlay (eds), *London 1500–1700. The Making of the Metropolis* (London and New York, 1986); E. A. Wrigley and R. S. Schofield, *The Population History of England 1541–1871. A Reconstruction* (London, 1981).

8. SCS, SDB, SDE, SLJ, SMA, SMC, SPC.

9. E. Cellier, 'A scheme for the foundation of a royal hospital . . . for the maintenance of a corporation of skilful midwives, and such foundlings, or exposed children as shall be admitted therein: . . . proposed . . . in the month of June, 1687', *Harleian Miscellany* (10 vols, London, 1808–13), vol. 4, 142–7.

10. *An Account of the General Nursery or Colledg of Infants, Set up by the Justices of Peace for the County of Middlesex with the Constitution and Ends Thereof* (London, 1686); *A short Account of the Work-house Belonging to the President and Governours for the Poor, in Bishopsgate-Street, London* (London, 1702).

11. Wrigley and Schofield, *Population History of England*, 77–83.

12. Cellier, 'A scheme for a royal hospital'; McClure, *Coram's Children*, 19; *The Guardian*, no. 106, 13 July 1713. The proportion of children brought into London from the surrounding area to be abandoned is not clear, although when mothers or relatives were traced and/or reclaimed foundlings they were from other London or Westminster parishes.

13. SCS *Register*, Burials, 2 Nov. 1656, 17 Dec. 1673, 15 Aug. 1724; SHB *Register*, Burials, 30 Sept. 1741.

14. V. Fildes, 'The English wet nurse and her role in infant care 1538–1800', *Med. Hist.*, 32 (1988), 142–73.

15. For example, SHB, SMMMS, SMW, Temple.

16. Temple *Registers*, Baptisms and Burials.

17. The common practice was to give the name of the parish as a surname and the name of the nearest saint's day as a Christian name. Others were named after the place in which they were abandoned. V. Fildes, 'The wet nursing of London's children, 1538–1800', in W. F. Bynum (ed.), *Living and Dying in London, 1500–1900* (London, forthcoming), Tables 1 and 2.

18. For example, SVFL *Register*, in June 1613, records the burial of three children, nursed in the parish, who were 'found in the p'ishe of Aldermary', but only one of the three is recorded in the SMA baptism register.

19. SLJ *Register*, Burials, 1700–9 *passim*; 'Ware parish register', HRO, D/P116 1/1–3.

20. E. H. Pearce, *Annals of Christ's Hospital* (London, 1908), 1–42.

21. *Christ's Hospital Admissions, passim.*

22. For example, SDB *Register*, 14 December 1567, baptized a foundling who was admitted 3 months earlier on 5 September 1567.

23. For example, SBA 'Parish clerks' memoranda books, 1583–1600', compared with SBA 'Parish register 1558–99'.

24. *Christ's Hospital Admissions*, 6–28, *passim.*

25. Finlay, *Population and Metropolis*, 37.

26. Pearce, *Annals of Christ's Hospital*, 37–41.

27. SBE *Vestry Minutes, passim*; SCS *Accomptes, passim*. These list, often in great detail, the clothing issued to foundlings who had just been discovered.

28. SMA *Register*, Baptisms, 2 Mar. 1659; SMW *Register*, Baptisms, 29 July 1677; SMOut *Register*, Baptisms, 13 May 1773.

29. SDE *Register*, Baptisms, 1699–1720.

30. A. Wilson, 'Participant or patient? Seventeenth century childbirth from the mother's point of view', in R. Porter (ed.), *Patients and Practitioners. Lay Perceptions of Medicine in Pre-industrial Society* (Cambridge, 1985), 129–44; and see his chapter (3) in this volume.

31. A. Dyer, 'Seasonality of baptisms: an urban approach', *Loc. Popul. Stud.*, 27 (1981), 26–34; J. Boulton, *Neighbourhood and Society. A London Suburb in the Seventeenth Century* (Cambridge, 1987), 49–59; Wrigley and Schofield, *Population History of England*, 286–95.

32. Finlay, *Population and Metropolis*, 37–42; Wrigley and Schofield, *Population History of England*, 289.

33. Ibid., 225.

34. O. H. Hufton, *The Poor of Eighteenth-century France 1750–1789* (Oxford, 1974), 335–6; Trexler, 'Foundlings of Florence', 266–8.

35. Martz, *Poverty and Welfare*, 225; Hufton, *The Poor of Eighteenth-century France*, 338; Delasselle, 'Abandoned Children', 48.

36. SHB *Register*, 'Addenda to baptisms', 418.

37. Cited in T. R. Forbes, *Chronicle from Aldgate. Life and Death in Shakespeare's London* (New Haven, 1971), 150–1.

38. L. Stone, *The Family, Sex and Marriage in England 1500–1800* (London, 1977), 70, 473–5, 640; De Mause, *The History of Childhood* 1–73; Wilson, 'Illegitimacy'.

39. K. Wrightson 'Infanticide in earlier seventeenth-century England', *Loc. Popul. Stud.*, 15 (1975), 10–22; R. W. Malcolmson, 'Infanticide in the eighteenth century', in J. S. Cockburn (ed.), *Crime in England 1550–1800* (London, 1977), 187–339; P. C. Hoffer and N. E. H. Hull, *Murdering Mothers: Infanticide in England and New England 1558–1803* (New York and London, 1981), 23–5, 107–11, 127–32, 166–70.

40. V. Fildes, *Breasts, Bottles and Babies. A History of Infant Feeding* (Edinburgh, 1986), 90.

41. Ibid., 98–133.

42. For example, SMW *Register*, Baptisms, 28 March and 28 Sept. 1698.

43. Ibid., 17 Sept. 1672, 29 Dec. 1677, 21 Apr. 1695, and see note 28 above.

44. SMF 'Examination book', 165a.

45. Ibid., 167.

46. Ibid., 168.

47. *Christ's Hospital Admissions*, 133, 185; SBE *Vestry Minutes*, 102.

48. S. Macfarlane, 'Social policy and the poor in the later seventeenth century', in Beier and Finlay, *London 1500–1700*, 252–77, p. 259.

49. Hufton, *The Poor of Eighteenth-century France*, 333, 335; Trexler, 'Foundlings of Florence', 266–7; Delasselle, 'Abandoned children', 70–4.

50. See note 10 above.

51. Trexler, 'Foundlings of Florence', 266–8.

52. Cited in W. Lempriere, *A History of the Girls' School of Christ's Hospital, London, Hoddesdon and Hertford* (Cambridge, 1924), 2.

53. *Christ's Hospital Admissions*, 174.

54. SCS *Register*, Baptisms, 20 March 1661.

55. *Christ's Hospital Admissions*, 18, 66, 200.

56. SCS *Accomptes*, 81; SDB *Register*, Baptisms, 17 Nov. 1650; SMF 'Examination book', 49.

57. SCS *Accomptes*, 81.

58. SMW *Register*, Baptisms, 23 Oct. 1698.

59. SMC *Register*, Baptisms, 1 June 1632; SCS *Accomptes*, 60.

60. SGP 'Churchwardens' accounts', 32; SBE *Vestry Minutes*, 170, 187.

61. Fildes, 'Wet nursing of London's children'.

62. Ibid.; SCS *Account Book*, 25, 26, 30, 41.

63. Fildes, 'Wet nursing of London's children'.

64. SBE *Vestry Minutes*, 141, 142, 227; SCS *Accomptes*, 79, 122; SGP 'Churchwardens' accounts', 12, 51, 53, 67.

65. *Christ's Hospital Admissions, passim.*

66. Ibid., *passim.*

67. Ibid., 67, 68, 148.

68. Ibid., 60, 75, 212–13, 220.

69. D. Marshall, *The English Poor in the Eighteenth Century*, (New York, 1969), 125–60; J. Hanway, *Letters on the Importance of the Rising Generation of the Labouring Part of our Fellow-subjects* (London, 1767); Fildes, *Breasts, Bottles and Babies*, 281–7.

70. SCD 'The Enfield book', 31 Aug. 1786; SCS *Register*, Baptisms, 8 Mar. 1733; SMC *Register*, Baptisms, 19 May and 18 Aug. 1749.

71. From the time the Foundling Hospital opened in 1741 until 1756, infants of a specific age were admitted in small numbers at set intervals. Although this may have had some effect on the numbers of children abandoned in the streets, it could not have greatly influenced the scale of abandonment in the capital until the period of General Reception 1756–60, during which all children brought to the institution had to be admitted. After this 4-year period, the hospital again took in very small numbers of children. See Wilson, 'Illegitimacy'.

72. J. E. Korbin (ed.), *Child Abuse and Neglect. Cross-cultural Perspectives* (Berkeley, 1981), esp. 1–12.

73. Shorter, *The Making of the Modern Family*, 170–203; De Mause, *The History of Childhood*, 1–74.

74. Fildes, *Breasts, Bottles and Babies*, 188–210, 281–7; J. Hanway, *An Earnest Appeal for Mercy to the Children of the Poor* (London, 1766); Hanway, *Letters on the Importance of the Rising Generation.*

75. Considering the vast numbers of women so employed, parish, hospital, and quarter-sessions records relate very few cases of abuse or neglect by these foster mothers; for an assessment of the care provided by the Foundling Hospital nurses, see V. Fildes, *Wet Nursing. A History from Antiquity to the Present* (Oxford, 1988), ch. 11.

76. Fildes, *Breasts, Bottles and Babies*, 188–210. Dosing with opiates and alcohol seems to have become common in the later seventeenth and eighteenth centuries. It is not mentioned in sixteenth- and early-seventeenth-century sources.

77. J. Graunt, *Natural and Political Observations on the Bills of Mortality. Much Enlarged*, 5th edn (London, 1676).

78. Fildes, *Breasts, Bottles and Babies*, 390–1.

79. Wrightson, 'Infanticide', 12, 16–18.

80. Ibid., 16; A. Macfarlane, 'Illegitimacy and illegitimates in English history', in P. Laslett, K. Oosterveen, and R. M. Smith (eds), *Bastardy and its Comparative History* (London, 1980), 71–85.

81. *Christ's Hospital Admissions*, 1.

82. Cited in Forbes, *Chronicle from Aldgate*, 199.

83. Cited in G. Clark, 'Nurse children in Berkshire', *Berks Old & New*, 2 (1985), 25–33.

84. SGP 'Churchwardens' accounts', 64.

85. W. J. Hardy (ed.), *Middlesex County Records. Calender of the Sessions Books 1689 to 1709* (London, 1905), 110.

86. E. G. Dowdell, *A Hundred Years of Quarter Sessions. The Government of Middlesex from 1660 to 1760* (Cambridge, 1932), 53–4.

87. Cited in J. Diprose, *Some Account of the Parish of Saint Clement Danes (Westminster) Past and Present* (2 vols, London, 1868), vol. 1, 193–4.

88. Ibid., 194.

89. Cited in Marshall, *The English Poor*, 99.

90. SMF 'Memoranda book', inside front cover; SMF 'List of poor', 658; see also M. D. George, *London Life in the Eighteenth Century* (Harmondsworth, 1966), 213–16, 371.

91. Fildes, 'The English wet nurse', 152–3.

92. Fildes, *Breasts, Bottles and Babies*, 280–1.

93. Although reports of physical abuse and neglect of older children (particularly apprentices) are much more common in parish and hospital archives. *Christ's Hospital Admissions, passim.*

94. De Mause, *The History of Childhood*; Shorter, *The Making of the Modern Family*, 170–203.

95. Marshall, *The English Poor*, 95–9; I. Pinchbeck and M. Hewitt, *Children in English Society* (2 vols, London, 1969), vol. 1, 176–7.

96. See her chapter (5) in this volume.

97. Pinchbeck and Hewitt, *Children in English Society*, 176–7; Fildes, *Breasts, Bottles and Babies*, cf. tables of wages on pp. 161 and 283.

98. SCD 'Payments for nursing children'; SMF, 'Annual lists of nurses and children'.

99. SBE *Vestry Minutes*, 170, 173, 180, 187; SCS *Accomptes*, 113, 116; Forbes, *Chronicle from Aldgate*, 195–6; see also *Christ's Hospital Admissions, passim.*

100. Cited in Forbes, *Chronicle from Aldgate*, 199.

101. *Christ's Hospital Admissions*; for mortality of infants (0–12 months) of Christ's Hospital, including legitimate and orphaned children as well as foundlings, see Fildes, 'Wet nursing of London's children', Table 1; C. Cunningham, 'Christ's Hospital: infant and child mortality in the sixteenth century', *Loc. Popul. Stud.*, 18 (1977), 37–40.

102. Temple, *Registers*, Baptisms and Burials, 1700–99.

103. H. Sloane, 'Letter to John Milner, vice-president of the Hospital for the maintenance and education of exposed and deserted young children, 28 October 1748', in J. Brownlow, *Memoranda: or, Chronicles of the Foundling Hospital* (London, 1847), 210–16.

104. Ibid., 211; Fildes, *Breasts, Bottles and Babies*, 281–7.

105. Fildes, 'English wet nurse', 168.

106. Fildes, *Breasts, Bottles and Babies*, 283–5.

107. Ibid., 262–306.

108. Hanway, *Earnest Appeal*; Hanway, *Letters on the Importance of the Rising Generation*, 1–67 *passim*. For a description of Hanway's work see also J. S. Taylor, 'Philanthropy and empire: Jonas Hanway and the infant poor of London', *Eighteenth Cent. Stud.*, 12 (1979), 285–305.

109. Fildes, *Breasts, Bottles and Babies*, ch. 11.

7

Conjugal love and the flight from marriage: poetry as a source for the history of women and the family

Mary Prior

When Dorothy McLaren researched wet nursing she often mused on how 'caring, gentle mothers' like Mary Verney could bring themselves to send their babies out to wet nurses.[1] The problem is part of a wider one, that of understanding the attitudes and emotions of wives in the early-modern period. Of all women, wives are the hardest to document, because on marriage a woman's legal identity was absorbed into that of her husband. Therefore any source which deals with married women is precious. Poetry concerns itself with attitudes and emotions, so the poetry of conjugal love seemed an obvious source to explore; and that written by both wives and husbands, for marriage is a partnership and attitudes and emotions within a marriage are the result of interaction.

Social historians have tended to shy away from literary evidence partly because it involves invasion into another discipline, and partly because the relationship of literature to reality is tenuous.[2] However, historians have to treat all their sources with caution, not only poetry. What could appear to be more matter of fact and straightforward than records of assize courts? Yet J. S. Cockburn has shown us that fact and fiction are uncomfortably confused in many indictments.[3]

The field had to be defined strictly so as to secure only poems by real husbands and wives. Musings on matrimony and the reactions of fictional husbands and wives were excluded. Such material could be used, at best, as supporting evidence. Some poems, apparently of conjugal love, were omitted because the authors appear to have been unmarried; and so were anonymous works and those which turned out on closer inspection to be addressed to God. Those which expressed a faltering love were included but poems of pure hate were not. Elegies and epitaphs were collected when it appeared they were the work of the grieving spouse, but eventually it was decided that they must be regarded as post-marital. Nevertheless, they have some value in this enquiry and, where relevant, note has been taken of them.

Although total coverage of the field would be impracticable, as large a sample of poems as possible was surveyed. Two sources provided initial access: anthologies, and Margaret Crum's *First-line Index* to manuscript poetry in the Bodleian Library,[4] which contains over 20,000 items of good and bad verse. [For the historian bad poetry is as important a source as good.] Additional material was found by following up leads in these works and those provided by other scholars. The emerging picture showed that late seventeenth- and eighteenth-century women poets were particularly poorly represented. With the aid of Janet Todd's *Biographical Dictionary*, a more strenuous search was made for poetry of this period.[5] A strict statistical analysis would be inappropriate because of the nature of the material but, even if the number of poems were greatly increased, the overall impression of the proportion of poems of conjugal love probably would not be radically altered. The number found was minute: just over 150 poems, written by just under forty poets. Most wrote only one poem to their spouse, but a handful wrote many. Sir John Harington wrote 26, Samuel Bishop 21, Judith Madan 16, Samuel Wesley the younger 10, Anne Bradstreet 9, Samuel Shepherd 8, and Anne Finch 6. The majority of the poems were rather bad. The poems of different periods have certain characteristics which will be explored. They can tell us something of the relationships of husbands and wives, of the nature of poetry and of the situations in which it is produced. However this chapter will concentrate largely on the first of these questions.

To the historian it may seem remarkable that there should be so few poems of conjugal love for, in the circles in which these poets moved, particularly those of the sixteenth and seventeenth centuries, many marriages were arranged. It was hoped that love would flower within marriage.[6]

Gender governed the types of love poetry which could be written. If we consider the possible relations of married and unmarried men and women as writers and recipients of love poetry, we can see in what relations it was acceptable for men and women to write poems to those of the opposite sex.

Taking men first we find that single and married men wrote poems to women regardless of whether the women were single or married. The double standard allowed men to sit lightly to the moral code here and, according to the most persistent conventions of courtly love, which powerfully influenced English poetry, true love had nothing to do with marriage. The one person to whom poetry was almost never addressed was the poet's wife. To write a poem to one's wife was to fly in the face of this inherited tradition.[7]

For women, on the other hand, to write anything at all was to flout convention, almost to defy morality, for the double standard imposed a chastity on women not expected of men. This chastity was expressed in modest behaviour. One must not draw attention to oneself. Silence was a form of modesty, and to write was to break silence.[8] It was immodest in the extreme for a single woman to write love poems to a man, married or unmarried,[9] and if she did so, they appeared anonymously. Elizabeth Barrett Browning[10] did not show Robert Browning her love poems until after marriage. The only man to whom a woman could write love poetry was her husband. The expression of devotion in an epitaph or elegy was acceptable.[11] Otherwise the one form allowed her was that not favoured by men. The whole poetic tradition rendered this almost absurd. When wives started to write love poems to their husbands there was no wealth of tradition to support them. The only form of poetry allowed to women was that to which inherited tradition assigned no value, and to which the rich resonances of the tradition did not apply.

The sixteenth century

Poems of conjugal love were uncommon in the sixteenth century. The poets shared certain common characteristics. None were women, all were influenced by the Renaissance, all had experience of the Continent, and of court circles. An important group were men holding high office in Church or state and strongly committed puritans.

The first poems we shall consider are 'The Epytaphe of Sir Gryffythe aprise' and 'The Lamentatyon of the ladye Griffythe'.

It is not entirely clear who wrote them, so they do not fall strictly into our category as we have defined it. The 'Epytaphe' deals with actual individuals. Sir Gryffythe is known to have been a knight who was present at the Field of the Cloth of Gold, and he was later stationed at Calais: the poems are thought to have been written between 1520 and 1540 but nearer the earlier date.[12] However, whether the poems were by Sir Gryffythe upon his deathbed, by his wife, or by a third party is far from clear. The purpose of the 'Epytaphe' was in part practical: to persuade his old comrades who had served Prince Arthur with him, to petition King Henry VIII to be 'good lord' to his widow. The 'Lamentatyon' follows very much the sentiment of that part of the 'Epytaphe' in which Sir Gryffythe farewells his wife, but is, in fact, an elegy. It seems likely that both poems were the work of the same hand.

We are on firmer ground with Surrey's poem 'The Complaynt of the absence of her louer being vpon the sea' in *Tottel's Miscellany*. Absence was a common subject of poems of both conjugal and courtly love. In this the poem breaks no new ground. Though it is written by the husband it is in an oblique mode, for it is written as if by the wife. It is no fiction, though, for a reference to 'T. his lytel son' is to Surrey's son Thomas.[13]

The poem speaks of the wife's grief in his absence, and of her dreaming of his return:

Then lyvelye doth he looke/ and saluith me agayne
and saith my deare how is it now/ that you haue all this
payne
wheare with the heavie cares/ that heapt are in my brest
breakes forth and me dischardgeth cleane/ of all my great
vnrest
butt when I me awake/ and fyndes it but a dreame
the angwyshe of my former woe/ beginneth more extreame

The fears and tears are projected on the wife. For a soldier such things would have been womanish.[14] That she should feel the loss rather than he would also be considered natural. Yet the poem's existence suggests that he also feels these emotions, though he does not admit to them.

The next poems form an interesting group. They were written by like-minded men with similar backgrounds and religious beliefs. Most knew each other personally. They were the civilian Walter Haddon; the Marian exile John Parkhurst, Bishop of

Norwich; Sir Nicholas Bacon,[15] Lord Keeper under Elizabeth (who had married Anne Cooke,[16] one of the learned daughters of the exiled Sir Anthony Cooke), and John Harington the elder.[17] Another with similar beliefs and background, Richard Cox, Bishop of Ely, falls naturally into this group, but as he only wrote epitaphs to his first wife he cannot be included.[18] All, save Parkhurst, were educated at Cambridge and most had a connection with the court at some time of their lives. As reformers their fortunes varied in Mary's reign. Haddon and Bacon were unscathed. Parkhurst and Cox escaped into exile with their wives. John Harington, who dedicated one of his works to Katharine Willoughby, Duchess of Suffolk, herself a noted reformer, was imprisoned for a period with Princess Elizabeth. His first wife, being a natural daughter of Henry VIII,[19] had been half sister to Elizabeth.

Like other reformers they believed in the marriage of the clergy, and sought a higher regard for matrimony, and for the status of women as their partners, though they still saw them as subordinate to men. They were all men of scholarly temperament. Some had been celibates, and in an earlier generation they might well all have been so. For them the Protestant ideal of marriage was still being shaped. In their poems we see them seeking to do so.

Walter Haddon's two linked poems in Latin on what the husband expects from his wife, and the wife from the husband, are essentially the same poem as John Harington's in English, though which is the original and which the translation is not certain.[20] The poems are described by Ruth Hughey as 'playfully domestic'. It is as if they were the outcome of an amused and amusing dialogue between husband and wife. In Harington's version of the wife's poem, 'Husband yf you will be my deare', the wife's viewpoint is given thus:

> T'observe your tymes, if tyme I chuse
> To know my tymes, you must take payne
> And how your frends, you wold I vse
> So, looke my frends, you entertaine . . .
>
> What so a wooer, you me behight
> NOWe husband good, performe as due
> Penelopes pathe, if I hold right
> Vlixes Steppes, see you tread trew

There was to be no double standard here.

Parkhurst was celebrated as a Latin epigrammatist, and he wrote four brief epigrams to his wife. One expresses the pleasure of a former celibate in marriage:

> Nil magis in votis est, quam ut possimus in una
> Esse domo, caste iungier atque thoro.
> [No more is there to pray for, than that we may in the house be together, united in a faithful marriage bed.]

However he then plunges from this elevated level into abuse of the 'two-horned crowd of shaven ones' who cannot endure 'so holy a work'. There is a certain cocking a snook in the conclusion: 'meanwhile let us seize our joys in private secrecy'.[21]

The single poem to his wife by the Lord Keeper, Sir Nicholas Bacon, is more sedate. 'Made at Wymbleton in his Lo: greate sicknes in the laste yeare of Quene Marye', it expresses his gratitude to his wife Anne (née Cooke) for nursing him in mind and body:[22]

> Thinkeinge alsoe with howe good will
> The Idle tymes whiche yrkesome be
> You have made shorte throwe your good skill
> In readeinge pleasante thinges to me,
> Whereof profitte we bothe did se,
> As wittenes can if they could speake
> Bothe your Tullye and my Senecke:

In the main these are the poems of men of very moderate poetic ability, and it is not surprising that they have not been anthologized, but they reflect very much the attitude of the first generation of the Elizabethan Church, an attitude to be found in Matthew Parker himself, the author of a book in defence of priests' marriages. Amongst the Parker Papers there is a small book printed by Richard Watkins entitled *Prosper his Meditation with his Wife*.[23] It is a poem by an early Roman bishop to his wife, presented with an English translation. This begins

> 'Come on O mate
> Inseparate
> Of all my lyffes affayres,
> Expende our state,
> Our brittle date
> Sweet joyes how dread appayres . . . '

It goes on to picture the couple joined in prayer and praise to God. A picture of his own relation to his wife comes from a bookseller's description of a new-year's gift of Matthew Parker's to his wife of a small book of prayers he had collected for her.[24] The poems of conjugal love of this early Elizabethan period reflected a strand of belief of a highly intelligent and articulate group of Protestants. None of their wives wrote poems of conjugal love, but nor did any other women of their period. Three women wrote epitaphs or elegies, and two of them moved in much the same circles as the men who wrote poems of conjugal love.

The three women were Mary Queen of Scots, who wrote an elegy for her first husband, Francis II of France:[25] Elizabeth Russell (née Cooke)[26] and Elizabeth Bullingham, wife of Bishop John Bullingham, who wrote one for her first husband, Charles Tredeneck. John Bullingham's brother, Bishop Nicholas Bullingham, had married into the Locke family, noted for its intelligent women.[27] One is left wondering what women's network may have connected the widow of Charles Tredeneck, buried in St Breock, in Cornwall, with such a circle.

John Harington and his son Sir John compiled over the years an important manuscript collection of verse which includes many which reflect an interest in marriage as a subject for poetry.[28] It is therefore not surprising that the son should be the poet who left the largest number of poems of conjugal love in the whole period studied. They are also the most varied in subject matter. Yet Sir John was a very different man from his father in his cast of mind. He was, above all, a courtier and perhaps is best remembered by some for his poems on 'Ajax' alias the jakes, by others for his *Briefe View of the Church of England*, with its thumb-nail sketches of various bishops. It shows him no friend of clerical wives, at whose expense he enjoyed himself, and not least when able to report witticisms of the Queen at their expense: for the Queen detested clerical marriage.[29] Sir John's position at court was privileged, owing to his parents' friendship with the Queen, and family connections. He was her godson and granted a licence unusual within the court.

The poetry of the court was essentially in the tradition of courtly love, adapted to the building up of the image of the virgin queen, who was the focus of the court, and who used poetry, as all the arts, to establish herself as an icon of divine authority. The court comprised her devotees, half courtly knights, half worshippers. Sex, power, and religion were smelted in the brilliance of this image.[30] Yet it was at this court that this worldly knight's poems of conjugal love passed from hand to hand, and were blessed by the Queen's approval.[31] The Queen was noted for disliking the marriage of her courtiers, whose undivided devotion she required, but this lover-like attitude would have been positively incestuous in her godson. From him the evidences of a happy marriage were acceptable. Perhaps even in the scandal-ridden court of her old age, in a period when there was also an outbreak of bastardy throughout the country, the poems came to the tired old woman as a model, witty enough to be acceptable in a sophisticated court.[32] Her patronage, as much as John Harington's happy marriage, was responsible for this spate of poems.

Although he wrote so many poems to her, Harington seems to have had less in common with his wife than did his parents with each other. He was much at court, and in a poem justifying his absence one sees him expressing the common view of separate spheres for husband and wife.[33]

> *Mall,* in my absence this ys still your song:
> 'Come home sweet heart, yov stay from home too long'
> That thow lov'st home, my love, I like yt well,
> Wives should be like thy Tortas in the shell.
> I love to seeke, to see, learn, know be knowne;
> Men nothing know, know nothing but their owne.
> 'Yes, but', you say to me, 'home homely is,
> And comely therevnto.' And what of this?
> Among wise men, they demed are but momes
> That allwayes ar abiding in their homes.
> To have no home, perhapps it is a curse;
> To be a prisoner at home 'tis worse.

The last lines must have been wounding.

He wrote in a cheery, teasing, patronizing tone on many matters: the birth of children; on female vanity; on whether a man could love his wife without lust ('But while of this chaste love thou dost devize, /And looks chaste babies in my wanton eyes');[34] on the absurdities of his mother-in-law; on her sorrow at parting at Chester; on her being 'sick of the sullens'. He lays down the law on such matters as a wife's duties; on withstanding the wiles of Catholics; on her high birth giving her an innate dignity that fine clothes could never give; on women's virtues, of the evil practice of 'partition' [separate estate] – 'For where there is my Lords, and that my Ladies, /There some, perhaps, think likewise of their babies.'[35]

Yet despite this heavy uxoriousness, how far apart their two worlds are is seen when he clumsily attempts to bridge the gap in 'To Mall, to Comforte her for the losse of her children'.[36] He compares her to one of her pet doves:

> When at the window thou thy doues art feeding,
> Then thinke I shortly my Doue will be breeding,
> Like will loue like, and so my liking like thee,
> As I to doues in many things can like thee . . .
> Both doe delight to looke your selues in Glasles,
> You both loue your own houses as it passes;
> Both fruitfull are, but yet the Doue is wiser,
> For, though she haue no friend that can aduise her,
> She, patiently can take her young ones losse,
> Thou, too impatiently doost beare such crosse.

With the high infant mortality in the early-modern period, the death of a baby was a grief few mothers were spared. Yet this totally inadequate poem is one of only two which attempts to comfort a wife. Its burden is, essentially, cheer up, there are more where that one came from.

The seventeenth century

Only six, possibly seven, husbands were discovered who wrote poems of conjugal love in this period. There was no continuing tradition. The small group of scholars, bishops, and public servants, with their blend of reformed theology and humanist learning, had gone, and the position of Harington had been unique. Elizabeth was no longer there to command the attentions of poets and courtiers. In the court of James I there was greater sexual freedom and experimentation. The tradition of courtly love modulated as the century progressed into libertinism.[37] Nor did Puritanism produce any great flowering. The repressive tone of such advice books as those of William Gouge and William Whateley does not suggest fertile ground.[38] The greatest poems of conjugal love in this century were addressed to dead wives, and fall outside this study.[39]

The husbands do not form a unified group. They were John Lilliat, a musician; John Donne; Thomas Beaumont;[40] James Graham, Marquis of Montrose; George Payler, and William Cavendish, Duke of Newcastle, and John Wilmot, Earl of Rochester.

Donne is the only major poet, and there is some doubt if any of his poems are in fact poems of conjugal love. Sir Herbert Grierson suggests that 'Sweetest love, I do not go', 'As virtuous men pass mildly away', 'A Valediction: of Weeping' and perhaps the sixteenth 'Elegy' were all addressed to his wife, but this has been disputed.[41] They are not explicitly so. The temper of the age made conjugal love, for the poet, 'the love that dare not speak its name'. Few were published in the seventeenth century. Many are still in manuscript. In 'To his Loving Wife, a welcome home', Lilliat actually compared the love of David and Jonathan, which according to the Bible, surpassed that of women, with 'Vesta's Love' – the love of man and wife, which he distinguished from 'Venus Love, whereof the poet's dream'. He was for Vesta's love, his wife being the clinching argument.[42] In 'My dear and only love', Montrose like Filmer compared a marriage to an absolute monarchy. Were his wife 'to hold a synod in her heart' he'd never love her more.[43] Rochester's extempore poem 'To my more than Meritorious Wife', written after 1666, shows the libertine wooing his neglected wife.[44]

The mid-century brought two husbands whose relationships with their wives show more intellectual interaction than was found earlier in the century. George Payler's poem attempts to comfort his wife, Mary Carey, for the loss of her children. She had just lost her fourth son and fifth child:

> Deare Wife, let's learne to get that Skill,
> Of free Submission to God's holy Will:
> He like a Potter is: & we like Clay,
> Shall not the Potter mould us his owne Way?
> Sometimes it is his Pleasure that we stand
> With pretty lovely Baby's in our hand:
> Then he in Wisdome turns the Wheel about,
> And drawes the Posture of those Comforts out;
> Into another Forme; either this, or that
> As pleases him: & 'tis no matter what:
> If by such Changes, God shall bring us in
> To love Christ Jesus, & to loath our Sin.[45]

This prefaced a series of poems in which Mary Carey attempted to fathom God's providence for her, and submit herself to it gratefully. The poem is the only poem apart from Harington's in which the husband seeks to comfort a wife mourning the loss of children, but it arose from a much closer interaction of husband and wife than was the case with the Haringtons. However, if Mary Carey did not have to try and present a cheerful face before her husband, she seemed to feel it was demanded before God:

> My dearest Lord, hast thou fulfill'd thy Will,
> Thy Hand-Maid's pleas'd, compleately happy still.

Even in the tragic poem 'Upon the Sight of my abortive birth the 31st of December 1657', with its desperate plea

> I am a Branch of the Vine, purge me therefore;
> Father, more Fruit to bring then heretofore,

she can end 'saith Maria Carey alwaies in Christ happy'. A masculine authority imposed a curb on natural feeling here, just as much as Harington attempted to do.[46]

William and Margaret Cavendish were an extraordinary couple.[47] Staunch royalists, they had followed Charles into exile, where they met and married. At the Restoration, feeling their loyalty insufficiently rewarded, they retired to their vast estates where, a mutual admiration society of two, they wrote in a variety of genres, Margaret with rather more energy than her husband. William wrote love poems to her during their courtship and a small number after marriage, but the poems written after marriage do not declare themselves explicitly. They are dated from the notebooks in which they appear.[48] These poems are less sedate than most poetry of conjugal love. One actually feels that, like the Parkhursts, they had fun. As well, he prefaced her *Poems and Fancies* with a ridiculously complimentary poem which begins:

> Your New-borne, sublime Fancies, and such store,
> May make our Poets blush, and write no more.[49]

With a confidence unusual in women in that age, she accepted it, and it was printed opposite her title-page. Margaret Cavendish died in 1673, William in 1676, and from then until 1715 I found no poem of conjugal love addressed to a wife.

Compared with men, women in the seventeenth century wrote very little indeed. Their published writings never reached as high as 2 per cent of the total output, but when it came to poems of conjugal love their output was larger than men's. Altogether five wives wrote twenty poems, whilst six or seven men wrote half that number. No doubt more by both men and women await discovery, but the very high proportion of wives' poems to that of husbands' in relation to their total output is unlikely to be seriously altered.

The reason women published so little was complex, as Crawford has shown.[50] The high level of illiteracy was one factor, as were social attitudes. For one thing, silence was seen as a virtue in women, and to write was to unsex oneself.[51] However, devotion to one's husband was also a wifely virtue, and to express it seems to have been seen as adequate reason for infringing the rule of silence. It would seem even that the presence of poems of conjugal love in a corpus of work was a sort of guarantee of virtue. Women's poems of conjugal love appeared first in mid-century, though not necessarily published then. Major female poets who were married wrote them. Their male counterparts did not.

Let us turn to the wives and their poems. Anne Bradstreet wrote nine, Anne Finch, Countess of Winchilsea, six (some perhaps in the eighteenth century), Katharine Philips three, the Hon. Gertrude Thimelby and Margaret Cavendish, Duchess of Newcastle, at least one (their whole works have not been examined).

Both the Puritan Anne Bradstreet and the Catholic Gertrude Thimelby wrote poems of unclouded wifely devotion. Anne Bradstreet saw herself in biblical terms as 'flesh of thy flesh, bone of thy bone'.[52] She wrote in poems grieving at her husband's frequent absence, for his journeys took him on lengthy and dangerous journeys from America to England, or through sparsely settled colonial America. Gertrude Thimelby wrote of a marriage in which 'No will is known 'till the other's mind.'[53] All this was highly acceptable. Katharine Philips compared herself and her husband in one poem to two watches keeping time:

> Now as in watches, though we do not know
> When the hand moves, we find it still doth go:
> So I, by secret sympathy inclin'd,
> Will absent meet, and understand thy mind.[54]

However, if her husband might be the 'Guardian' of her heart, as she put it, they differed politically. She was a Royalist, he a Parliamentarian. In 'To Antenor on a Paper of mine which J.J. threatens to publish', she declares indignantly, 'Must then my crimes become thy scandal too?':

> My love and life I must confess are thine,
> But not my errors, they are only mine,
> And if my faults must be for thine allow'd,
> It will be hard to dissipate the cloud:
> For Eve's rebellion did not Adam blast,
> Until himself forbidden fruit did taste.[55]

Though it was a poem of wifely devotion it denied the current view of the unity of husband and wife which had been expressed early in the century by Lady Elizabeth Carew, in her play *The Tragedie of Mariam, the faire queene of Jewry*. Here the chorus asks rhetorically:

> When to their Husbands they themselues doe bind,
> Doe they not wholy giue themselues away?
> Or giue they but their body not their mind,
> Reseruing that though best, for others pray?[56]

For Margaret Cavendish and Anne Finch, the question of different points of view did not arise, for both retreated with their husbands from the wider world, husband and wife united in their disapproval.[57] We have seen already how Margaret and William Cavendish lived in retirement from the Restoration court. Anne Finch and her husband lived in a similar internal exile. Anne Finch had been one of Mary of Modena's maids of honour, and, from loyalty to her, retired to the country on the accession of William and Mary. Here they lived a quiet, studious life with congenial friends and relatives.[58] In this self-made world, isolated from contemporary attitudes and expectations, like the Cavendishes they developed a marriage of great personal affection and intimacy. Anne Finch was the only wife whose poems of conjugal love were written between 1676 and 1715. If more are to be found it will probably be amongst those living out of the fashionable world of that period.

In a somewhat similar way persecution and exile probably affected dissident groups from the Marian exiles to the Quakers. The letters and Latin poems of Mary Mollineux, the Quaker, written for her husband in gaol, may reflect her affection, but the poems are no more poems of conjugal love than is 'Fight the good fight'.[59] If we were to include them simply because they were made for his benefit we might as well include an apple pie made for a husband's birthday dinner.

The reaction against marriage

The silence of these years was not fortuitous. In this period women mounted an attack on marriage and the double standard. It was slow to come to a head. Discontent may be seen in Katharine Philips in the 1650s or early 1660s; the focus is not yet very sharp. In 'An Answer to another persuading a Lady to Marriage', she compares the position of the marriageable girl, extravagantly courted, with that of the married woman:

> She is a publick deity,
> And were't not very odd
> She should depose herself to be
> A petty household god?[60]

To 'Alexis in Answer to his Poem against Fruition', Aphra Behn inveighed against the libertinism which sought only conquest and saw nothing but tediousness in lasting relations.[61] Mary Astell presented the case most cogently in *Some Reflections on Marriage* which appeared in 1700. Anti-marriage poems appeared. Lady Mary Chudleigh wrote:

> Wife and servant are the same,
> But only differ in the name:
> For when that fatal knot is tied,
> Which nothing, nothing can divide,
> When she the word *Obey* has said,
> And man by law supreme has made,
> Then all that's kind is laid aside,
> And nothing left but state and pride . . .
> Then shun, oh shun that wretched state,
> And all the fawning flatt'rers hate.
> Value yourselves, and men despise:
> You must be proud, if you'll be wise.[62]

Sarah Fyge Egerton wrote in much the same vein in 'The Emulation'.[63] Even the happily married Anne Finch protested against the double standard in 'The Unequal fetters':

> Mariage does but slightly tye Men
> Whilst close Pris'ners we remain,
> They the larger Slaves of Hymen
> Still are begging Love again
> At the full length of their chain.[64]

This dissatisfaction with marriage was not purely literary. It was a general mood. In 1673 a contemporary observer noted 'there being almost all over England, a spirit of madness running abroad, and possessing men against marrying, choosing rather to have mistresses'.[65] Celibacy was seen as an option. In the 1690s the Kemeys sisters established a 'kind of female nunnery' in Somerset;[66] others were mooted; Mary Astell wrote her *Serious Proposal to the Ladies* supporting a scheme taking women's education seriously.

The age of marriage rose. Few good poets married, and the number of men and women generally who never married had risen during the seventeenth century.[67] The word spinster took on its present meaning.[68] By the mid-eighteenth century, however, the number of those never marrying fell to a low level.[69]

The eighteenth century

The men who wrote poems of conjugal love in the eighteenth century were very different in education and social standing from those of the sixteenth century. Four out of six of the earlier group were educated at Oxford or Cambridge; in the later period, only three out of thirteen are known to have studied there. They were overwhelmingly middle class, and only one was an aristocrat. In the earlier period all had some court connection, though they were not necessarily of aristocratic birth. In both groups some were clerics, but whilst in the sixteenth century the clerics were bishops, none was so in the later period. Many of the poets belonged to the common ground of religion where moderate Anglicanism and early nonconformity met.[70]

Their poems were all more or less a reaction to the attitudes of the preceding years. For some the reaction was simply to re-iterate the authoritarianism so many of the anti-marriage poems had attacked, presumably on the grounds that 'what I say three times is true'. At the other extreme was a small group of poems written by husbands celebrating their wives' achievements. Both these reactions appear in 1715. The cult of sensibility was a somewhat later response, repudiating the hard-nosed cynicism of the bleak years, but not necessarily its assumption of authoritarianism. Men invaded what had formerly been seen as women's province. Womanish feelings were cultivated, and men discovered domesticity. All too often it was the reiteration of patriarchy in disguise, the annexing of the realm formerly given over to women. Let us treat them in order.

The first type was foreshadowed by Samuel Wesley the elder, the father of John Wesley. In a poem which does not fall strictly within our definition of a poem of conjugal love, Samuel Wesley described the qualities of the good wife, and her wifely obedience in his account of the relationship of the Virgin Mary and Joseph.

> Nor did I for her *Care ungrateful* prove,
> But only us'd my *Pow'r* to show my *Love.*
> What e'er she *askt* I gave, without *reproach* or *grudg*[e],
> For still she Reason askt – *and I was Judg*[e].[71]

In 1715 two poems of conjugal love broke the long silence, and Samuel Wesley, the younger, the eldest son of Samuel and Susanna Wesley, and the brother of John Wesley, was the author of one of them. Altogether he wrote ten poems to his wife.[72] Whilst full of love and admiration, they insist, almost to the point of insult, that his love is based not on passing beauty but on moral worth, and that worth was highly domestic. He exhibits a patriarchalism like his father's. In a poem, 'The December day',[73] composed for her birthday, he wrote:

> No silks unpaid-for rustle here,
> No foreign frippery we import;
> No velvets or brocades appear;
> But (what few birthdays see at court)
> Friendship unbought and love display
> Their beams on this December day.
> Not sharp and ever-during pain
> Her cheerful constancy can move
> From toil incessant to refrain,
> To slight her duty or her love . . .

These rather oppressive poems do not seem to have been entirely appreciated. Like his father, Samuel saw the man as 'judge', and nowhere more than in his relations with his sister Mehetabel Wright.

Mehetabel, or Hetty, had been married off, after a youthful indiscretion, to a plumber and glazier, William Wright. The marriage was unsuited to a girl of great ability and considerable education, and they did not get on.[74] In a pathetic poem to him she implores

> Tell me *why* I do not please.

She has tried to please him, and to hide her grief:

> I oft have wiped these watchful eyes,
> Concealed my cares, and curbed my sighs,
> In spite of grief, to let thee see
> I wore an endless smile for thee.[75]

Matters did not improve, and her 'Wedlock: a satire' is very bitter,[76] and brought a stinging rejoinder from Samuel, ending:

> Repent, renounce all wicked wit:
> Think not your pride I bear too hard on.
> So may the world your flights forget,
> And God forgive, and Willy pardon.[77]

Patriarchy was ordained by God. She must submit.

Hetty Wright did not die as Virginia Woolf imagined Shakespeare's sister Judith, whom she saw committing suicide and being buried at a crossroads. Rather, her life was, according to the epitaph she wrote for herself, 'a living death, a long despair'.[78] The work of the two Samuel Wesleys represents an Evangelical reaction to the onslaught on marriage.

The other poem written in 1715 was the work of Thomas Rowe and celebrated his wife's achievement. Thomas and his wife Elizabeth Rowe were writers, as united in their interests as the Cavendishes or the Finches. Both wrote on literary and religious subjects. Both came from nonconformist backgrounds but they were on friendly terms with both Bishop Ken and the Thynnes of Longleat, who also knew the Finches well.[79] Thomas Rowe died in 1715, and before his death wrote a poem to his much-admired wife who was his elder by 15 years. In this he saw himself watching over her from the lower reaches of heaven

195

during the remainder of her life, then ascending to God, the fount of their happiness, to sing the songs she taught him.[80] His wife wrote two elegies on his death, considered at the time of 'infinite pathos'.

Aaron Hill and Barton Booth also admired their wives' abilities. Both men had connections with the stage, and their poems appeared in the 1720s and 1730s. Aaron Hill, who was a manager, dramatist, poet, and projector, married a woman known to us only as 'Miranda'. Her own poems in manuscript were praised by Richard Savage.[81] Hill wrote two short poems to her during her life, one accompanying Locke's *Treatise on Education* for use in bringing up their children. His finest poem, however, deals with revisiting an inn after her death and recalling past happiness.[82] Barton Booth, the actor-manager, married an actress, reputed to have been mistress to the Duke of Marlborough. He wrote two poems to her, one expressing his good fortune at having married her, the other, 'On Myra dancing', a tribute to her as a dancer. At the end of the eighteenth century the politician James Charles Foxe turned a few lines for his wife, the actress, formerly his mistress, Mrs Armstead.[83] These however express only gratitude for the happiness she has brought him.

We now come to poems which show the influence of the cult of sensibility. As in the seventeenth century, eighteenth-century husbands found it easier to cope with dead wives in verse than living ones. The poet whose verse had the greatest impact was George Lyttleton, later Lord Lyttleton. He had written poems to his wife Lucy in courtship, and also one joyful one after marriage; but the Monody which he wrote when, after a short marriage, she died in childbirth, caught the mood of the period.[84] The poem appeared in 1747, at the time when the cult of sensibility was about to find a name.[85] In 1768, when the wives of John Langhorne, John Scott of Amwell, and Cuthbert Shaw all died in childbirth, each wrote a Monody for which Lyttleton's was the model.[86]

Most of the remaining poems deal with domestic virtues in pedestrian verse. Nathaniel Cotton, physician and friend of Cowper, wrote of domestic happiness in 'The Fireside', and of watching together children growing up.[87] The favourite form of poem was the rather formal birthday, or New Year poem, or one on a wedding anniversary. Samuel Bishop wrote nineteen for his wife's birthday, which was also their wedding anniversary.[88]

The poems accompanied gifts, whose appropriateness was always linked to compliments to her appearance, taste, or virtues. Thus, of a paste buckle:

> On Merit's ground proud diamonds go,
> As we should say – 'Thus we bestow!'
> Paste comes to you on terms less vain,
> Not to bring beauty, but to gain.[89]

In the eighteenth century the literary output of women was impressive. Writing was opening up as a profession for women. Much of it took the form of highly romantic novels where the cult of sensibility flourished. Yet despite particularly strenuous efforts, comparatively few poems of conjugal love by wives were found. Six, including Hetty Wright, wrote poems to their husbands. It is as if they no longer needed such poems to establish their respectability, and, as professionals, found the presence of family an embarrassment – like old-fashioned dons taking family in to lunch in a modern college.

The earliest and most prolific was Judith Madan, aunt to William Cowper, and correspondent of Pope. It was a love marriage, and her husband, a soldier, was often absent on service. A large body of their letters exist. The poems extend from just after her marriage at the end of 1723 to 1734. They express an ardent devotion, but remain largely unpublished.[90]

On the whole though the poems expressed less romantic feeling than the novels of the period. Mrs Tonnereau – so far unidentified – wrote of moving house,[91] Mrs Barbauld begged her husband to take a break from his books,[92] a subject on which Anne Finch had also written; Mrs Darwall wrote one poem on a wedding anniversary, another at her husband's request, on connubial love.[93] Mrs Cobbold wrote a valentine to her elderly husband, mocking current notions of love poetry:

> A Wife send a Valentine! Lord, what a whim!
> And then of all people to send it to him![94]

Only Elizabeth Hands, formerly a housemaid, wrote a poem of any depth of feeling, and this poem's inclusion is a bit of a cheat because it is more to God than to her husband. 'On the Author's Lying-in, August, 1785' is a poem of thanksgiving. It is radiant with a joy of achievement not found elsewhere.

> I live! my God be prais'd, I live,
> And do most thankfully receive,
> The bounty of my life:
> I live still longer to improve,
> The fondest husband's tender love,
> To the most happy wife.
>
> I live within my arms to clasp,
> My infant with endearing grasp,
> And Feel my fondness grow.[95]

The poem would have delighted Dorothy McLaren with its fresh and spontaneous feeling. It would have been seen as further proof of the difference between the attitude of ordinary working women to their infants and that of the well-to-do. The rest of the poets and their spouses were from higher levels of society. Here, though, we may find some clues to the behaviour of a Mary Verney. In the poems of Sir John Harington and Mary Carey and her husband we find that when their babies died the wives' feelings were to be repressed in conformity with the authority of the husband or of God himself. They must, like Hetty Wright, wear an endless smile.

Conclusion

There are few poems of conjugal love, and none are great poetry. Traditional poetry reinforced the workings of the double standard and the doctrine of separate spheres for men and women. These supplied men with a language for the free expression of emotion without marriage, but not within. Women, breaking silence late, were free to express wifely devotion, but traditional poetry of love provided no models, and they were denied the rich resonances of that poetry.

Men attempted to write poetry of conjugal love when they sought to rework the basis of marriage both in the sixteenth century (when wives had yet to find their voice), and in the eighteenth century, when women had started to criticize marriage. When wives started to write poems of conjugal love, though their poems were full of wifely devotion, they validated their subversive actions, for to write, and write for publication, was to flout womanly modesty.

The later part of the seventeenth century and the early-eighteenth century were inimical to the expression of conjugal love in poetry. Only aristocrats living in private worlds of their own creation wrote such poems. Between 1676 and 1715 there were no poems by men, and Anne Finch was the sole woman to find a voice.

This silence is an aspect of the flight from marriage which marked this period. Evidence is mounting to show that Stone was wrong in seeing this period as marked by the development of closer and warmer conjugal relations.[96] Woman's criticisms of marriage were an influential reaction to the bleakness of current attitudes to marriage. Mary Astell was not a woman born out of her time. Yet the celebration of domestic virtues which marked the second half of the eighteenth century was in part a reassertion of patriarchal values in the face of criticism by women.

Acknowledgements

I would like to thank the following for discussing this chapter, suggesting sources, or answering queries: Roger Lonsdale, Helen Philips, Patricia Crawford, Norman Davis, Nigel Smith, Alan Brissenden, and Valerie Fildes. Any mistakes are mine.

Notes

1. D. McLaren, 'Marital fertility and lactation 1570–1720', in M. Prior (ed.), *Women in English Society 1500–1800* (London, 1985), 26.

2. L. Martines, *Society and History in English Renaissance Verse* (Oxford, 1987), vii.

3. J. S. Cockburn, 'Early modern assize records as historical evidence', *J. Soc. Arch.*, 5 (1975), 215–31.

4. M. Crum (ed.), *First-line Index of English Poetry, 1500–1800, in Manuscripts of the Bodleian Library, Oxford* (2 vols, Oxford, 1969). Only poems which appeared to deal with conjugal love in the first line could be identified using this index.

5. J. Todd, *A Biographical Dictionary of British and American Women Writers 1660–1800* (London, 1984).

6. R. A. Houlbrooke, *The English Family 1450–1700* (London, 1984), 105; Lawrence Stone, *The Family, Sex and Marriage in England 1500–1800* (London, 1977), 104.

7. K. V. Thomas, 'The double standard', *J. Hist. Ideas*, 20 (1959). The length of the period from puberty to marriage may well explain

the amount of poetry written before marriage, but it does not in itself explain the falling away afterwards: J. R. Gillis, *For Better, For Worse* (New York and Oxford, 1985), 11–83: S. H. Mendelson, 'Debate: "The weightiest business": marriage in an upper-gentry family in seventeenth-century England', *P & P*, 85 (1979), 128–35.

8. P. Crawford, 'Women's published writings 1600–1700', in Prior (ed.), *Women in English Society*, 214–15.

9. Love poems by a single woman could only appear pseudonymously. This was the case with Ephelia's *Female Poems on Several Occasions* (London, 1679).

10. *D.N.B.*

11. M. E. Lamb, 'The Cooke sisters' attitudes towards learned women', in M. P. Hannay (ed.), *Silent but for the Word: Tudor Women as Patrons, Translators, and Writers of Religious Works* (Kent, Ohio, 1985), 119–20.

12. A. R. Benham and R. M. Padelford, 'The songs of Rawlinson MS. C.813', *Anglia* 31 (1908), 309–10, 347–50.

13. H. E. Rollins (ed.), *Tottel's Miscellany 1557–1587* (2 vols, Cambridge, Mass., 1965), vol. 1, 18–19; R. Hughey (ed.), *The Arundel Harington Manuscript of Tudor Poetry* (2 vols, Columbus, Ohio, 1960), vol. 1, 132; vol. 2 110–13.

14. W. Shakespeare, *Macbeth*, Act 4, sc. 3.

15. On Haddon, Parkhurst, and Bacon, see *D.N.B.*

16. Lamb, 'Cooke sisters', 107–25.

17. *D.N.B.*, subsumed under Sir John Harington.

18. CCCC, MS. 168.

19. N. E. McClure (ed.), *The Letters and Epigrams of Sir John Harington* (Philadelphia, 1930), 4–7.

20. Hughey, *Arundel Harington Manuscript* vol. 1, 95–6, vol. 2, 30–3.

21. J. Parkhurst, *Ludicra siue epigrammata iuuenilia* (London, 1573), 141. I am grateful to Dr J. F. Matthews for this translation.

22. Sir N. Bacon, *The Recreations of His Age* (Oxford, 1919), 26–8.

23. R. I. Page, 'Matthew Parker's copy of "Prosper his meditation with his wife"', *Trans. Camb. Bibliog. Soc.*, 8 (1983), 342–9.

24. 'Matthew Parker's New Year's Gift to his Wife', listed in T. Kerslake, *Catalogue of Literary Curiosities Including the Remains of an Ancient Library Originally Belonging to Doctor William Turner* (Bristol, n.d.).

25. B. Travitsky, *The Paradise of Women: Writings of English Women of the Renaissance* (Connecticut and London, 1981), 192–3.

26. Travitsky, *Paradise of Women*, 23–4.

27. W. F. Carter, *The Records of King Edward's School, Birmingham*, vol. 1, (1924), xlvii; P.R.O., STAC 5 B11/66; STAC 5 B38/10; PROB 11/60/42; P. Collinson, 'The role of women in the English Reformation illustrated by the life and friendship of Anne Locke', *Stud. Church Hist.*, 2 (1965), 258–72.

28. Hughey, *Arundel Harington Manuscript*, 27–8, 63–7.

29. Sir J. Harington, *A Briefe View of the Church of England as It Stood in Q. Elizabeths and King James His Reigne to the Yeere 1608*, (ed.), J. Chetwind (London, 1653), 1–4, 27–8, 63–4, 110–21; M. Prior,

'Reviled and crucified marriages: the position of the Tudor bishops' wives', in Prior, *Women in English Society*, 134–5.

30. F. A. Yates, *Astraea: The Imperial Theme in the Sixteenth Century* (London, 1985), 29–110.

31. McClure, *Letters and Epigrams*, 96–8.

32. P. Laslett, *Family Life and Illicit Love in Earlier Generations* (Cambridge, 1977), 111–20. This would presuppose a remarkable ability to grasp the situation of the nation. However, this was as much one of Elizabeth's characteristics as its absence was one of Mary's. There is room for a feminist life of Elizabeth and her ability to control a court in which all power, save hers, was masculine.

33. McClure, *Letters and Epigrams*, 304.

34. Ibid., 307.

35. Ibid., 254.

36. Ibid., 239.

37. A. J. Smith, 'The failure of love: love lyrics after Donne', in *Metaphysical Poetry*, ed. M. Bradbury and D. J. Palmer (New York, 1970), 41–71; McClure, *Letters and Epigrams*, 28–34.

38. K. Davies, 'Continuity and change in literary advice on marriage', in R. B. Outhwaite (ed.), *Marriage and Society* (London, 1981), 63–6.

39. None of the poems of conjugal love can compare with, for instance, Henry King's 'Exequy', or Milton's 'Methought I saw my late espoused Saint'.

40. BodL, MS Malone 18, p. 90.

41. Sir H. Grierson (ed.), *The Poems of John Donne* (London 1933), xix; P. Cruttwell, 'The love poetry of John Donne: Pedantique Weedes or Fresh Invention', in Bradbury and Palmer, *Metaphysical Poetry*, 22–3.

42. BodL, MS Rawl. poet. 148 fol. 107.

43. H. J. C. Grierson and G. Bullough, *The Oxford Book of Seventeenth Century Verse*, (London, 1934), 585–6.

44. K. Walker (ed.), *The Poems of John Wilmot, Earl of Rochester* (Oxford, 1984).

45. BodL, MS Rawl. D. 1308, p. 177.

46. Ibid., 179, 215–22.

47. S. H. Mendelson, *The Mental World of Stuart Women: Three Studies* (Brighton, 1987), 12–61.

48. D. Grant (ed.), *The Phanseys of William Cavendish Marquis of Newcastle Addressed to Margaret Lucas and Her Letters in Reply* (London, 1956), xxix–xxxii, 91–4.

49. M. Cavendish, Duchess of Newcastle, *Poems and Fancies* (London, 1653).

50. Crawford, 'Women's published writings', 214–17.

51. Ibid., 219–20.

52. J. R. McElrath Jr and A. P. Robb (eds), *The Complete Works of Anne Bradstreet* (Boston, 1981), 181.

53. A. Dyce, *Specimens of British Poetesses* (London, 1827), 443–4.

54. G. Sainsbury (ed.), *Minor Poets of the Caroline Period* (3 vols, Oxford, 1905–21), vol. 1, 551–2.

55. Ibid., vol. 1, 535.

56. E. C. [Lady Elizabeth Carey], *The Tragedie of Mariam, the Faire Queene of Jewry* (Oxford, 1914), lines 1237–40.

57. Cf. Smith, 'Failure of love', 70–1.

58. M. Reynolds (ed.), *The Poems of Anne Countess of Winchilsea* (Chicago, 1903), xxiii–xxix.

59. For the attitudes of John Parkhurst and his wife see R. A. Houlbrooke (ed.), *The Letter Book of John Parkhurst, Bishop of Norwich 1571–5*, (Norwich, 1974 and 1975), 71, 80, 84, 143.

60. L. Bernikow (ed.), *The World Split Open* (London, 1979), 63.

61. Ibid., 71.

62. R. Lonsdale (ed.), *The New Oxford Book of Eighteenth Century Verse* (Oxford, 1984), 36.

63. Ibid., 37.

64. Reynolds, *Countess of Winchilsea*, 150–9.

65. J. Thirsk and J. P. Cooper (eds), *Seventeenth-century Economic Documents* (Oxford, 1972), 742; Outhwaite, 'Introduction', in Outhwaite (ed.), *Marriage and Society*, 12–13.

66. B. Hill, 'A refuge from men: the idea of a Protestant nunnery', *P & P* 117 (1987), 107–130.

67. E. A. Wrigley and R. S. Schofield *The Population History of England 1541–1871* (London, 1981), 259–65. Figures are not yet definitive.

68. Widows describing themselves as spinsters in their wills can still be found until the 1670s.

69. Wrigley and Schofield, *Population History*, 259–65.

70. Based on *D.N.B.*

71. S. Wesley, *The Life of Our Blessed Lord and Saviour Jesus Christ* (London, 1693), 40.

72. S. Wesley, jun., *Poems on Several Occasions*, ed. J. Nichols (London, 1862).

73. Ibid., 232–3.

74. A. Clarke, *Memoirs of the Wesley Family Collected Principally from Original Documents* (London, 1823), 486–91.

75. Ibid., 491–3.

76. Lonsdale, *New Oxford Book of Eighteenth Century Verse*, 165.

77. Wesley, *Poems*, 554–6.

78. Clarke, *Memoirs of the Wesley Family*, 503–4.

79. *D.N.B.*; Thomas Rowe is subsumed under his wife Elizabeth Rowe; Reynolds, *Poems of Anne Countess of Winchilsea*, xxxix–xl. There is no evidence that the Rowes and Finches were close friends though. Any influence must have been through mutual friends.

80. T. Rowe (ed.), *The Miscellaneous Works of Mrs Elizabeth Rowe*, to which are added 'Poems on several occasions', by Thomas Rowe (2 vols, London, 1739), vol. 2, 297–302.

81. *The Poetical Works of Aaron Hill*, in R. Anderson, M.D. (ed.), *A Complete Edition of the Poets of Great Britain* (14 vols, London, 1794), vol. 8. 656.

82. *Poetical Works of Aaron Hill,* 'To Miranda after marriage with Mr Lock's Treatise on Education', 697; 'Alone at an inn at Southampton', ibid., 696.

83. P. H. Highfill, Jr., K. A. Burnim, and E. A. Langhans, *A Biographical Dictionary of Actors, Actresses etc. in London 1660–1800* (12 vols, Carbondale and Edwardsville, Illinois, 1973–87), vol. 2, 222–8, for the Booths; ibid., vol. 1, 98 for Mrs Armstead and Foxe.

84. *The Poetical Works of George Lyttelton,* in Anderson (ed.), *Complete Poets,* vol. 10. 244, 262–5. Smollett composed a parody on it.

85. Janet Todd, *Sensibility, an Introduction* (London, 1986), 6–9.

86. *The Poetical Works of John Langhorne, M.D.* in Anderson (ed.) *Complete Poets,* vol. 11, 213–14, 249; *The Poetical Works of John Scott esq,* in Anderson (ed.) *Complete Poets,* vol. 11. 720, 735–6; C. Shaw, *Monody to the Memory of a Young Lady Who Died in Child-bed* (3rd edn, London, 1770). This last was dedicated to Lord Lyttelton.

87. *The Poetical Works of Nathaniel Cotton,* in Anderson (ed.), *Complete Poets,* vol. 11, 1139–40.

88. S. Bishop, *Poetical Works* (2nd edn, 2 vols, London, 1800), vol. 2, 3–71.

89. Ibid., vol. 2, 14.

90. F. Madan, *The Madan Family* (Oxford, 1933), 85–91.

91. BodL, MS Eng. poet.e.28, pp. 340–1.

92. C. Bax and M. Steward (eds), *The Distaff Muse* (London, 1949), 36–7.

93. M. Darwall, *Poems on Several Occasions* (2 vols, Walsall, 1794), vol. 2, 55–7, 123–4.

94. E. Cobbold, *Poems with a Memoir of the Author* (Ipswich, 1835), 7–8.

95. E. Hands, *The Death of Ammon, a Poem, with an Appendix Containing Pastorals, and Other Poetical Pieces* (Coventry, 1789), 123–4.

96. Stone, *The Family, Sex and Marriage,* 361–2.

Bibliography

The works listed are restricted to those concerned with English motherhood prior to the nineteenth century. More general works are included only where they contain a significant amount of information pertaining to England in this period.

Pregnancy and childbirth

Boucé, P. -G. (1987) 'Imagination, pregnant women, and monsters in eighteenth-century England and France', in G. S. Rousseau and R. Porter (eds) *Sexual Underworlds of the Enlightenment*, Manchester, 86–100.

Carter, J. and Duriez, T. (1986) *With Child. Birth through the Ages*, Edinburgh.

Crawford, P. (1978) 'Attitudes to pregnancy from a woman's spiritual diary, 1687–8', *Loc. Popul. Stud.* 21: 43–5.

Eshleman, M. K. (1975) 'Diet during pregnancy in the sixteenth and seventeenth centuries', *J. Hist. Med.* 30: 23–39.

Forbes, T. R. (1988) 'A jury of matrons', *Med. Hist.* 32: 23–33.

Fox, C. E. (1966) 'Pregnancy, childbirth and early infancy in Anglo-American culture, 1675–1830', Ph.D. dissertation, University of Pennsylvania, Univ. Microfilms 67/7838.

Graham, H. (1960) *The Mystery of Birth and the Customs that Surround It*, London.

Lewis, J. S. (1986) *In the Family Way. Childbearing in the British Aristocracy, 1760–1860*, New Brunswick.

Medvei, V. C. (1987) 'The illness and death of Mary Tudor', *J. Roy. Soc. Med.* 80: 766–70.

Pereira-Pennisi, D. (1987) 'Childbirth as depicted in British fiction of the period 1658–1768', *Hist. Nurs. Grp. Roy. Coll. Nurs. Bull.* 2: 8–16.

Riley, M. (1968) *Brought to Bed*, London.

Schnucker, R. V. (1974) 'The English Puritans and pregnancy, delivery and breastfeeding', *Hist. Childh. Quart.* 1: 637–58.

Sorel, N. C. (1984) *Ever Since Eve. Personal Reflections on Childbirth*, New York.

Wilson, A. (1985) 'Participant or patient? Seventeenth century childbirth from the mother's point of view', in R. Porter (ed.) *Patients and Practitioners. Lay Perceptions of Medicine in Pre-industrial Society*, Cambridge, 129–44.

——(forthcoming) *A Safe Deliverance: Ritual and Conflict in English Childbirth 1600–1750*, Cambridge.

Midwives, obstetrics, and gynaecology

Aveling, J. H. (1872) *English Midwives. Their History and Prospects*, London.

Boss, B. and Boss, J. (1983) 'Ignorant midwives – a further rejoinder', *Bull. Soc. Soc. Hist. Med.* 33: 71.

Crawford, P. (1981) 'Attitudes to menstruation in seventeenth-century England', *P & P* 91: 47–73.

Delaney, J., Lupton, M. J., and Toth, E. (1976) *The Curse. A Cultural History of Menstruation*, New York (rev. edn, Champaign, Illinois, 1988).

Dewhurst, J. (1980) *Royal Confinements: A Gynaecological History of Britain's Royal Family*, London.

——(1984) 'The alleged miscarriages of Catherine of Aragon and Anne Boleyn', *Med. Hist.* 28: 49–56.

——(1985) 'Royal obstetrics of early England', *Mat. Child Hlth*, 10: 216–18, 245–7, 272–4, 299–302, 339–40.

Donnison, J. (1977) *Midwives and Medical Men. A History of Inter-professional Rivalries and Women's Rights*, London (2nd edn, 1988).

Eccles, A. (1977) 'Obstetrics in the 17th and 18th centuries and its implications for maternal and infant mortality', *Bull. Soc. Soc. Hist. Med.* 20: 8–11.

——(1982) *Obstetrics and Gynaecology in Tudor and Stuart England*, London.

Forbes, T. (1962) 'Midwifery and witchcraft', *J. Hist. Med.* 17: 265–83.

——(1966) *The Midwife and the Witch*, New Haven.

——(1971) 'The regulation of English midwives in the eighteenth and nineteenth centuries', *Med. Hist.* 15: 352–62.

Harley, D. N. (1981) 'Ignorant midwives – a persistent stereotype', *Bull. Soc. Soc. Hist. Med.* 28: 6–9.

Jordanova, L. J. (1985) 'Gender, Generation and science: William Hunter's obstetrical atlas', in W. F. Bynum and R. Porter (eds) *William Hunter and the Eighteenth-century Medical World*, Cambridge, 385–412.

Lane, J. (1987) 'A provincial surgeon and his obstetric practice: Thomas W. Jones of Henley-in-Arden, 1764–1846', *Med. Hist.* 31: 333–48.

McLaren, A. (1981) '"Barrenness against nature": recourse to abortion in pre-industrial England', *J. Sex Res.* 17.

——(1985) 'The pleasures of procreation: traditional and biomedical theories of conception', in W. F. Bynum and R. Porter (eds) *William Hunter and the Eighteenth-century Medical World*, Cambridge, 323–41.

McLaren, D. (1979) 'Emmenologia: a curse or a blessing?', *Bull. Soc. Soc. Hist. Med.* 25: 65–7.

Oakley, A. (1984) *The Captured Womb. A History of the Medical Care of Pregnant Women*, Oxford.

Peckham, C. H. (1935) 'A brief history of puerperal infection', *Bull. Hist. Med.* 3: 187–212.

Porter, R. (1987) '"The secrets of generation display'd": *Aristotle's Masterpiece* in eighteenth-century England', in R. P. Maccubbin (ed.) *'Tis Nature's Fault. Unauthorised Sexuality during the Enlightenment*, Cambridge, 7–21.

Rowland, B. (ed.) (1981) *The Medieval Woman's Guide to Health: The First English Gynaecological Handbook*, London.

Schnorrenberg, B. B. (1981) 'Is childbirth any place for a woman? The decline of midwifery in eighteenth-century England', *Stud. Eighteenth-Cent. Cult.* 10: 393–408.

Shorter, E. (1983) *A History of Women's Bodies*, London.

——(1985) 'The management of normal deliveries and the generation of William Hunter', in W. F. Bynum and R. Porter (eds) *William Hunter and the Eighteenth-century Medical World*, Cambridge, 371–83.

Smith, H. (1976) 'Gynaecology and ideology in seventeenth century England', in B. Carroll (ed.) *Liberating Women's History*, Urbana, 97–114.

Speert, H. (1973) *Iconographia Gyniatrica. A Pictorial History of Gynecology and Obstetrics*, Philadelphia.

Spencer, H. R. (1927) *The History of British Midwifery from 1650 to 1800*, London.

Stark, J. N. (1908) 'An obstetric diary of William Hunter', *Glasg. Med. J.* 70: 167–77, 241–56, 338–56.

Towler, J. and Bramall, J. (1986) *Midwives in History and Society*, London.

Versluysen, M. C. (1981) 'Midwives, medical men and "Poor women labouring of child": lying-in hospitals in eighteenth-century London', in H. Roberts (ed.) *Women, Health and Reproduction*, London, 18–49.

Wilson, A. (1983) 'Ignorant midwives – a rejoinder', *Bull. Soc. Soc. Hist. Med.* 32: 46–9.

——(1985) 'William Hunter and the varieties of man-midwifery', in W. F. Bynum and R. Porter (eds) *William Hunter and the Eighteenth-century Medical World*, Cambridge, 343–70.

Maternal mortality

Loudon, I. (1986) 'Deaths in childbed from the eighteenth century to 1935', *Med. Hist.* 30: 1–41.

——(1991) *Obstetric Care and Maternal Mortality 1700–1900*, Oxford.

Schofield, R. (1986) 'Did the mothers really die? Three centuries of maternal mortality in "The world we have lost"', in L. Bonfield, R. Smith, and K. Wrightson (eds) *The World We Have Gained*, Oxford, 231–60.

Willmott Dobbie, B. M. (1982) 'An attempt to estimate the true rate of maternal mortality, sixteenth to eighteenth centuries', *Med. Hist.* 26: 79–90.

Breastfeeding, fertility, and birth control

Biller, P. P. A. (1982) 'Birth-control in the west in the thirteenth and fourteenth centuries', *P & P* 94: 3–26.

Fildes, V. A. (1986) *Breasts, Bottles and Babies. A History of Infant Feeding*, Edinburgh.

——(1987) 'Breastfeeding in Tudor and Stuart England', *Mid. Chron.* 100: 157–60.

——(1988) 'Historical changes in patterns of breastfeeding', in S. Teper, P. Diggory, and D. M. Potts (eds) *Natural Human Fertility. Social and Biological Determinants*, Basingstoke and London, 118–29.

Finlay, R. A. P. (1979) 'Population and fertility in London 1580–1650', *J. Fam. Hist.* 4: 26–38.

——(1981) *Population and Metropolis. The Demography of London 1580–1650*, Cambridge.

McLaren A. (1984) *Reproductive Rituals: The Perception of Fertility in England from the Sixteenth Century to the Nineteenth Century*, London.

McLaren, D. (1978) 'Fertility, infant mortality and breastfeeding in the seventeenth century', *Med. Hist.* 22: 378–96.

——(1979) 'Nature's contraceptive. Wet nursing and prolonged lactation: the case of Chesham, Buckinghamshire 1578–1601', *Med. Hist.* 23: 426–41.

——(1985) 'Marital fertility and lactation 1570–1720', in M. Prior (ed.) *Women in English Society 1500–1800*, London, 22–53.

Ranum, O. and Ranum, P. (eds) (1972) *Popular Attitudes towards Birth Control in Pre-industrial France and England*, New York.

Schnucker, R. V. (1974) 'The English Puritans and pregnancy, delivery and breastfeeding', *Hist. Childh. Quart.* 1: 637–58.

——(1975) 'Elizabethan birth control and Puritan attitudes', *J. Interdisc. Hist.* 5: 655–67.

Taylor, J. (1969) 'The duty of nursing children', in *The Nursing Mother. Historical Insights from Art and Theology*, repr. from *Child and Fam.* 8: 19–29.

Varenkov, H. (1969) 'The nursing madonna: a cultural motif', in *The Nursing Mother. Historical Insights from Art and Theology*, repr. from *Child & Fam.* 8: 8–18.

Wilson, C. (1982) 'Marital fertility in pre-industrial England, 1550–1840', unpub. Ph.D. thesis, University of Cambridge.

——(1984) 'Natural fertility in pre-industrial England, 1600–1799', *Popul. Stud.* 38: 225–40.

——(1986) 'The proximate determinants of marital fertility in England 1600–1799', in L. Bonfield, R. Smith, and K. Wrightson (eds) *The World We Have Gained*, Oxford, 203–30.

Wrigley, E. A. (1966) 'Family limitation in pre-industrial England', *Econ. Hist. Rev.*, 2nd series, 19: 82–109.

——(1978) 'Marital fertility in seventeenth-century Colyton: a note', *Econ. Hist. Rev.* 31: 429–36.

——(1981) 'Marriage, fertility and population growth in eighteenth-century England', in R. B. Outhwaite (ed.) *Marriage and Society*, London, 137–85.

Infant care

Bel Geddes, J. (1966) *Small World. A History of Baby Care from the Stone Age to the Spock Age*, London.

Caulfield, E. (1931) *The Infant Welfare Movement in the Eighteenth Century*, New York.

Crawford, P. (1986) '"The sucking child": adult attitudes to childcare in the first year of life in seventeenth-century England', *Cont. & Change* 1: 23–54.

Dick, D. (1987) *Yesterday's Babies. A History of Babycare*, London.

Fildes, V. A. (1980) 'Neonatal feeding practices and infant mortality in the 18th century', *J. Biosoc. Sci.* 12: 313–24.

——(1982) 'The age of weaning in Britain 1500–1800', *J. Biosoc. Sci* 14: 223–40.

——(1986) 'Infant care in Tudor and Stuart England', *Mid. Hlth Vis. Comm. Nurse* 22: 79–84.

——(1986) 'The early history of artificial feeding', *Mat. Child Hlth* 11: 222–7, 259–63.

——(1986) '"The English disease": infantile rickets and scurvy in pre-industrial England', in J. Cule and T. Turner (eds) *Child Care through the Centuries*, Cardiff, 121–34.

Rendle-Short, J. (1960) 'Infant management in the 18th century with special reference to the work of William Cadogan', *Bull. Hist. Med.* 34: 97–122.

Wilson, A. F. (1979) 'The enlightenment and infant care', *Bull. Soc. Soc. Hist. Med.* 25: 44–7.

Child care and child rearing

Bayne-Powell, R. (1939) *The English Child in the Eighteenth Century*, London.

Beekman, D. (1977) *The Mechanical Baby. A Popular History of the Theory and Practice of Child Raising*, New York.

Byman, S. (1978) 'Child raising and melancholia in Tudor England', *J. Psychohist.* 6: 67–92.

Carlton, C. (1986) *Royal Childhoods*, London.

Charlton, K. (1988) '"Not publike onely but also private and domesticall": mothers and familial education in pre-industrial England', *Hist. Educ.* 17: 1–20.

Cule, J. and Turner, T. (eds) (1986) *Child Care through the Centuries,* Cardiff.

De Mause, L. (ed.) (1976) *The History of Childhood,* London.

Gordon, E. C. (1986) 'Child health in the middle ages as seen in the miracles of five English saints, A.D. 1150–1220', *Bull. Hist. Med.,* 60: 502–22.

Gransden, A. (1972) 'Childhood and youth in medieval England', *Nott. Med. Stud.* 16: 3–19.

Hanawalt, B. (1977) 'Childrearing among the lower classes in late medieval England', *J. Interdisc. Hist.* 8: 1–22.

Hardyment, C. (1983) *Dream Babies. Child Care from Locke to Spock,* London.

Hughes, M. J. (1984) 'Child-rearing and social expectations in eighteenth-century England: the case of the Colliers of Hastings', in O. M. Brack (ed.) *Studies in Eighteenth-century Culture,* Madison, Wisconsin, 79–100.

Illick, J. E. (1976) 'Child-rearing in seventeenth-century England and America', in L. De Mause (ed.) *The History of Childhood,* London, 303–50.

Jewell, H. M. (1982) '"The bringing up of children in good learning and manners": a survey of secular and educational provision in the north of England, 1350–1550', *North. Hist.* 18: 1–25.

Johansson, S. R. (1987) 'Centuries of childhood/centuries of parenting: Phillippe Aries and the modernization of privileged infancy', *J. Fam. Hist.* 12: 343–65.

King-Hall, M. (1958) *The Story of the Nursery,* London.

Latham, J. (1974) *Happy Families. Growing up in the Eighteenth and Nineteenth Centuries,* London.

McCracken, G. (1983) 'The exchange of children in Tudor England: an anthropological phenomenon in historical context', *J. Fam. Hist.* 8: 303–13.

Orme, N. (1984) *From Childhood to Chivalry. The Education of the English Kings and Aristocracy, 1066–1530,* London.

Pelling, M. (1988) 'Child health as a social value in early modern England', *Soc. Hist. Med.* 1: 135–64.

Piercy, S. L. (1982) *The Cradle of Salvation: Children and Religion in Late Sixteenth and Early Seventeenth Century England,* Santa Barbara.

Pinchbeck, I. and Hewitt, M. (1969) *Children in English Society,* 2 vols, London.

Pollock, L. A. (1983) *Forgotten Children. Parent–child Relations from 1500 to 1900,* Cambridge.

——(1987) *A Lasting Relationship. Parents and Children over Three Centuries,* London.

——(forthcoming) '"Teach her to live under obedience": the making of women in the upper ranks of early modern England', *Cont. & Change.*

Radbill, S. X. (1974) 'Pediatrics', in A. G. Debus (ed.) *Medicine in Seventeenth-century England,* Los Angeles, 237–82.

Ruhrah, J. (1925) *Pediatrics of the Past*, New York.

Ryerson, A. (1960) 'Medical advice on child rearing 1550–1900', unpub. D.Ed. thesis, Harvard University.

Simon, J. (1979) 'Childhood in earlier seventeenth-century England', in K. Dent (ed.) *Informal Agencies of Education*, Leicester, 1–27.

Somerville, C. J. (1978) 'English Puritans and children: a social-cultural explanation', *J. Psychohist.* 6: 113–37.

Stickland, I. (1973) *The Voices of Children 1700–1914*, Oxford.

Still, G. F. (1931) *The History of Paediatrics*, London.

Tennant, D. F. (1984) 'Anabaptist theologies of childhood and education: (2) child rearing', *Bapt. Quart.* 30: 348–66.

Tucker, M. J. (1976) 'The child as beginning and end: fifteenth and sixteenth century English childhood', in L. De Mause (ed.) *The History of Childhood*, London, 229–57.

Wilson, S. (1984) 'The myth of motherhood a myth: the historical view of European child-rearing', *Soc. Hist.* 9: 181–98.

Wooden, W. W. (1982) 'The topos of childhood in Marian England', *J. Med. Ren. Stud.* 12: 179–94.

Wet nursing, parish nursing, and the country nursing of foundlings

Caulfield, E. (1932) 'The Countesse of Lincolne's nurserie', *Am. J. Dis. Child.* 43: 151–62.

Christ's Hospital Admissions 1554–1599 (1937) London.

Clark, G. (1985) 'Nurse children in Berkshire', *Berks Old & New* 2: 25–33.

——(1987) 'A study of nurse children 1550–1750', *Loc. Popul. Stud.* 39: 8–23.

Cule, J. (1986) 'John Jones physition on The Preservation of Bodie and Soule 1579', in J. Cule and T. Turner (eds) *Child Care through the Centuries*, Cardiff, 195–209.

Cunningham, C. (1977) 'Christ's Hospital: infant and child mortality in the sixteenth century', *Loc. Popul. Stud.* 18: 37–40.

Dulley, F. (1982) 'Nurse children: a forgotten cottage industry', *Herts Count.* 37: 14–15.

Fildes, V. A. (1986) *Breasts, Bottles and Babies: A History of Infant Feeding*, Edinburgh.

——(1988) *Wet Nursing. A History from Antiquity to the Present*, Oxford.

——(1988) 'The English wet nurse and her role in infant care 1538–1800', *Med. Hist.* 32: 142–73.

——(forthcoming) 'The wet nursing of London's children 1538–1800', in W. F. Bynum (ed.) *Living and Dying in London 1500–1900*, London.

——(forthcoming) 'The wet nurses of the London Foundling Hospital 1756–1767', *Cont. & Change*.

George, M. D. (1966) *London Life in the Eighteenth Century*, Harmondsworth, ch. 5: 'Parish children and poor apprentices', 213–61.

Jones, A. (1978) 'The Foundling Hospital and its arrangements for country nursing 1756–67. Illustrated by examples from Hertfordshire', unpub. dissertation for Extension Diploma in History, University of London.

Lewis, T. (1984) 'Parish poor children and nurse children in Enfield', *Loc. Popul. Stud.* 33: 65–6.

McClure, R. K. (1981) *Coram's Children. The London Foundling Hospital in the Eighteenth Century*, New Haven.

McLaren, D. (1979) 'Nature's contraceptive. Wet nursing and prolonged lactation: the case of Chesham, Buckinghamshire 1578–1601', *Med. Hist.* 23: 426–41.

Nichols, R. H. and Wray, F. A. (1935) *The History of the Foundling Hospital*, London.

Osborn, M. L. (1979) 'Hired mothering through the ages', in J. G. Howells (ed.) *Modern Perspectives in the Psychiatry of Infancy*, New York, 593–616.

Pearce, E. H. (1908) *Annals of Christ's Hospital*, London.

Rowe, V. A. (1983) *The Bluecoat Children at Ware, 1564–1761*, Ware.

Taylor, J. S. (1979) 'Philanthropy and empire: Jonas Hanway and the infant poor of London', *Eighteenth Cent. Stud.* 12: 285–305.

Infanticide and child abuse

Baron, F. X. (1979) 'Children and violence in Chaucer's *Canterbury Tales*', *J. Psychohist.* 7: 77–103.

Coleman, E. (1976) 'Infanticide in the early middle ages', in S. Stuard (ed.) *English Women in Medieval Society*, Philadelphia.

Damme, C. (1978) 'Infanticide: the worth of an infant under law', *Med. Hist.* 22: 1–24.

Forbes, T. R. (1986) 'Deadly parents: child homicide in eighteenth- and nineteenth-century England', *J. Hist. Med.* 41: 175–99.

Hair, P. E. H. (1972) 'Homicide, infanticide, and child assault in late Tudor Middlesex', *Loc. Popul. Stud.* 9: 43–6.

Helmholz, R. H. (1974) 'Infanticide in the Province of Canterbury during the fifteenth century', *Hist. Childh. Quart.* 2: 379–90.

Hoffer, P. C. and Hull N. E. H. (1981) *Murdering Mothers: Infanticide in England and New England 1558–1803*, New York.

Hopkirk, M. (1949) *Nobody Wanted Sam. The Story of the Unwanted Child, 1530–1948*, London.

Johansson, S. R. (1987) 'Neglect, abuse and avoidable death: parental investment and the mortality of children in the European tradition', in R. J. J. Lancaster and J. Lancaster (eds) *Child Abuse and Neglect: Biosocial Dimensions*, Chicago.

Kellum, B. A. (1974) 'Infanticide in England in the later middle ages', *Hist. Childh. Quart.* 1: 367–88.

Langer, W. (1974) 'Infanticide: a historical survey', *Hist. Childh. Quart.* 1: 353–65.

Lawrence, A. (1989) 'British women's psychological disorders in the seventeenth century', in A. Angerman, G. Binneman, A. Keunen,

V. Poels, and J. Zirkzee (eds) *Current issues in Women's History*, London.

Malcolmson, R. W. (1977) 'Infanticide in the 18th century', in J. S. Cockburn (ed.) *Crime in England. 1500–1800*, London, 187–209.

Murphy, T. R. (1986) '"Woful childe of parents rage": suicide of children and adolescents in early modern England, 1507–1710', *Sixteenth Cent. J.* 17: 259–70.

Ober, W. B. (1986) 'Infanticide in eighteenth-century England. William Hunter's contribution to the forensic problem', *Path. Ann.* 21: 311–19.

Radbill, S. X. (1968) 'A history of child abuse and infanticide', in R. E. Helfer and H. Kempe (eds) *The Battered Child*, Chicago, 3–17.

Rodin, A. E. (1981) 'Infants and gin mania in 18th-century London', *J. Am. Med. Ass.* 245: 1237–9.

Ryan, W. B. (1862) *Infanticide: Its Law, Prevalence, Prevention and History*, London.

Wrightson, K. (1975) 'Infanticide in earlier seventeenth-century England', *Loc. Popul. Stud.* 15: 10–22.

——(1982) 'Infanticide in European history', *Crim. Just. Rev.* 3: 1-20.

Marriage and family life

Altschul, M. (1965) *A Baronial Family in Medieval England: The Clares, 1217–1314*, Baltimore.

Amussen, S. D. (1988) *An Ordered Society. Gender and Class in Early Modern England*, Oxford.

Ashley, M. (1964) *The Stuarts in Love, with some Reflections on Love and Marriage in the Sixteenth and Seventeenth Centuries*, New York.

Beier, L. M. (1985) 'In sickness and in health: a seventeenth century family's experience', in R. Porter (ed.) *Patients and Practitioners. Lay Perceptions of Medicine in Pre-industrial Society*, Cambridge, 101–28.

Bennett, H. S. (1932) *The Pastons and their England*, 2nd edn, Cambridge.

Berlatsky, J. (1978) 'Marriage and family in a Tudor elite: familial patterns of Elizabethan bishops', *J. Fam. Hist.* 3: 6–22.

Brodsky, V. (1989) *Mobility and Marriage: The Family and Kinship in Early Modern London*, Oxford.

Chaytor, M. (1980) 'Household and kinship: Ryton in the 16th and early 17th centuries', *Hist. Workshop J.* 10: 25–60.

Cowgill, U. M. (1970) 'Marriage and its progeny in the city of York, 1538–1751', *Kroeber Anthrop. Soc. Pap.* 42: 47–87.

Crawford, P. (1984) 'Katharine and Philip Henry and their children: a case study in family ideology', *Trans. Hist. Soc. Lancs Chesh.* 134: 39–73.

Davidoff, L. and Hall, C. (1987) *Family Fortunes. Men and Women of the English Middle Class, 1780–1850*, London.

Davies, K. M. (1981) 'Continuity and change in literary advice on marriage', in R. B. Outhwaite (ed.) *Marriage and Society*, London, 58–80.

Durston, C. (1988) '"Unhallowed wedlocks": the regulation of marriage during the English revolution', *Hist. J.* 31: 45–59.
——(1988) *The Family and the English Revolution*, Oxford.
Emmison, F. (1964) *Tudor Food and Pastimes. Life at Ingatestone Hall*, London.
Flandrin, J. -L. (1979) *Families in Former Times. Kinship, Household and Sexuality*, trans. R. Southern, Cambridge.
Gillis, J. R. (1981) 'Peasant, plebeian, and proletarian marriage in Britain 1600–1900', in D. Levine, (ed.) *Proletarianization and Family History*,
——(1985) *For Better, for Worse: British Marriages, 1600 to the Present*, New York.
Harris, B. J. (1982) 'Marriage sixteenth-century style: Elizabeth Stafford and the third Duke of Norfolk', *J. Soc. Hist.* 15: 371–82.
Houlbrooke, R. A. (1984) *The English Family 1450–1700*, London.
——(1988) *English Family Life 1560–1725. An Anthology of Diaries*, Oxford.
Ingram, M. (1985) 'The reform of popular culture? Sex and marriage in early modern England', in B. Reay (ed.) *Popular Culture in Seventeenth-century England*, London, 129–65.
——(1987) *Church Courts, Sex and Marriage in England, 1570–1640*, Cambridge.
Larminie, V. (1984) 'Marriage and the family: the example of the seventeenth-century Newdigates', *Midland Hist.* 9: 1–22.
Laslett, P. (1977) *Family Life and Illicit Love in Earlier Generations*, Cambridge.
——(1979) *The World We Have Lost*, 2nd edn, London.
——(1983) *The World We Have Lost Further Explored*, London.
Laslett, P. and Wall, R. (eds) (1972) *Household and Family in Past Time*, Cambridge.
Lorence, B. W. (1974) 'Parents and children in eighteenth-century Europe', *Hist. Childh. Quart.* 2: 1–30.
Macfarlane, A. (1970) *The Family Life of Ralph Josselin, a Seventeenth-century Clergyman. An Essay in Historical Anthropology*, Cambridge.
——(1986) *Marriage and Love in England. Modes of Reproduction 1300–1840*, Oxford.
Marshall, D. (1926) *The English Poor in the Eighteenth Century*, London (repr. New York, 1969).
Mendelson, S. (1979) 'Debate: "The weightiest business": marriage in an upper gentry family in seventeenth-century England', *P & P* 85: 128–35.
Menefee, S. (1981) *Wives for Sale. An Ethnographic Study of British Popular Divorce*, Oxford.
Mertes, K. (1988) *The English Noble Household, 1250–1600*, Oxford.
Mueller, G. J. W. (1957) 'Inquiry into the state of a divorceless society: domestic relations, law and morals in England from 1660–1857', *Univ. Pittsburgh Law Rev.* 18: 545–78.
Outhwaite, R. B. (ed.) (1981) *Marriage and Society: Studies in the Social History of Marriage*, London.

Pollock, L. (1987) '"An action like a strategem": courtship and marriage from the middle ages to the twentieth century', *Hist. J.*, 30: 483–98.

Porter, R. (1985) 'Marriage, sex and the family in England, 1660–1800. An essay review', *Med.Hist.* 29: 442–5.

Powell, C. L. (1972) *English Domestic Relations, 1487–1653*, New York.

St Clare Byrne, M. (ed.) (1981) *The Lisle Letters*, 6 vols, Chicago.

Sharpe, J. A. (1981) 'Domestic homicide in early modern England', *Hist. J.* 24: 29–48.

——(1986) 'Plebeian marriage in Stuart England: some evidence from popular literature', *Trans. Roy. Hist. Soc.*, 36.

Shorter, E. (1977) *The Making of the Modern Family*, Glasgow.

Slater, M. (1984) *Family Life in the Seventeenth Century. The Verneys of Claydon House*, London.

Stone, L. (1961) 'Marriage among the English nobility in the sixteenth and seventeenth centuries', *Compar. Stud. Soc. Hist.* 3: 182–214.

——(1977) *The Family, Sex and Marriage in England 1500–1800*, London.

Trumbach, R. (1978) *The Rise of the Egalitarian Family. Aristocratic Kinship and Domestic Relations in Eighteenth Century England*, London.

Winchester, B. (1955) *Tudor Family Portraits*, London.

Wolfram, S. (1987) *In-laws and Outlaws. Kinship and Marriage in England*, London.

Housework and the home

Bayne-Powell, R. (1956) *Housekeeping in the Eighteenth Century*, London.

Bradley, R. M. (1912) *The English Housewife in the Sixteenth and Seventeenth Centuries*, London.

Davidson, C. (1982) *A Woman's Work is Never Done. A History of Housework in the British Isles 1650–1950*, London.

Davis, D. (1966) *A History of Shopping*, London.

Filbee, M. (1980) *A Woman's Place. An Illustrated History of Women at Home. From the Roman Villa to the Victorian Townhouse*, London.

Fussell, G. E. and Fussell, K. R. (1953) *The English Countrywoman. Her Life in Farmhouse and Field from Tudor times to the Victorian Age*, London (repr. 1981).

Hole, C. (1949) *English Home Life 1500–1800*, London.

——(1953) *The English Housewife in the Seventeenth Century*, London.

Lofts, N. (1976) *Domestic Life in England*, London.

McKendrick, N. (1974) 'Home demand and economic growth: a new view of the role of women and children in the industrial revolution', in *Historical Perspectives: Studies in English Thought and Society*, London, 152–210.

St Clare Byrne, M. (ed.) (1949) *The Elizabethan Home. Discovered in Two Dialogues by Claudius Hollyband and Peter Erondell*, London.

Shammas, C. (1981) 'The domestic environment in early modern England and America', *J. Soc. Hist.* 14: 3–24.

Working mothers

Bennett, J. M. (1986) 'The village ale-wife: women and brewing in fourteenth-century England', in B. A. Hanawalt (ed.) *Women and Work in Preindustrial Europe*, Bloomington, 20–36.

Chamberlain, M. (1981) *Old Wives' Tales. Their History, Remedies and Spells*, London, part 1.

Clark, A. (1919) *Working Life of Women in the Seventeenth Century*, London (repr. 1982).

Earle, P. (1989) 'The female labour market in London in the late-seventeenth and early-eighteenth centuries', *Econ. Hist. Rev.* 42.

Hanawalt, B. A. (1986) 'Peasant women's contribution to the home economy in late medieval England', in B. A. Hanawalt (ed.) *Women and Work in Preindustrial Europe*, Bloomington, 3–19.

Hutton, D. (1985) 'Women in fourteenth century Shrewsbury', in L. Charles and L. Duffin (eds) *Women and Work in Pre- industrial England*, London, 83–99.

Kowaleski, M. (1986) 'Women's work in a market town: Exeter in the late fourteenth century', in B. A. Hanawalt (ed.) *Women and Work in Preindustrial Europe*, Bloomington, 145–64.

Lacey, K. E. (1985) 'Women and work in fourteenth and fifteenth century London', in L. Charles and L. Duffin (eds) *Women and Work in Pre-industrial England*, London, 24–82.

Middleton, C. (1985) 'Women's labour and the transition to pre-industrial capitalism', in L. Charles and L. Duffin (eds) *Women and Work in Pre-industrial England*, London, 181–206.

Pinchbeck, I. (1930) *Women Workers and the Industrial Revolution 1750–1850*, London (repr. 1981).

Roberts, M. (1985) '"Words they are women, and deeds they are men": images of work and gender in early modern England', in L. Charles and L. Duffin (eds) *Women and Work in Pre-industrial England*, London, 122–80.

Stuart, D. M. (1946) *The English Abigail*, London.

Tilly, L. A. and Scott, J. W. (1978) *Women, Work, and Family*, New York.

Willen, D. (1988) 'Women in the public sphere in early modern England: the case of the urban working poor', *Sixteenth Cent. J.* 19: 559–75.

Wright, S. (1985) '"Churmaids, huswyfes and hucksters": the employment of women in Tudor and Stuart Salisbury', in L. Charles and L. Duffin (eds) *Women and Work in Pre-industrial England*, London, 100–21.

Wyman, A. L. (1984) 'The surgeoness: the female practitioner of surgery 1400–1800', *Med. Hist.* 28: 22–41.

Unmarried mothers

Hair, P. E. H. (1966) 'Bridal pregnancy in rural England in earlier centuries', *Popul. Stud.* 20: 233–43.

——(1970) 'Bridal pregnancy in earlier rural England further examined', *Popul. Stud.* 24: 59–70.

Laslett, P. and Oosterveen, K. (1973) 'Long-term trends in bastardy in England. A study of the illegitimacy figures in the parish registers and in the reports of the Registrar General, 1561–1960', *Popul. Stud.* 27: 255–86.

——and Smith, R. M. (eds) (1980) *Bastardy and its Comparative History. Studies in the History of Illegitimacy and Marital Nonconformism in Britain, France, Germany, Sweden, North America, Jamaica and Japan,* London.

Meteyard, B. (1980) 'Illegitimacy and marriage in eighteenth-century England', *J. Interdisc. Hist.* 10: 479–89.

Oosterveen, K., Smith, R. M., and Stewart, S. (1980) 'Family reconstitution and the study of bastardy: evidence from certain English parishes', in P. Laslett, K. Oosterveen, and R. M. Smith (eds) *Bastardy and its Comparative History,* London, 86–140.

Quaife, G. R. (1979) *Wanton Wenches and Wayward Wives. Peasants and Illicit Sex in Early Seventeenth-century England,* London.

Wilson, A. (1989) 'Illegitimacy and its implications in mid-eighteenth-century London: the evidence of the Foundling Hospital', *Cont. & Change* 4: 103–64.

Widowed mothers

Brodsky, V. (1986) 'Widows in late Elizabethan London: remarriage, economic opportunity and family orientations', in L. Bonfield, R. Smith and K. Wrightson (eds) *The World We Have Gained,* Oxford, 122–54.

Carlton, C. (1978) 'The widow's tale: male myths and female reality', *Albion* 10: 118–29.

Clark, E. (1985) 'The custody of children in English manor courts', *Law Hist. Rev.* 3: 338–9.

Holderness, B. A. (1984) 'Widows in pre-industrial society: an essay upon their economic functions', in R. M. Smith (ed.) *Land, Kinship and Life-cycle,* Cambridge, 423–42.

Holman, J. R. (1975) 'Orphans in pre-industrial towns – the case of Bristol in the late seventeenth century', *Loc. Popul. Stud.* 15: 40–4.

Kettle, A. J. (1984) '"My wife shall have it": marriage and property in the wills and testaments of later mediaeval England', in E. M. Craik (ed.) *Marriage and Property,* Aberdeen, 89–103.

Laslett, P. (1974) 'Parental deprivation in the past: a note on the history of orphans in England', *Loc. Popul. Stud.* 13: 11–18.

Todd, B. J. (1985) 'The remarrying widow: a stereotype reconsidered', in M. Prior (ed.) *Women in English Society 1500–1800,* London, 54–92.

Walker, S. S. (1976) 'Widow and ward: the feudal law of child custody in medieval England', *Fem. Stud.* 3: 104–16.

Works on women which contain information on the role of mothers in pre-industrial England

André, C. S. (1981) 'Some selected aspects of the role of women in sixteenth century England', *Int. J. Wom. Stud.* 4: 76–88.

Angerman, A., Binneman, G., Keunen, A., Poels, V., and Zirkzee, J. (eds) (1989) *Current Issues in Women's History*, London.

Badinter, E. (1981) *The Myth of Motherhood. An Historical View of the Maternal Instinct*, trans. R. De Garis, London.

Bennett, J. M. (1987) *Women in the Medieval English Countryside. Gender and Household in Brigstock before the Plague*, Oxford.

Bridenthal, R. and Koonz, C. (eds) (1977) *Becoming Visible: Women in European History*, Boston.

Brown, I. Q. (1982) 'Domesticity, feminism and friendship: female aristocratic culture and marriage in England 1660–1760', *J. Fam. Hist.* 7: 406–24.

Charles, L. and Duffin, L. (eds) (1985) *Women and Work in Pre-industrial England*, London.

Crawford, P. (1984) 'From the woman's view: pre-industrial England, 1500–1750', in P. Crawford (ed.) *Exploring Women's Past. Essays in Social History*, Sydney, 49–85.

Ehrenreich, B. and English, D. (1973) *Witches, Midwives and Nurses. A History of Women Healers*, London.

Fell, C. (1984) *Women in Anglo-Saxon England and the Impact of 1066*, London.

Fraser, A. (1984) *The Weaker Vessel. Woman's Lot in Seventeenth-century England*, London.

Hanawalt, B. A. (ed.) (1986) *Women and Work in Preindustrial Europe*, Bloomington.

Hill, B. (1986) *Eighteenth Century Women. An Anthology*, London.

Hill, G. (1986) *Women in English Life from Medieval to Modern Times*, 2 vols, London.

Kanner, B. (ed.) (1980) *The Women of England from Anglo-Saxon Times to the Present. Interpretive Bibliographical Essays*, London.

Labarge, M. W. (1986) *Women in Medieval Life*, London.

McLaren, D. (1979) 'The individualism of good mothering', *Bull. Soc. Soc. Hist. Med.* 24: 36–8.

MacLean, I. (1980) *The Renaissance Notion of Woman*, Cambridge.

Mendelson, S. (1987) *The Mental World of Stuart Women. Three Studies*, Brighton.

Power, E. (1975) *Medieval Women*, ed. M. M. Postan, Cambridge.

Prior, M. (ed.) (1985) *Women in English Society 1500–1800*, London.

Smith, H. (1982) *Reason's Disciples. Seventeenth-century English Feminists*, Urbana.

Stenton, D. M. (1957) *The English Woman in History*, London (repr. New York, 1977).

Stuard, S. (ed.) (1976) *English Women in Medieval Society*, Philadelphia.

Thompson, R. (1974) *Women in Stuart England and America*, London.

Travitsky, B. S. (1980) 'The new mother of the English renaissance: her writings on motherhood', in C. N. Davidson and E. M. Broner (eds) *The Lost Tradition. Mothers and Daughters in Literature*, New York, 33–43.

Wall, R. (1981) 'Woman alone in English society', *Ann. Démog. Hist.* 303–17.

Willen, D. (1984) 'Guildswomen in the city of York, 1560–1700', *Historian* 46: 204–18.

General and demographic works which include material relevant to the study of mothers in pre-industrial England

Bashar, N. (1983) 'Rape in England between 1550 and 1700', in *The Sexual Dynamics of History*, London, 28–46.

Bonfield, L., Smith, R. and Wrightson, K. (eds) (1986) *The World We Have Gained. Histories of Population and Social Structure*, Oxford.

Bynum, W. F. (ed.) (forthcoming) *Living and Dying in London. 1500–1900*, London.

——and Porter, R. (eds) (1985) *William Hunter and the Eighteenth-century Medical World*, Cambridge.

Drummond, J. C. and Wilbraham, A. (1958) *The Englishman's Food. A History of Five Centuries of English Diet*, rev. edn, London.

Emmison, F. G. (1973) *Elizabethan Life: Morals and the Church Courts Mainly from Essex Archdiaconal Records*, Chelmsford.

Finlay, R. A. P. (1978) 'Gateways to death? London child mortality experience 1570–1653', *Ann. Démog. Hist.*: 105–34.

Fletcher, A. and Stevenson, J. (eds) (1985) *Order and Disorder in Early Modern England*, Cambridge.

Glass, D. V. and Eversley, D. E. C. (eds) (1974) *Population in History. Essays in Historical Demography*, London.

Hollingsworth, T. H. (1965) 'The demography of the British peerage', *Popul. Stud. Suppl.* 18.

——(1974) 'A demographic study of the British ducal families', in D. V. Glass and D. E. C. Eversley, (eds) (1974) *Population in History. Essays in Historical Demography*, London, 354–78.

Jarrett, D. (1974) *England in the Age of Hogarth*, Frogmore, Herts.

Jones, R. E. (1976) 'Infant mortality in rural North Shropshire, 1561–1810', *Popul. Stud.* 30: 305–17.

——(1980) 'Further evidence on the decline in infant mortality in pre-industrial England: North Shropshire 1561–1810', *Popul. Stud.* 34: 239–50.

Langer, W. L. (1972) 'Checks on population growth: 1750–1850', *Scient. Am.* 226: 92–9.

Levine, D. (1987) *Reproducing Families. The Political Economy of English Population History*, Cambridge.

MacDonald, M. (1981) *Mystical Bedlam. Madness, Anxiety, and Healing in Seventeenth-century England,* Cambridge.

Marcy, P. T. (1981) 'Factors affecting the fecundity and fertility of historical populations. A review', *J. Fam. Hist.* 6: 309–26.

Mechling, J. (1975) 'Advice to historians on advice to mothers', *J. Soc. Hist.* 9: 44–63.

Nair, G. (1988) *Highley 1550–1880: The Development of a Community,* Oxford.

Porter, R. (1982) *English Society in the Eighteenth Century,* Harmondsworth.

Reynolds, G. (1979) 'Infant mortality and sex ratios at baptism as shown by reconstruction of Willingham, a parish on the edge of the fens, in Cambridgeshire', *Loc. Popul. Stud.* 22: 31–7.

——(1986) 'Rape – does it have a historical meaning?', in S. Tomaselli and R. Porter (eds) *Rape,* Oxford, 216–36.

Rodgers, B. (1949) *Cloak of Charity. Studies in Eighteenth Century Philanthropy,* London.

Rousseau, G. S. and Porter, R. (eds) (1987) *Sexual Underworlds of the Enlightenment,* Manchester.

Schofield, R. S. (1970) 'Perinatal mortality in Hawkshead, Lancashire, 1581–1710', *Loc. Popul. Stud.* 4: 11–16.

——and Wrigley, E. A. (1979) 'Infant and child mortality in the late Tudor and early Stuart Period', in C. Webster (ed.) *Health, Medicine and Mortality in the Sixteenth Century,* Cambridge, 61–95.

Slack, P. (1988) *Poverty and Policy in Tudor and Stuart England,* London.

Smith, R. M. (1981) 'Fertility, economy and household formation in England over three centuries', *Popul. Dev. Rev.* 7: 595–622.

——(ed.) (1984) *Land, Kinship and Life-cycle,* Cambridge.

Snell, K. D. M. (1985) *Annals of the Labouring Poor. Social Change and Agrarian England, 1660–1900,* Cambridge.

Stone, L. (1965) *Crisis of the Aristocracy 1558–1641,* Oxford.

——and Stone, J. F. (1984) *An Open Elite? England 1540–1880,* Oxford.

Thomas, K. (1961) 'The double standard', *J. Hist. Ideas* 20: 195–216.

West, F. (1974) 'Infant mortality in the East Fen parishes of Leake and Wrangle', *Loc. Popul. Stud.* 13: 41–4.

Wilson, A. (1980) 'The infancy of the history of childhood: an appraisal of Philippe Aries', *Hist. & Theory,* 19: 147–50.

Wrightson, K. (1982) *English Society 1580–1680,* London.

Wrigley, E. A. (1987) *People, Cities and Wealth,* Oxford.

——and Schofield, R. S. (1981) *The Population History of England 1541–1871. A Reconstruction,* London.

——(1983) 'English population history from family reconstitution: summary results 1600–1799', *Popul. Stud.* 37: 157–84.

Index